WAR
NERD

GARY BRECHER

WAR NERD

Soft Skull Brooklyn

Library of Congress Cataloging-in-Publication Data

Brecher, Gary.
War nerd / Gary Brecher.
p.cm.
ISBN-13: 978-0-9796636-8-0
ISBN-10: 0-9796636-8-7
1. War and society.   2. World politics–1989–   I. Title.
HM554.B74 2008
303.6'6–dc22
2007046876

Cover design by Goodloe Byron
Interior design by Pauline Neuwirth, Neuwirth & Associates, Inc.
Printed in the United States of America

Soft Skull Press
An Imprint of Counterpoint LLC
2117 Fourth Street
Suite D
Berkeley, CA 94710

www.softskull.com
www.counterpointpress.com

Distributed by Publishers Group West

10   9   8   7   6   5   4   3   2   1

CONTENTS

**WAR
NERD**

INTRODUCTION

I'M A WAR nerd. A backseat sergeant. I know what I am. All I have to do is look down at the keyboard and there's my hairy white gut slopping over it, and there's crumbs between the keys from the fake homemade soft 'n' chewy big cookies in the vending machine downstairs. I mean, they made me pay for the last keyboard because I spilled Diet Coke all over it. Diet Coke, the most fattening drink in the world. Every Web pig in the world is swimming in it, farting off the side of the swivel chair, aroma-free carbonation farts, or at least you hope they are.

So I'm unhealthy. No shit, Sigmund. I live in Fresno, which is a death sentence already, and I do about fifteen hours a day at this desk. Six or seven entering civilian numbers for the paycheck and the rest surfing the war news.

War is the only good thing in my life. In fact, war is great. You're not supposed to say that, but it is. You think so yourself. People used to admit that they loved war. It's worth remembering that, so you can tell the peaceniks they're the freaks, not us.

Pick any tribe you want, and you'll find their heroes were warriors. It wouldn't occur to them that there was any other kind of hero: hero and warrior are the same thing. Not even the peaceniks want to give back what war gave them: the house they live in, the streets they drive down. Think about the city you live in. Whose was it three hundred years ago? If you live in America, you live on land that was taken by conquest. I guess I'm supposed to think that Gandhi is a hero. If you think that, stop smudging up my book. You're in the wrong shelf.

Besides, war is fun. That's another big lie, that war is nothing but tragedy for everybody. The Russians have a saying that has a little more truth to it: War is a mother to some and a stepmother to others. I've talked to a few old guys who were in WWII and I noticed the older they got, the less they wanted to talk about their civilian lives. Not even the wife and kiddies meant that much to them compared to those few years in uniform.

And that's natural because war is and always has been how you show you really care. Say it with blood. You want that piece of land? Be ready to die for it. Better yet, as Patton would say, kill for it.

War is also the mother of invention. Peacetime clogs people's brains worse than Thanksgiving dinner. War is like a 150-mm alarm clock right there in your bedroom. When the walls get blown out and the roof starts falling, people show what they can do. And they get braver, they get smarter, they go from nowhere to glory. Take U. S. Grant. Our finest war lifted him from town drunk to commanding officer of the Potomac, the finest force the world has ever seen.

It happens everywhere, every century. If the Mongols hadn't decided to make the whole world their back pasture, then Subotai, the greatest general who ever lived, would've wasted his life pulling sheep across creek beds. That's peacetime: slopping around in the mud with the sheep. I just don't see how people think that's better than conquering the world.

And ladies, this is not some men's club here. Ever hear of Joan of Arc? She was all woman, baby, and she could smite with the best of 'em. If she'd stayed at home to bake bread, you never would've heard of her.

So there are all kinds of reasons to learn about war. Like it's just naturally the coolest thing humans have ever done or ever will do. Like it's the truth behind all the vanilla preaching, like it shows what people can accomplish, what people can survive—what people do when everything is on the line.

It's also as funny as Hell. I guess I'm not supposed to say that either, but it's true. Right now (January 12, 2008), you can't turn on the TV without seeing U.S. Navy footage of some Iranian speed-boats doing a few waterskiing moves around an American frigate in the Persian Gulf. The soundtrack is some foreign accent saying, "I am coming to blow you up!"

If you don't know anything about war like most people don't, you're sitting there in Iowa with your knees knocking, sure that these Iranian Evinrudes are just about to come crashing into your living room. If you're a serious war nerd, you know better. Sure enough, it's just come out that the scary foreign voice on that soundtrack didn't come from any of the Iranian Bayliners. It was a "prank" by this guy local sailors call Filipino Monkey, who's been harassing every tramp steamer to come through the gulf within the last fifteen years.

That's the first level of comedy. If you know a little history, there's also the way this is like a bad sequel to the Tonkin Gulf Resolution back in 1964, when the U.S. Navy helped get us into 'Nam by saying it had been mugged by a North Vietnamese destroyer. Naturally, the Navy volunteered the U.S. Army to fix the situation by sacrificing sixty thousand GIs in an Asian land war.

And then there's the really scary part of the joke, which is that the U.S. Navy really could be in big trouble if the Iranians decide to use those speedboats in a low-tech swarm attack. You see, way back in 2002, we staged the Millennium Challenge War Games in the Persian Gulf. The American officer who was supposed to be playing the Iranians managed to sink two-thirds of the U.S. fleet with a swarm of cheap improvised weapons, including Cessnas and civilian motorboats.

Once you've learned to read a war the way I'll teach you, you'll be able to watch footage like that, separate the bullshit from the serious threats, and enjoy the comedy of war, even while you're seeing the truth behind each side's propaganda.

So why get a life when you've got a war?

Part 1

THE
AMERICAS

COLOMBIA:
A HUNDRED YEARS OF SLAUGHTERTUDE

AMERICA KEEPS GETTING deeper into the shit in Colombia. We're airlifting planeloads of cash on the Colombian army—$1.5 billion is what the Defense Department admits, so you gotta assume it's more like $10 billion, with the rest squeezed through the usual CIA laundries. Colombia's gung ho president, Alvaro Uribe, says whatever Washington likes to hear; he's going to ratchet up the war against the rebels. Washington will give Colombia anything it wants, if only to annoy Hugo Chavez, who's right next door in Venezuela.

The big rebel group, FARC (Fuerzas Armadas Revolucionarios de Colombia), has the same bring-it-on attitude. The rebels are always on the lookout for new ways to kill people. They even hired three ex-IRA guys to show 'em how to make remote-launched mortars, and learned so fast they damn near blasted el presidente right off the platform at his own inauguration.

So with everybody ready to party, seemed like a good time to give you a little briefing on Colombia, our new pal. But I have to warn you: Colombian history is as messy as a slaughterhouse floor in a blackout. So I'll give you a choice: the short version (for MTV victims with thirty-second attention spans) or the long version for serious military buffs.

First, the short version:

Colombian History and Culture in Three Easy Steps
- *Step 1:* Rent *Scarface.*
- *Step 2:* Fast-forward to that scene where Al Pacino and

his friends try a coke deal with some Colombians. The Colombians want to take the money and keep the coke. They try to persuade Pacino to tell them where the money is by handcuffing him and his buddy to the wall, revvin' up a chainsaw and sawing off his friend's arms and legs till the whole room is so splattered with blood you can't see who's killing who anymore.

- *Step 3:* Replay this scene over and over for four hundred years.

And that, kids, is the history and culture of Colombia.

OK, now a more detailed version.

Say Latin America's a psych ward (which it pretty much is, anyway). Panama would be the sociopath con man. Argentina'd be this suicidally depressed old bag. Brazil would be a classic nympho whore . . . and Colombia would be the guy all the other psychos are scared of, the guy in the triple-locked cage at the end of the high-security corridor, who used to barbecue his victims and make "Kiss the Cook" aprons out of their skin.

Colombians have been killing each other since the Spanish came ashore and got to work hacking the local Indians into extinction. Between 1819 and 1900, Colombia had fifty rebellions and eight full-scale civil wars. Some of the rebellions were quick little coups with only double-digit casualties, but some were serious bloodbaths. In the War of a Thousand Days (1899–1901), those hardworking Colombian killers managed to knock off 100,000 of their fellow citizens. They kept at it and hit some kind of peak in the 1940s with *la Violencia*, a free-for-all that notched up at least 300,000 dead.

One interesting thing about Colombian killing is they do it both ways: solo and in groups. There are some nationalities that turn into psycho killers once they put on a uniform, but wouldn't even run a yellow light once they're back in civvies, two classic examples being the Japanese and Germans. The Japanese did things in China that'd make Jeffrey Dahmer puke. Beheading contests, sword practice on pregnant Chinese, hacky sack with babies and bayonets. But those Japs went home and instantly morphed into salary-men who wouldn't even jaywalk. Same with the Germans: let 'em loose in a gray helmet and they go crazy, but back home in Dusseldorf, they'd die before they'd drop an ice cream stick on the sidewalk.

Then there are the countries that kill real well in private life, but won't fight in uniform—Italians, say. Mean fuckers on the street, in the alley, but put one in a uniform, and he can't wait to throw away his rifle and find a nice, cozy cellar to hide out in.

But Colombians are multi-event killers. They're like the Bo Jackson of killing: They can do it all. In uniform or out, home games or away, on the street or the battlefield. Men, women, children, dogs—if it moves, Colombians'll kill it. For any reason. Or no reason. For money, fun, the revolution, the counterrevolution, or just for practice.

Killing is like the only way you can make a point in Colombia. Take soccer. We all know foreigners get weird about soccer—hooligans, riots, all that. But Colombians do it their way—none of that noise and drunken chair-throwing crap you get with English hooligans. Colombians say it with bullets. In the 1994 World Cup, Colombia lost out because a player named Andrés Escobar scored an "own goal." Escobar flew back to Colombia expecting to get a hard time. But nobody yelled at him. That wouldn't be the Colombian way. All that happened was that as soon as Escobar stepped out of his house, a man walked up and emptied a whole 9-mm clip into him. I mean, that's what you call fan feedback.

Before they got guns, Colombians settled life's little problems with machetes. I read about this pretty damn cool custom they had in Colombian villages: If two men have a disagreement, they don't shout, they don't sue, they don't bore everybody with long arguments. Nope. Two guys just take up their machetes, and then each grabs one end of a serape. When the ref blows his whistle, they start chopping each other up. The first guy to let go of the serape loses. Usually because he's dead.

The winner, who's probably bleeding to death himself, walks away covered with glory—and a few quarts of arterial blood. The goat or chicken or whatever it was the fight was about belongs to him, and he staggers off just as happy as a Colombian can be, down to the coffin shop to see if he can trade the goat for an upgrade to the deluxe mahogany model.

The historians I've been reading—typical bleeding-heart college professors—all try to say Colombians aren't really violent. Oh no! It's America's fault, or it's the United Fruit Company's fault, or it's the cocaine trade, or whatever.

Yeah. Reminds me of this "cultural education" visitor we had when I was in ninth grade in Long Beach—this huge Samoan lady who stomped in and told us she was going to "break the stereotype" that Samoans were violent. She sang some Samoan poem and showed us a flower arrangement, which was supposed to prove to us Samoans were the gentlest people ever to walk the earth. Our mullet-hair dyke teacher stood next to her, all nodding and clapping and going, "Oh, how true!"—and when big Samoan lady finally shut the Hell up, the dyke reached out to try to hug her. Except she couldn't get her little arms around far enough. It was funny, and about half the class sort of laughed. Samoan lady didn't like that. She put out one big nonviolent Samoan hand about the size of a catcher's mitt on the dyke's chest and shoved her halfway across the room. Then the bell rang and the rest of us squeezed around Samoan lady to see if we could make it to the vending machines before Sammy Faumina. Sammy was this peaceful, gentle Samoan guy who weighed about five hundred pounds, liked bouncing white kids' heads off their lockers, and could shake us down for our lunch money.

So how about a little truth for once? As in: Colombians kill. They've done it nonstop for four hundred years. They'll do it for another four hundred. That's part of the reason it's hard to explain the current wars in Colombia, because they're just a little episode in one long war that will never end.

I say "wars" because there are at least three rebel armies and God knows how many death squad paramilitary groups fighting right now in Colombia. The three rebel armies have some things in common: They all talk more or less like Commies. They all say they're for the peasants, and they talk about cooperating—but they'd kill each other in a second if they weren't too busy fighting the government.

The three groups go by initials, natch: FARC, M19, and ELN. The biggest, by far, is the FARC, with around eighteen thousand combat troops. That may not seem like a lot by U.S. or Russian army standards, but you have to remember, most guerrilla groups are real small. They have to be. They need to be mobile, keep their logistics simple, and be able to disappear fast. For that kind of fighting, you don't really need too many combat troops.

There are guerrilla groups with only a couple of dozen troops that work damn well. In fact, one of the weirdest war stories I ever heard was about a guerrilla army consisting of three guys. They were survivors of a Japanese platoon stranded in the Philippines, and their leader, this hard-ass sergeant, refused to surrender. He decided that it was his duty to the emperor to kill anyone who entered his territory. For thirty years, these three guys controlled a huge chunk of jungle, killing any of the locals who entered their domain. The Philippine army couldn't find them; the villagers got the message and left them alone. In other words, the little group was an effective military force—with three men.

So eighteen thousand men makes the FARC a huge army, by guerrilla standards. They're by far the most aggressive of the three groups. Like most Latin American guerrilla armies, they have an elite command group who are almost all middle- or upper-class boys 'n' girls, commanding troops who are almost all *campesinos*. (That's the way Colombia's army looks, too: rich elite command, poor peasant troopers. It's the way Colombians split the money down there, too: Four hundred families own half the crummy country, and everybody else lives on beans and rice.)

The two other rebel armies, ELN and M19 (the oldest group) haven't been run as well as FARC; they're seen as less powerful and clever and are just holding on. But the FARC really believes it's gonna defeat the Colombian National Army. This is unique, if you think about it, because it's been a long time since a Maoist peasant army won anything. The Khmer Rouge were the last to do it, and that was over a quarter-century ago. In 1950, the world was jammed with groups like the FARC, but now, only in a few weird, fucked-up corners like Nepal and Colombia do they count for anything.

The FARC's last big push was supposed to take the big cities—the old Maoist battle plan, where you strangle the cities and then march in. It failed. FARC lost a lot of soldiers and retreated to its backwoods power bases. The only city in Colombia where FARC has any control is Medellin, Pablo Escobar's ol' stomping ground. The slums of Medellin are FARC territory. But when the offensive failed, most of the eighteen thousand FARC men dispersed again back to the big tracts of jungle and scrub FARC run.

The army and its paramilitary allies are even harder to sort out than the rebel groups. For starters, you've got the official Colombian National Army, which is estimated at 55,000 to 90,000 combat troops—not nearly enough for the ten-to-one ratio you usually need for counterinsurgency warfare. They're not world-class soldiers, but there's an old military rule that mediocre troops are adequate for defense, not attack, and that's what the Colombian army realized. It holds the cities and leaves the search-and-destroy mission to the paramilitary gangs.

The paramilitary groups—and there are at least a half-dozen operating in Colombia now—are right-wing militias. Their job is killing anybody who even smells like a rebel, with a little torture thrown in for fun. They're set up and paid by the army or the rich families that really run the country. The paramilitary are recruited mostly from the army, so the whole army-paramilitary divide isn't so clear. A guy can be a government soldier all day, doing the nice-nice stuff like guarding a bridge, waving to the tourist buses that go by—then go home, change into civilian clothes, hop on a pickup, and go off to kill villagers as a paramilitary.

You can respect the army and the FARC, but the paramilitaries—the more I read about them, the more I wanted to see them all dead. They don't settle for killing; they play with people, popping out eyeballs, cutting off tits, real sick stuff.

In fact, the only really fun part of the Colombian wars is that when the urban offensive failed, FARC decided to go for the paramilitaries instead. The army was trying to run a kind of Vietnamization program, get the paramilitaries to do some actual fighting. The army thought it could turn these sick fucks into soldiers. Didn't happen. The FARC trapped big paramilitary forces in towns all over the country and wiped them out. Turned out the paramilitaries didn't like fighting people who had guns. They were great at beating unarmed peasants to death, but fled like sissies when they ran into FARC.

The rebels got a lot more popular when they whacked the paramilitaries, because nobody likes those fuckers, not even the army. Though the army uses the paramilitary, it still hates the sick little bastards. So FARC is riding pretty high right now.

It's also set on the money front. Guerrilla groups have to buy their weapons in the black market, and that's incredibly expensive. But don't think FARC has to worry about that. It's the richest guerrilla group this side of Fatah, thanks to its own coke-'n'-opium growing and shipping business in the areas it controls. In fact, the Bush press whores like to say FARC is responsible for all the coke killing our kids, blah-blah-blah. Bullshit. Every group in Colombia grows, processes, ships, and sells coke and opium: the army, the paramilitaries, the rebels, not to mention a whole lot of poor, scared peasants who just want to make a little money.

It might seem weird that a just semibig country like Colombia can have all these armies and dope-growers running around at once without running into each other. It's a matter of geography. The geography of Colombia is as fucked-up as everything else about the place. Basically, there's the Andean highlands, where the big families and most of the other people live. Then there's the hot, swampy coast, where the people are black and a little less bloodthirsty, by all accounts. And there's the llanos, big, flat swamps full of anacondas to the east, and the jungles south of the highlands and sometimes right in between mountain ranges. A few miles as the crow flies may mean going from sea level to ten thousand feet.

If that seems confusing, it is. In fact, confusion is maybe the best word to describe the whole military history of the place. One confusion-causing tactic that's very important in Colombia is the false-flag massacre. *False flag* means inventing a fake group that goes out and kills people so the real killers, the army or the rebels, don't get the blame. So soldiers dress up as rebels, go into a pro-rebel village shouting, "*Viva la Revolucion! Viva Che!*" and kill pro-rebel villagers. The idea is to break down the trust between the villagers and the guerrillas. Next time the real rebels come to the village asking for food and info, they're not going to get a friendly reception. (You see the same thing in Algeria, where a lot of those weird massacres by "Islamic militants" are done by soldiers dressed up like imams to discredit the Islamic parties.)

Of course, the false-flag deal works both ways, so sometimes the rebel groups put on government uniforms and kill a few people, just to keep the peasants from trusting the government.

Are you beginning to get the impression that the life of a Colombian villager is not that restful? They probably piss their pants with fear every time they hear a truck coming toward the village: Which anthem should they sing when it pulls up? "*Madre de dios,* do we put up the Che Guevara poster or the crucifix?"

Killing poor, dumb peasants, pulling out their teeth with pliers—that's what the war in Colombia comes down to. It's the kinda stuff that gives war a bad name. And we're supposed to send American GIs to wade into this stinking Manson Family of a country? It's not like the Colombians need our help to kill each other. They do it just fine on their own—always have, always will.

SHINING PATH:
THE COMEBACK TOUR

SOMETHING KIND OF surprising happened in Peru in July 2003. An army patrol was ambushed by Shining Path guerrillas in the Ayacucho Valley, a patch of nearly vertical jungle on the east side of the Andes. The ambush wasn't much in classic military terms, seven soldiers killed and another ten wounded out of a thirty-man patrol. It was over in a few minutes. The troops didn't see anybody and probably didn't hit a single guerrilla. Not the kind of battle war buffs like to reenact. But it could be the start of something big.

I'm not sure if anybody still remembers the Shining Path these days. It was always a weird bunch of people, even by guerrilla warfare standards, but it was big back in the late 1980s to early 1990s. For a while, Shining Path guerrillas were on the attack all over Peru.

Then in 1992, the government finally grabbed their leader. He turned out to be an ex-professor named Abimael Guzman. Shining Path without Guzman was like the Doors without Jim Morrison: totally worthless. Guzman ranted and raved for a few weeks, and then, surprise-surprise, he saw the light and decided to work with the government for a peaceful solution. I wonder how many of his fingernails they had to pull out before he changed his mind.

Peruvian Psy-Ops officers figured that Guzman was so important to Shining Path that they hired fashion designers—I'm not kidding here—to make clothes that'd make him look totally stupid when they put his trial on TV. These designers noticed Guzman had gotten fat—all those years of hiding out, no exercise. So they put him in big, wide, horizontal stripes. I've seen the video of him on trial. He looks like a big fat Latino bumblebee. And that did the trick. Nobody would follow him once they saw him in those horizontal stripes. I'm telling you, life's not easy for a fat man.

For ten years, Shining Path was quiet. You may remember that in 1996, some guerrillas raided the Japanese ambassador's house in Lima and took hostages. Well, that wasn't Shining Path. It was this other revolutionary group, Tupac Amaru. No, not the dead rapper. Tupac Amaru was an Inca king who fought the Spanish. The rapper was named after the Inca, not the other way around—got it, all you ignorant MTV casualties out there?

By all accounts, the Tupac Amaru rebels are the nice, easygoing type of guerrillas. It sure seems that way, considering what happened at the Jap's house. After a couple of months, some specially trained "Peruvian Special Forces" smashed their way in, killed all the Tupac guerrillas, and set everybody free.

It wouldn't have turned out so nice if Shining Path had been holding the hostages. They were always the not-nice type of guerrilla. More the kill-everybody-and-their-dog type. In fact, Shining Path used dogs to announce its debut. When Guzman decided the time was right to start military operations, he told his cadre to hang dead dogs from all the lampposts in every city in Peru. It was some kind of secret sign that he got out of Chairman Mao, something about "running dogs of Imperialism." It made quite an impression, but it seems like a pretty crummy thing to do to the dogs. The way I see it, people have it coming, but dogs deserve a break. Poor bastards.

Guzman started way back, back in the 1960s. He was one of those hippie professors who was poisoning kids' heads with Mao and Marx, but one thing you have to give him: He read his Little Red Book a lot more carefully than all the other campus Maoist types did. He got Mao's biggest message, which is patience. Take your time. Be nice to the peasants. Win 'em over. Live in their stinking huts, eat their rotten food, show respect, and so on.

People don't realize how long it takes to organize a guerrilla war. I get letters saying, "Just stick to the military stuff!" Well, that may work with conventional war, but most of the wars going now are as irregular as a bear that raided an Ex-lax warehouse. And you can't stick to the military side in irregular warfare. It hardly even matters. Mao lost a lot of territory to Chiang, to the Japs. But he had a little poem that explained his philosophy:

"Keep men, lose land–
Land can be taken again.
Keep land, lose men–
Land and men both lost."

So Mao is the original advocate of the so-called Hearts and Minds
Strategy. Guzman learned his lesson and worked on organization
for fifteen years before his guerrillas fired a shot. He took all his
radical students out to the villages where the Inca peasants lived;
he hunkered down with the villagers and won them over.

To see how that could happen, you have to realize how bad these
people were living. Peru just never had one good day in history,
ever. The Incas were just plain weird, with their rope notes and
rope bridges and whatever. And then Pizarro comes in and, with
a few dozen Spanish soldiers, kills the Inca emperor, steals all the
gold, and puts the peasants to work in the gold and silver mines
as slaves. No pay, no nothing, just the whip if you slow down and
the sword if you complain. Nobody knows how many Indians died
in those mines, but it's well into seven figures. Then it's the usual
Latin American transition from Spanish rule to the local Mestizos
taking over–except the locals treat the Indians just as bad as the
Spanish did and nothing changes.

Hell, at the altitude some of those Quechua live, you can't even
say, "The air is free," because there's barely enough oxygen to
go around. Life is corn and potatoes and not much of either. All
they've got is the coca leaves–they chew 'em with a piece of coal
and go around drooling big, black ropes of cocaine spit. If somebody
calls you an Indian (*indio*) in Peru, you're supposed to be ashamed.
If you're a Quechua who wants to move up, George and Weezie
Jefferson style, you turn into a *cholo*. (That sure ain't what *cholo*
meant where I come from, but hey . . .)

So it made a big impression on the Inca peasants when all these
rich, shiny white people from the cities came to their villages and told
them about a workers' paradise, where everybody would be equal.

By the time Guzman gave his cadre the word to start the war in 1980, he had a big, strong network in place all over Peru. The revolution hit high gear around 1985. For five or six years, Shining Path looked unbeatable. It was strong in the cities as well as the villages. And the members were smart, adaptable guerrillas who added some techniques of their own. Like shawls and dynamite. One thing Peru has plenty of is dynamite—all those mines means a lot of blasting. And the other thing it has is Quechua women in big shawls. So Shining Path taught women how to turn their shawls into slings. They'd light a stick of dynamite, throw it in their shawls, whirl it to get some torque, and let fly at the target. They bombed embassies, ambushed army units, killed villagers who didn't want to join and just generally raised Hell all over Peru. It wasn't pretty, but it was working.

Then the cops found Guzman, and the movement just seemed to collapse. Now, that's a little odd. A lot of revolutionary movements have kept going after the big, charismatic leader gets captured. So why the sudden collapse after they got Guzman? Maybe it was the way Psy-Ops (with some CIA help) made Guzman look so lame in his bumblebee suit. But maybe it goes back further. If you remember learning about the Incas in elementary school (do they still make kids do that in California? I sure had to), you might recall that once the Inca himself, the emperor, got captured, everything stopped dead. No more resistance. From then on, the Spanish were able to order millions of Inca peasants around like cattle. So maybe the way Shining Path stopped dead after Guzman was captured is just the way Inca culture works.

Or maybe they can find a new Guzman, a new Inca. It's happened before. The Spanish killed Atahualpa, the Inca emperor, in 1532. But Tupac Amaru started a revolt against the Spanish in 1780. That's right—250 years after the conquest, right when America was fighting the British, the Incas were still fighting the Spanish.

These people are patient. You can stomp them for a while, but like Ah-nold, they'll be back. Maybe in another 250 years or so, they'll finally win one.

HAITI: THE BIG HATE

HAITI'S GOT TO be the most amazing, blood-soaked, heroic, messed-up story in the Western Hemisphere: slave armies defeating Napoleon's troops; huge castles built in the middle of the jungle; endless three-cornered war between whites, blacks, and mulattos . . . it's just incredible. In fact, it's so wild and complex that the whole story could fill a book. I'll start by covering Haiti up to independence in 1803; then I'll bring it from there to the present.

You might remember we had Haiti all fixed up back in the Clinton days. Our boy was Jean-Bertrand Aristide, a "slum priest" who went around sharing lice with the po' folks and generally out-holying Mother Theresa. Except Mother Theresa never lived in Haiti. If she had, she'd have been more like the lady who started the Lord's Resistance Army in Uganda—she'd have told her followers to go out there and spread the word with Kalashnikovs and pangas.

That's what happened to Bill Clinton's tame saint, this Aristide. He won the elections; then the local thugs dumped him. And instead of letting Haiti do things the good old Haitian way, Clinton sent in U.S. troops in 1994 to put Aristide back in charge.

Well, it's more than ten years later, and Haiti's still Haiti. Just a few years ago, in 2004, there was a classic story: Some gang calling itself a resistance army took over Gonaives, which one story billed as "the fourth-largest city in Haiti." Whoa, there's a slogan to bring the tourists running: fourth-largest city in Haiti.

This "army" said it was fighting against Aristide's government, which it accused of incompetence, brutality, and corruption. In other words, acting like every other Haitian government in history.

Then it came out that the heroic Revolutionary Artibonite Resistance Front just went through a little PR makeover of its own. Yup, it seems they used to call themselves the Cannibal Army. That was probably the perfect name for stage one of a Haitian revolution: Scare the Hell out of everybody. By getting their name changed to the Resistance Front, they were just doing what comes naturally: trying to put a shine on the ol' machetes, make the struggle look noble.

In a way, the only sad thing about Haiti is the way we keep trying to make it into Ohio. Because it never will be, and we only look ridiculous trying, giving the local killers fancy, democratic names. If we just let Haiti be Haiti—a crazy, brave, blood-soaked voodoo kingdom—people might learn to respect the place. I have, after reading up on it. Haiti has one of the wildest histories I've come across anywhere, and it's not just killing, either. A lot of Haitian leaders were brilliant guys who weren't afraid of anybody—not Napoleon, not Jesus, not nobody. They were self-made, black Roman emperors. They came up the hard way, out of slavery in the cane fields, and beat the European armies that tried to take the place back. French, British, Spanish—the Haitians took them all on and put the fear into them. The only people Haitians can't beat is themselves, and that's nothing for soldiers to be ashamed of.

We've made them ashamed, though, by telling them the only way to be worth anything in this world is by working in offices, wearing dress shirts, and watching TV. Goddamn, does my life suck: If I had a little more of a tan, then Haiti and a job in the Cannibal Army would look like a pretty good career option.

Unfortunately for me, they don't want white guys. Jean-Jacques Dessalines, one of the scariest men who ever ruled Haiti with a bloody machete, said it pretty clearly when it came to racial policy: "For the Haitian declaration of independence, we should use a white man's skin for parchment, his skull for an inkwell, his blood for ink, and a bayonet for a pen!"

It kinda reminds me of what it was like going to high school in Long Beach, Mister White Minority, aka punching bag. Every time a rerun of *Roots* was going to be shown on TV, I'd stay home sick—sick of getting the crap beat out of me in the halls.

I'd probably make a good parchment—you know, lots of room for any added clauses the lawyers want you to put in at the last minute—but even data entry has got to be better than having a Haitian committee writing on my back with a bayonet.

Of course, there's lots of big racial talk in the world, and not much of it means anything. That's what I respect about Haiti: They mean every goddamn word. Take Dessalines; his men killed every paleface they could catch. They were following a good Haitian tradition, dating back to the big slave rebellions, when the black rebels used a white baby stuck on a pike as their flag. Now that's serious people. You see where all this Cannibal Army stuff comes from.

And they've got reasons to be pissed off. Once you start getting into Haitian history, you find out why people play rough down there: because somebody else played way rough with them. Play the tape as far back as you want, and there's always some badder gang moving in and stomping the Haitians into hamburger.

It was going on when Columbus arrived. Hispaniola, the island that Haiti and the Dominican Republic share, was a paradise when he got there. The locals were a tribe called the Taino, a branch of the Arawaks, who were by all accounts these cool, relaxed people who believed in free love, the Dick Gregory Bahamian diet, and hanging out on the beach. Like stone-age hippies. Columbus hated to leave—for one thing, the Arawaks had no problem handing over their wives to the Europeans for a week or so—but he had to report back to Isabella, so he left some men, who started building a settlement. By the time he got back, the place was burned to the ground by the Caribs, a cannibal tribe that thought *Arawak* meant "barbecue." They ate Columbus's men too—a little white meat for variety—and moved on. Soon there were so few Arawaks left that the price per pound was too high, even for a Carib planning a big backyard cookout. And in a couple of generations, there were no Arawaks at all.

Then instant karma kicked in, when the Spanish came back with more men and more guns and wiped out the Caribs. The Caribs went out in style: The last few just jumped off cliffs instead of letting the Europeans capture them and put them to work on the sugar cane plantations they were setting up.

Well, that meant a shortage of free labor, which cut into the profit margin. So the plantation owners started buying Africans.

Lots and lots of Africans. Nobody's sure how many, but it's well into seven figures. Most of them died on the voyage, or under the whip, or from disease, but there were enough left to keep the cane plantations going.

And that was important, not just to the local colonists but to France, which ruled the whole island back then. You have to remember, the Europeans were focused on the West Indies in those days. They didn't think much of North America at the start of the 1700s. It was just a big, cold wilderness with no gold and no potential for raising the tropical crops that really made money. Barbados meant more to England than Virginia did, and Hispaniola meant more to France than Canada meant.

Cotton hadn't come in yet. It was sugar cane that made the big money. And sugar is a really labor-intensive crop. It's also some of the worst work in the world, by all accounts. One ex-cutter said harvesting sugar cane was like trying to cut fiberglass poles all day with your bare hands. You come home full of slashes, cuts, bits of bamboo jammed into your hands and arms and face.

Twelve, fourteen, hours of that a day, every day, with a white guy on a horse whipping your enthusiasm up every time you stop to wipe the sweat out of your eyes. And then, lucky you, you get to go home to a cage and a bowl of corn mush before sacking out for a few hours. Then it's up at the crack of dawn, or rather the whip, and back into the fields.

That was life for black Haitians for a long, long time. And it got them seriously pissed off. The revolts started early and just kept on coming.

Now this is a weird thing, the way the Haitian slaves kept on fighting back. Because—and I'm sorry to be so un-PC here, but it's the truth—slaves in the British possession didn't revolt much. There never was a big, serious slave revolt in the U.S. South, for example. Not even when the Union troops got close. Even then the slaves did what their masters told them to do.

But the French didn't do as good a job of breaking down the new slaves. The English in Jamaica, Barbados, and the Southern colonies of North America made sure the slaves from different tribes were mixed up. The Brits made it punishable by flogging or worse to speak African languages, and they forced the blacks to find Christ or die. (Ah, you gotta love those evangelical assholes!)

The French were sloppy. They let slaves from the same tribes stay together and speak their African languages. They let escaped slaves set up their own villages way inside the tropical forests. They let the slaves keep up African religions—that's what voodoo is. And they started up a separate mulatto class.

The mulattos are the hardest thing for Americans to understand about Haiti. The thing is, everybody's racist, everybody in the damn world—but different countries are racist in different ways. Example: I was watching *Da Ali G Show*, and he's messing with some stuffed-shirt Oxford guy who says to Ali, "Well, you're only saying that because you're black." I'm watching, thinking, "He's not even brown. He's barely tan!" Well, that's because the U.K. has its own rules for racism, where I guess anybody who's not totally white is black.

American racism down South was kind of like that. If you had any black blood, you were black. That was it, period. You were a nigger, and not a person.

The French didn't do it that way. They had this half-and-half class, the mulattos, who were free, could get rich, could even get educated. And the French treated them sort of like semi–human beings. So the mulattos started identifying with the French, trying to be French, and then getting mad when they were kept out of power. Sometimes they backed the French, sometimes the slaves. They were the wild card—they could go either way.

So when the rebellions started around 1750, you had this wild, amazing, totally messed-up little island full of crazy people who were all going crazy in different ways. Out in the forests are escaped slaves still speaking African languages, doing voodoo, and sharpening their machetes. On the plantations are hundreds of thousands of black slaves getting worked to death under the whip—and they've got machetes, too. In the cities and in little towns are the mulattos, who speak French and wear those George-Washington three-cornered hats and want a bigger piece of the pie. On top of them is a thin layer of jumpy French colonists who have a shoot-first-ask-questions-later attitude with any slave who gets an attitude. And on top of them are a few French government types who keep trying to put the whole mess back under control and make it a nice, comfortable French province.

Guess what? It blowed up. It blowed up real good. The first big explosion was in 1751. When a voodoo priest stirred up the escaped slaves in the forest, they attacked the settlements. The field slaves joined them, and six thousand people died before the French captured the voodoo priest and burned him at the stake. And what saved the French was that this time, the mulattos weighed in against the rebels. The mulattos didn't like these crazy African voodoo guerrillas any more than the French did. They just wanted to eat their croissants and talk about *l'amour* with the white folks.

Things were quiet for a while—that is, just slaves being whipped to death, runaway slaves burning down isolated settlements, small stuff. Then came the French Revolution. Kaboom! All Hell breaks loose, not just in Europe, but everywhere the French had colonized. The radicals in Paris order that any mulatto who owns land can vote and be a citizen. The local colonists say no way.

So this time it's the mulattos who revolt, in 1790. And the funny part is that this time, the black slaves get payback on their light-skinned ex-friends by joining the French to stomp the rebel mulattoes. See what I mean? A three-sided fight is a *lot* more complicated than a simple two-man bout, and all the Haitian wars were three-sided.

Then in 1791, just one year after they helped the French crush the mulatto rebellion, the blacks started their own. It was the big one, with a half-dozen brilliant guerrilla commanders, some of them noble and decent men like Toussaint-Louverture, and others just plain scary, like Jeannot, the guy whose armies marched with a white baby on a pike as their flag.

They had a simple policy: Kill every white you find, and burn everything. They torched the whole island. Ships at sea said the place was smoking, literally, for months.

Then the vultures dropped in: The Spanish and British landed to take advantage of the chaos and divide the island between them. By this time, everybody was killing everybody. There were even black slaves fighting to restore the French king. Toussaint, the smartest of the rebellion's leaders, decided Haiti would be better off making a deal with the radicals in Paris than with the Spanish and British, who'd reestablished slavery everywhere they went. He joined the French forces, kicked the Spanish and British out, and beat the mulattos under Rigaud. He was in charge until Napoleon came into power.

Napoleon had plans for the island. And he had a surplus brother-in-law, Charles LeClerc, who he was sick of seeing around the home office in Paris. So it was the old story: The boss sends his useless brother-in-law on a long business trip to get him out of sight. LeClerc landed in Haiti in 1802 with twenty thousand men. Toussaint, who was definitely the noblest man in the whole mess, surrendered to avoid more slaughter. The French made him a lot of promises, broke them in about five seconds, and sent Toussaint to France in chains, where he died in a freezing dungeon a couple of years later.

And that was the last good guy in the story. From here on, it's just bad guys versus worse guys, versus even worse guys, versus guys who would scare Charles Manson.

But there was one last twist before the next cycle of killing. Haiti got its independence after all, in 1803, only a year after Toussaint was tricked and captured. LeClerc's army was vanishing, dying in hundreds from every tropical disease. LeClerc himself died of yellow fever. Meanwhile, Napoleon was getting ready to kick some major ass in Europe, and he lost interest in America. It was right then, if you recall, that he sold Louisiana to Jefferson for three cents an acre, a good buy except for Mississippi, which I personally wouldn't pay even one cent per square mile for.

With Louisiana sold off and his army dead or dying, Napoleon cut his losses. LeClerc's replacement fled to Jamaica with what was left of his troops—he figured he was safer surrendering to the British than to the Haitians. Haiti was—ta-da!—a free country.

Oh, but the fun was just starting. Haitian history just won't stop happening. Aristide, Clinton's great black hope, was booted out. By 2007, René Préval was president, but if you don't like him, just wait; another dude'll be along in a minute.

Whatever's happening now in Haiti, whatever happens there next week, it's all happened before. Usually a dozen times before. The names and the casualty figures change, but the basic plot never does.

Here's an example—a news story on Haiti. You tell me the date: "A revolt began in the provinces . . . The city of Gonaives was the first to have street demonstrations and raids on food-distribution warehouses. From October to January, the protests spread to six other cities . . . By the end of that month, Haitians in the south had revolted . . . "

If you guessed sometime in 2007, you lose. This story was from 1986. There are others a lot like it from other years, going back a long, long time. Whatever's happening in Haiti, it's happened before and never did any good. This is one place where things can always get worse, but never better.

Weird how nobody remembers. Not even me. I was watching TV back in 1986, paying pretty close attention to foreign military news. In fact, I wasn't doing much else. And I remember lots of big news stories from back then. But whatever they showed about Haiti, I must've just shrugged it off. And we'll all forget this latest ruckus just as fast. A few months from now, you can win any trivia contest by asking "Who was Aristide?" I guarantee, nobody'll remember his name.

Right now, the United States is still pretending to care about what happens to the Haitians, talking a lot of crap about establishing democracy. And we're doing something we've also done lots of times before: sending in the marines.

Nobody remembers that the U.S. Marines were the most stable, long-term government Haiti ever saw. They were in charge from 1915 to 1934. It was Woodrow Wilson, one of our all-time do-gooder presidents and a big backer of little nations, who sent them to Haiti. Things had just gotten a little too bloody for Woody to tolerate.

The Haitians were having one of their more colorful periods. In 1912, the president of Haiti was blown up in an explosion that may or may not have been accidental. The next four contenders died or fled, leaving the presidential chair vacant just long enough for a really crazy specimen named Vilbrun Guillaume Sam, who grabbed it in March 1915.

Sam was not what you'd call a champion of democratic process. Within four months, he'd rounded up 167 personal enemies. Then he had them shot.

The people took to the streets looking for Sam's hide. He hid behind the drapes at the French embassy. The French were still trying to explain the details of international law to the mob when they broke in, dragged Sam out from behind the potted plants, and tore him limb from limb. You don't get much chance to use that phrase, "limb from limb," and really mean it. But that's what they did. They were so proud of themselves they had a parade, with Sam's arms, legs, head, and torso like Rose Bowl floats.

Wilson, one of these sour, serious Presbyterian types, was appalled. He forgot all his talk about nonintervention and told the marines to go down there and give the Haitians order and democracy if they had to crack every head in the country to do it.

From 1915 to 1934, the U.S. commander ruled the country with a figurehead Haitian as president. For almost twenty years, the marines kept Haiti more peaceful and prosperous than it had ever been. They wiped out malaria; built a bunch of roads, bridges, and other U.S. Army Corps of Engineers trademark boondoggles; and kept the hotheads under control.

But the locals weren't totally happy. For one thing, the white American troops didn't discriminate the way the "Haitian elite" expected. The "elite" was mulatto and spoke French. They considered themselves way superior to the "blacks," the pure-African peasants who spoke Creole and did all the actual work. Naturally, these mulattos expected to collaborate with the foreign whites to keep the blacks down where they belonged, and the so-called elites were outraged when the marines made it clear that as far as the Americans could see, everybody in Haiti was just plain black.

This is what they call poetic justice, I guess. It got a lot less poetic, though, when the marines left in 1934. A creep named Vincent took power, made up a new constitution naming him King of Everything for Life, and started sleazy dealings with an even bigger creep named Rafael Trujillo, who was King for Life in the Dominican Republic, on the east side of the island.

This Trujillo was a classic 1930s fascist. He used more skin lightener than Michael Jackson and decided that he and his fellow Dominicans were Aryans, whereas those dirty Haitians across the border were nothing but a bunch of uncivilized blacks.

In 1937, just when Hitler was shifting into high gear in Europe, Trujillo decided to have a little holocaust of his own. He ordered the Dominican army to kill all the Haitians they could catch in the border zone. One of the ways they could tell they had Haitians was when they asked people to say *perejil*. If you couldn't trill your *r*'s like they taught you in Spanish class, you got the chop. Literally, because Trujillo told his soldiers to use machetes, not rifles. That way, he could say it was enraged local peasants who did the killing. And besides, bullets cost money.

Nobody cared about all those dead Haitians. Didn't even notice. The world was too worried about what was going on in Europe. (This was back when Europe actually mattered.) And to put it cold-bloodedly, nobody ever has cared much what happens to the Haitians, anyway. The United States demanded that Trujillo pay reparations, which he bargained down to $500,000, which if my calculator is right comes to $25 per head.

The Americans who tried to fix Haiti up were no idiots. After all, Franklin Roosevelt wrote the Haitian constitution when he was secretary of the navy, and Woodrow Wilson was an impressive guy, kind of like Jimmy Carter with testicles. But it just didn't take. After the marines left in 1934, the Haitian army was about the only thing that was still running properly.

From 1934 to 1957, Haiti was even messier than usual. It was Coups "R" Us, with more name changes than the Golden State Warriors' coaching staff. And about as much success, too.

A humble, smiling, little black country doctor, François Duvalier, was the one man who figured out a way to bring the whole country under his control.

Problem number one was the army, because it could and did overthrow any president who got uppity. Problem number two was bonding with the big "black" population, who didn't know or care who was running the cities. Duvalier started by courting the black peasants. He talked a lot of "black and proud" stuff and got officially interested in voodoo, which made the peasants feel like he was a homeboy and scared the Hell out of them as well, since Duvalier let it be known that he was in touch with some very scary spirits.

Then he took on the army. It had put him in charge; now he wanted to make sure it could never take him out. He announced that he was president for life, but that didn't impress anybody. He was the eighth Haitian to claim that title. It meant about as much as a Don King title bout.

Duvalier wasn't just woofing, though. He took two classic power-consolidating steps—so any of you wannabe dictators out there, get your Palm Pilots out and take notes. First, he set up a presidential guard, separate from the army and packed with his own men. Second, he started a second armed force, a counterweight to the army. Think Saddam's Republican Guard, Khomeini's Islamic Revolutionary Guard/Pasdaran, or Mao's Red Guard.

Duvalier's group was just as ruthless as any, but a lot more horror-movie fun. He'd done his homework in Haitian voodoo stories, and he organized a gang he called the Tonton Macoute, which means "bogeyman." The Macoutes fanned out through the cane fields, became something between a protection racket, a voodoo cult, and a Duvalier private army. They were the coolest, scariest thing to hit rural Haiti since George Romero moved the zombie movie north. Every red-blooded Haitian boy wanted to be a boogeyman. There weren't too many other exciting career options: cut cane all day in the heat, come home to a one-room shed, catch a simple cold and die for lack of medicine. You can see why getting to be a voodoo disciple/ninja assassin kind of had appeal.

While the Macoutes kept the countryside terrified, the presidential guard rode herd on Port-au-Prince. And "Papa Doc" ruled over all of it, smiling for the cameras and killing anybody who even looked cross-eyed at him. He did away with at least thirty thousand people—and the peasants still loved him.

They gave him the ultimate compliment any dictator can get: He died in power. And the system he'd set up was so strong that even his idiot fat son, Jean-Claude, managed to survive in power for fifteen years. He would've died in office, too, but he was so stupid he married a snotty mulatto girl the peasants hated, then spent $3 million on the wedding while sugar prices were falling through the dirt floor.

In 1986, it finally boiled over. A rising started in . . . Can you recall which city? Right: Gonaives. It spread south, right on cue. The Americans urged the Haitian president to leave. He fled the country, and a new regime came in, proud as punch, promising to "rid Haiti of corruption."

See what I mean? You don't need to write a new Haiti news story. Just take the old ones and change the dates.

MASSACRES PAID YOUR MORTGAGE, DUDE

WHERE DO YOU live? Now answer fast: Who lived there three hundred years ago? The reason you can live there without asking some chief's permission is that your tribe wiped out their tribe. Primitive warfare paid the mortgage on your house, dude. And it happened every bit as cold-bloodedly as it's happening in Africa right now.

Take Montana. Now it's vacation land for every Hollywood leftie, but 150 years ago, it was up for grabs. As the Anglos muscled in on them, North American tribes fought, negotiated, or ran. Those who fought lost. They won some battles along the way, but they were little tribes against the Anglos, the biggest and scariest tribe in the world. The tribes that negotiated knew from the start that the stronger tribe always takes what it wants, sooner or later. Those who ran faced the same old problem: The only places you could run to were already claimed by other tribes. The only solution, in the simple, hard rules of primitive warfare, was to wipe out the other tribe.

That was how the Sioux decided to wipe out the Crow in 1860. The Sioux were fierce people. Don't believe that Kevin-Costner-*Dances-with-Wolves* bullshit. The Sioux ate wolves for breakfast. They took what they wanted—land, horses, slaves—from anybody they could. But they were already beginning to realize they couldn't fight the white men. Basically, it was the Navajo versus Ute story on a bigger scale: Farmers always beat hunters in the long run, because agriculture can feed so many more mouths. The nomadic, buffalo-hunting Sioux were some of the finest light irregular cavalry in the world—Genghis Khan would've admired them. But they couldn't cope with the sheer numbers of white farmers overrunning the Sioux lands on the plains.

The Crow tribe's country, in eastern Montana and Wyoming, was still beyond the range of the whites, so the Sioux decided to wipe out the Crow and take their land. The Sioux chief made a speech setting out the strategic goals of primitive warfare with classic simplicity:

> Today when the sun sets, there will be no more Absarokee [Crow] left! We will kill all their warriors and even the old men; we will save their young boys and raise them to become Dakota [Sioux] warriors, and we shall marry their wives and daughters to raise more warriors to fight the whites when they follow us to our new land.

It was a sound plan. It failed because the Crow got word of it. They were waiting when the Sioux attacked. There was a battle—

which wasn't part of the Sioux plan—at Pryor Creek near where Billings, Montana, is now, and the Sioux were beaten. One of the ironies of the battle is that Pryor Creek feeds the Bighorn River, where the Sioux would later win their greatest victory against the whites, wiping out Custer's entire force, sixteen years after losing at Pryor Creek.

Even if the Sioux had taken the Crow's lands, it wouldn't have done them much good; by 1900 the Crow, the Sioux, and all the other Plains tribes were destroyed. The mismatch was too complete. In a classic primitive-warfare scenario like those in Africa, the Sioux would have been wiped out, with a few boys spared to be raised as members of the conquering tribe. And that's pretty much what happened: The remnants of the tribes were corralled and pushed onto the least desirable land anybody could find, with their kids sent to U.S. government boarding schools to learn Anglo culture.

The famous massacres, like the one at Wounded Knee in 1890, where three hundred uncorralled Sioux were shot down by the Seventh Cavalry (which was still a little steamed about Custer), are usually treated as shocking, evil things, senseless outbreaks of savagery. That's just nonsense. Massacre is standard primitive-warfare policy for handling prisoners from defeated tribes, especially if they get ornery.

The Sioux who died at Wounded Knee were hard to handle. They were followers of the new Ghost Dance religion. Religion is the last refuge of defeated tribes. The Byzantines spent their last days praying, when the Turkish cannons were blasting down the walls of the city. The Sioux turned to Wovoka, a Ute "messiah" who had the word from God that if the Plains Indians danced the Ghost Dance, their ancestors would return, wipe out the whites, and put the Indians back in total control.

If you read what the Ghost Dancers were preaching, you can see that they saw the situation in classic primitive-warfare terms: wiping out the other side totally. If they could've done it militarily, they would've; instead, they dreamed about it.

Wovoka's vision was counter-genocide, pure and simple: God

was going to create a new layer of soil thirty feet deep, and all the whites were going to be buried under it—instant fossilization. The new soil would make excellent grazing—lots of paleface fertilizer down there—for the buffalo that God was going to spread across the prairies, and the Indians would inherit the earth.

In other words, both sides were talking genocide, because that's the point of all primitive warfare.

We Americans can't seem to face facts like that. We're not as consciously cold-blooded or clearheaded as the Brits, who did hundreds of Wounded Knees all over the world without flinching or losing any sleep, either.

We had to lie to ourselves about it—first one lie, then the opposite one. Right after the "battle" of Wounded Knee, Congress went into a frenzy of patriotic bullshit. It handed out more than a dozen Congressional Medals of Honor, the highest decoration our country has, to troopers who died in the "fight," even though most accounts of the battle agree that the Cav's casualties were almost certainly caused by friendly fire. The troopers had made one of the most basic mistakes you can make in an ambush. They surrounded the Sioux encampment from all sides, so when they started firing, anything that missed its target (and that included two Hotchkiss rapid-fire cannon that could get off almost a round per second) was likely to hit the troopers across the way.

Then, a few generations later, when the Plains were safely turned into farmland, the media started telling the opposite lie, turning the Sioux into heroes and the Seventh Cav into monsters.

It really pisses me off, the way these Kevin Costner types romanticize rebel tribes, once they're safely annihilated. It's been happening for hundreds of years, too. The Brits totally wiped out the Scottish Highland tribes—and they were tribes—after they rebelled in 1745. It was merciless, classic primitive warfare: men hanged on the battlefield, farms burned to the ground, kids dragged away to be trained as Englishmen, the native Scottish language and songs forbidden by law. And then, once England was sure the Highlanders were gone, it started romanticizing everything about them, even those dumb skirts the Highland men wore because they were too dumb to make pants that fit.

When I was growing up, my teachers tried to make the Sioux into saints and the Seventh Cav into murderers. I had to read *Bury My Heart at Wounded Knee* in high school, and if my teacher had heard me even hint that it wasn't a good-versus-evil story, she'd have expelled me on the spot. Everybody had a great time crying for the poor Indians—but I noticed nobody said anything about giving them California back.

A BOY NAMED DOROTEO:
THE LIFE AND WARS OF PANCHO VILLA

EVERYBODY'S SCREECHING ABOUT beefing up the Mexican border, but if they knew a little more about the long history of Gringo-Mexican scuffles, they'd realize this is one of the quieter times along the Rio Grande. The really serious border panic was back in 1916, when irregular Mexican troops commanded by a bandit (or guerrilla, depending on your team loyalties) named Pancho Villa raped and pillaged a whole New Mexico town, overran a U.S. cavalry encampment, and forced President Woodrow Wilson to station seventy-five thousand troops along the border. Compare that with the piddling five thousand that G.W. Bush wants to commit to border patrol, and you can see how much scarier things were back when Pancho was our Spanish-speaking Osama on horseback.

Of course, there've been tribal rumbles between Anglos and Mexicans for hundreds of years, and so far, we've won most of them. That's why the border's on the Rio Grande instead of, say, Arkansas: We pushed it way west and south in what we call *the* Mexican War of 1846–1848. Most war buffs know at least a little about that war, but people seem to know more about German or British military history than they do about the guerrilla war run by the great Pancho. And as for the Mexican Civil War that drove Villa to become a border outlaw, hardly anybody knows anything about it, even though the decisive battle of that war, Celaya, rates as the third-bloodiest battle ever fought in the Western Hemisphere.

Villa commanded the losing side at that battle, and it was his defeat at Celaya that started him on his comeback career harassing Gringos along the Rio Grande. Pancho had already come a long way by the time he gambled and lost at Celaya. He started life with a lot of minuses, such as being born a Mexican peasant in the northern deserts of Durango, and being christened "Doroteo Arango." You can't blame him for wanting out.

Little Doroteo tried working in the fields and didn't like it. So he took the one available road to stardom: becoming a bandito. Of course, later on his fans said he'd only become an outlaw after killing a landlord who'd raped his sister, but you get that kind of story about Jesse and Frank James, too. Whenever a country boy went on to glory as a highwayman in 1800s America (north or south of the border), people started making up campfire songs and stories about him as a Robin Hood-meets-Mother Theresa who just happened to shoot people, which was their own fault anyway for getting between him and the money.

Doroteo joined up with a local outlaw band that happened to be led by a guy named . . . Pancho Villa. And when the original gangsta Pancho was killed in a shootout, Doroteo not only took over the gang but decided that Pancho wouldn't be needing his name any more, and took that, too.

He'd made the right career choice. Banditry was the only growth industry in Mexico in early-twentieth-century Mexico. It was a bad time even by local standards. Not that there have been a lot of Golden Eras in Mexico, but 1910-1920 was a total mess, thanks to a 1910 revolution against the dictator Diaz. The revolution started with a lot of talk about "the people" and "democracy" and turned, naturally, into bloody chaos with a lot of little warlords who were in the habit of burning and looting villages that didn't pay them protection money. All this was in the name of Declarations and Coalitions and other PR, but what was really going on was betrayal after betrayal; a dude named Huerta had another dude named Madero shot, and then this guy Carranza had Huerta exiled, and so on.

At ground level, it all meant that Mexico was in nonstop combat, with a phase they called Civil War (1910–1914) sliding smoothly into Phase Two, the Revolucion, from 1915 to 1920. It was a great time to be a young, heavily armed egomaniac like our Pancho. Even if they'd had an aptitude counselor in his village, no standardized test could have offered him a better option than *pistolero*. He rose fast in the business; by 1914, his little gang of desert bushwhackers had grown into a huge force called the Division del Norte. Most of the division's strength was its cavalry, but it also had its own artillery, infantry, and even a medical corps operating out of specially equipped railway cars.

That force structure tells you something about what a strange form of warfare was going on in Mexico. Cavalry had already been blown off the battlefield in Europe by 1915, but it was still the most powerful arm in Mexico, a huge country with lousy roads. But these horseback armies also had machine guns, the weapon that had wiped cavalry off the Western Front, and a railway-based medical service.

Celaya was like the slogan those Mexican tourist brochures use: "Mexico, where old meets new." The old—cavalry, machismo, charisma—met the new: machine guns and concertina wire. Unfortunately for Pancho, he was representin' old-school: machismo on horseback vs. overlapping fields of fire.

Celaya was definitely one of the weirdest, longest battles on record. It's unlike any other battle I've studied. But then, every great battle has its own flavor. Just take some of the most familiar bouts from our Civil War. The first Bull Run was almost comic, with carriages full of scared D.C. ladies whipping the horses, trying to outrun the Federal infantry back to town. The comedy turned to pure gorefest at Antietam, an all-day stabfest, like a Scorsese film of two guys stabbing each other in an alley from sunrise to sunset. Or take the ironclads' duel in Hampton Roads; that one was like a Japanese monster flick, with the *Monitor* as Godzilla and the *Merrimack* as Mothra duking it out in Tokyo Harbor.

Celaya combines the gory comedy of the First Bull Run with the antifun, hard lessons of WW I trench warfare. The new-school dude who'd learned the lessons of the Western Front was Villa's opponent, lvaro Obregón. Obregón started out as a small farmer in Sonora—Indian country, home of the Mayo and Yaqui tribes. He came from immigrant stock; "Obregón" started out as "O'Brien"; Obregón was the grandson of an Irish railroad worker. He sure looks it in the old photos—a very un-Mexican-looking dude, pale with one of those droopy moustaches that make everybody look like Stephen Stills.

Obregón didn't act like a Mexican guy, either. Most Mexican guys I've known are—how can I say this nicely?—not exactly shy about promoting themselves. They believe in showing *muchos cajones*, which after a couple of Coronas, translates into pretty much nonstop bragging.

Pancho Villa was the ultimate Mexican braggart; Obregón was modest. In his memoirs, instead of bragging about his early heroics, Obregón curses himself for not joining the fight against the Diaz dictatorship sooner, and says his excuses—he had a family to raise, etc.—were nothing but "cunning lies."

That's a real un-Mexican thing to do, accusing yourself like that. Instead of bragging after he beat Villa, he joked that the reason he won is that "fortunately, Villa led the attack personally."

Like most good lines, that was basically true, too. Obregón won at Celaya because he dealt with Villa's macho ways, galloping around Mexico leading cavalry charges, cool-headedly. While Villa was swaggering around making himself a living legend, Obregón was doing his groundwork. Unlike most Spanish-speaking, white-looking Mexicans, he respected the Indios who lived in his part of Sonora. He learned to speak the Mayo and Yaqui languages—and it paid off big in battle, when the Yaquis, big, tough, silent marksmen, became his best and most loyal troops.

He also listened to his German military adviser, Maximilian Kloss. Obregón put Kloss in charge of his heavy weapons, machine guns, and artillery. That was also a very un-Mexican thing to do.

All the big players circa 1915–Villa, Zapata, Carranza–kept a few German military advisers around for show, but only Obregón bothered to listen to what his tame German had to say. So Obregón was the only commander in Mexico who understood that the era of grand cavalry charges–Villa's trademark move, his version of Tyson's right hook–was over, finito, or as Herr Kloss would have said, kaput.

But Obregón's best weapon was a real unglamorous one: barbed wire. People don't appreciate what a powerful device that stuff is. Not the ranchers' version, the kind I used to rip my jeans on climbing fences, but military-issue coils of razor wire. Obregón confiscated 632 rolls of the stuff from a U.S. expeditionary force that briefly occupied Veracruz, and when he gave it to Herr Kloss, the German's eyes just lit up. Give a German officer that much barbed wire, some machine guns, and four batteries of French field artillery, and you can pretty much sleep through the rest of the battle, tell your aides to wake you when it's time for the victory parade.

Ever since the first Scythian got his leather-pants ass up on a horse and realized he could tear around the steppes sticking pedestrians like frogs, infantry commanders have been desperately trying to come up with ways of coping with the striking power of cavalry charges. Along the way, they've invented some nasty, effective devices. My favorite is the caltrops, which looks like a big, sharp-tipped version of the jacks girls used to play with. (Do girls still play with those? Dunno. Kids tend to shy away from me.)

Caltrops were carried in sacks and sown like landmines in front of infantry positions likely to be charged by cavalry. When those tanklike warhorses thundered toward the shield wall, they'd step on a few caltrops and be instantly transformed from Hellbeasts to whinnying ponies, rearing up and throwing their riders, like mechanical bulls during a power surge. It must have just made your average man-at-arms's day, seeing those knights in their expensive armor suddenly grounded, ripe for throat slitting.

But caltrops, and the jumbo versions of them made of sharpened logs, were hard to lug around, heavy, and labor-intensive. Barbed wire was light, expandable—think of a Slinky that would disembowel the kids enjoying its progress downstairs—and lethal to the sort of mass cavalry charge that had made Pancho Villa a legend.

Pancho's men were cowboys, see, real Norteños—*muy macho*, none too bright. A lot of people don't get how different the different parts of Mexico are. Zapata, another big player in the civil war/revolution, came from the far south, where the Indio peasants were submissive plantation slaves. Other Indios, like Obregón's Yaquis, a foot taller and nobody's slaves, would sooner die than kneel down. Then there are the northern desert provinces, Villa's country, where it's like a Mex-Tex world, as full of macho bullshit as the West Wing crew in Crawford.

That macho crap won Pancho a lot of battles, because let's be honest here, a lot of the regular Mexican troops he faced were skittish Indio draftees who barely spoke Spanish and didn't exactly burn with morale. A few hundred bold riders galloping at them full speed with a mile-high dust cloud behind them were enough to make that sort of cannon fodder toss their rifles and hide in the nearest arroyo.

That was the lesson Villa had learned. The lesson he hadn't learned was why good commanders keep a big part of their forces in reserve. Now this is an interesting idea, the reserve, one that kids and amateurs don't get. I admit, when I was a kid, I never got this "reserve" thing, either. Why wouldn't you commit everything to battle? Why keep part of your strength back there, those rectangles with a diagonal line and "R" marking them on battle maps?

The answer's simple: Without a reserve, a commander can't exploit enemy weaknesses that develop in the course of a battle, or bolster his own weak points in time. Pancho found that out the hard way at Celaya.

To be fair, Villa wasn't the only military mind with an "Everybody charge!" fixation. Every major army, circa 1914, was convinced that defense was for pussies and pure élan would win out every time. The French motto was "*L'Audace, toujours l'audace*," meaning basically, "Charge those Kraut machine guns till your intestines are draped across the barbed wire like Christmas tinsel!"

But by 1915, some commanders—not, unfortunately, the ones leading the British, Russian, French, or German armies—had figured out that wire and automatic weapons meant *"l'audace"* translated into *"l'idiotisme!"* and accepted that military tech now favored defense over attack. Obregón, who read everything he could about the Western Front, knew it. Villa, who could barely sign his name, hadn't. Uh-oh, Spaghetti-Os, if you happened to be one of Pancho's cowboys, riding *"Ándale, ándale, arriba, arriba!"* into the machine guns.

Obregón chose defense right off, occupying and fortifying the town of Celaya, about halfway between Guadalajara and Mexico City. The country was perfect for a defender with plenty of ammunition and barbed wire: flat farmland with few trees but lots of ditches and irrigation canals, ready-made trenches for the sort of WW I–style fighting Obregón had in mind.

Just as Obregón had hoped, Villa decided to attack. His smarter aides begged him not to. They pointed out that Obregón had twelve thousand defenders to Villa's eight thousand attackers, a far cry from the textbook three-to-one advantage attackers hope to have. For Villa, macho to the last, it was a matter of pride. He said he had to *"pegarle el Perfumado." El Perfumado* was his term for Obregón, sort of like "wuss," with a hint of "faggot."

Obregón was happy to be underestimated like that. He was counting on it.

Even so, Villa's cavalry won the first round. Obregón had made a big mistake, staking a two-thousand-man force too far outside his lines. Villa's Division del Norte smashed it so hard Obregón had to personally lead an armored train, accompanied by his remaining cavalry, in a rescue mission. The train distracted Villa's men from hunting down Obregón's surviving outpost garrison, but at the end of the first day of battle, April 6, 1915, Obregón sent a gloomy message to HQ, saying his cavalry screen was totally gone.

Villa's troopers drove Obregón's men back into their own lines and followed them in, shooting everything that moved. Obregón had to commit his reserves, and even his own bodyguards, to the lines before Villa's horsemen were pushed back. The tide started to turn as Villa's hotheads kept charging the wire, meeting Kloss's carefully plotted overlapping fields of machine-gun fire.

That night, Villa got the boys together and announced the plan. It was dead simple, way too simple: At dawn, everybody attacks. That was it. When some cooler heads mentioned that their ammunition trains still hadn't arrived, Villa replied, "Our courage will be our ammunition." Here's a helpful hint: If you ever find yourself under a commander who talks like that, flee. The night doesn't belong to Michelob; it belongs to deserters. Just wait till it's nice and dark, and head for the hills, because anyone who says courage is your ammo is just going to get you killed.

Villa's men had guts, though. At dawn they charged the machine guns, got mowed down, and came back for more. When you imagine the battlefield, remember that horses make huge targets, and after an hour, there were so many dead and dying horses in front of Obregón's lines that Villa's men found it hard to pick their way over the mounds of bleeding, shitting, screaming shot horses. I always feel sorry for the horses. I mean, we deserve it—people deserve everything they get—but the horses don't. One thing you have to say for mechanized warfare, it saved a lot of horses from horrible deaths. Tanks don't scream in agony when they get hit.

After a few hours, Villa's charges started to weaken Obregón's lines near the railway. This is exactly where a reserve could have won the battle for Villa. Except the fool didn't have any. Villa saw the weakness, screamed at his men to go for it—but they were busy attacking all along four miles of defensive perimeter, and there was no way they could concentrate their forces on the weak point. Obregón, on the other hand, was able to plug the gap with his reserves. Then, while Villa was galloping around encouraging his boys, he was stunned to see Obregón's cavalry enveloping his right flank, followed by an infantry advance crushing his left.

By midafternoon, Villa had no choice but to retreat. He'd lost three thousand men in two days of fighting. Obregón's losses were much smaller, about six hundred dead. Villa's legend of invincibility was gone.

That should have been the end of the Battle of Celaya. But it was just getting started, thanks to Villa's incredibly swollen ego. Unwilling to admit that he'd lost to "el Perfumado," he went back to bragging. Believe it or not, Villa actually sent a letter to all the Mexican newspapers, all the foreign embassies, and everybody on his Xmas card list, announcing in all-caps rant style that he, Francisco Villa, would fall upon the town of Celaya in three days, sweeping all before him. Obregón must have danced an Irish jig when he got the note. Not only had Villa committed his army to more human-wave slaughter, but he'd actually been considerate enough to tell the enemy when he was coming. Obregón and Kloss had three whole days to go over the field, adjust their fields of fire, and tinker with ways of flooding the fields and otherwise making advance impossible. Obregón even had telephone lines installed, connecting all his subcommands with his HQ.

If you're getting the idea that a twentieth-century army was about to meet a nineteenth-century one, you're right.

By the time battle resumed on April 13, Obregón's forces were about the same size as Villa's, each about thirty thousand men. But Obregón's defenses were much, much stronger. His lines encircled the whole town of Celaya in a twelve-mile perimeter. That afternoon, Villa attacked the western sector, with the usual results: His men were slaughtered, but their pressure did tell on the defenders after a couple of hours. But again, Obregón had the reserves to plug the gaps. In fact, this time he kept a full 40 percent of his force in reserve. Villa, as usual, was unclear on the whole concept and had no reserves at all.

The second day, April 14, was another bloody stalemate, a lot bloodier for Villa's cavalry than Obregón's entrenched infantry. The day ended with heavy rain that delayed the counterattack Obregón was planning.

The next day, Villa's tactical imagination really extended itself: Instead of renewing the attack on Obregón's western perimeter, he decided to hit the southeastern part of the perimeter. As usual, his guys were brave, and then dead, in that order. And as usual, their courage gained them some ground, which was plugged—as usual—by Obregón's reserves. And then came the biggest instant replay of all: While Villa was leading the cheers for his cavalry charges, the rest of Obregón's huge reserve, led by his cavalry, enveloped Villa's left flank—just like it had in the first battle of Celaya, a week earlier. Villa was not a man to learn from his mistakes.

Seeing themselves surrounded again, Villa's men finally figured out that their leader was a conceited fool, and they took the smart option: Drop your rifle and run. Villa's elite bodyguards, the Dorados, were so offended at these *maricones* that they turned their machine guns on the fleeing troops. But it's a funny thing I've noticed about battles: When a rout really takes hold, men will be braver fleeing than they ever were advancing. Villa's men ran through the Dorados' fire just to get away from Obregón's cavalry.

What was left of Villa's army just watched, stunned, as Obregón's men surrounded them. The Villistas surrendered by the thousand—eight thousand prisoners were taken in one day, along with thirty artillery pieces (more than twice what Obregón had). During the second battle, one of Villa's cannon had blown off Obregón's arm, but he survived. It was Villa who was broken as a contender for power. Villa rode back north with what was left of his hard-core Dorados. His only comment was, "I'd rather have lost to a Chinaman than Obregón." 'Scuse me, Pancho, but I believe "Asian American" is the preferred nomenclature.

You can't help but like Villa, though. He's like a cross between Homer Simpson and Spartacus. For instance, when Villa made it back up to Chihuahua to regain his old territory, he found out that the scrip his army made everybody use for money was now worthless. Pancho solved that problem brilliantly, by ordering a printing company in Texas he'd worked with before to print more money.

So far, Villa was chummy with the United States, always willing to buy or sell a little contraband across the border. But after Celaya, that killjoy Woodrow Wilson decided no American firms were allowed to sell weapons to Villa. Wilson was cozying up to the winners at Celaya, distancing himself from the loser in the usual way. Pancho didn't like that, and liked it even less when Obregón's forces closed in on him with the help of U.S. railroad trains. He was in a bad mood already, and this interference by the gringos was getting on his nerves. So in early 1916, he tried to express his dissatisfaction by having a troop of his riders stop a train, drag off eighteen Texans working in Mexico, and shoot them.

This was a big hit with the local peasantry. And remember, irregular warfare like this is closer to scripting a TV show than to classical conventional war. It's all about winning over the local peasants, who thought the idea of all those big-talking Texans pulled off a train and shot was hilarious. So Villa decided to take his act on the road: On March 9, 1916, he and his riders attacked a whole town in New Mexico, a little place called Columbus. They raped, pillaged, looted, and burned in classic irregular-cavalry style. I mean, this is what irregular cavalry units do best: Roar into town screeching, shooting off their pistols and terrorizing the locals. Actually, Villa's men were wimps compared with classic mounted hordes like the Huns or Mongols; only eight civvies were killed in the Columbus raid. Penny-ante stuff, by Genghis Khan standards, but enough to outrage American politicians. After all, it's not every day a mainland American town gets overrun by foreign hordes.

Villa wasn't completely impulsive and improv, though. He'd had spies check out the place long before he brought in his main force. And word had gotten out to the local Mexicans, most of whom found reasons to leave town before the raid. The Anglos never saw it coming, though. The idea that a foreign military force would attack anywhere in the lower forty-eight just didn't occur to them, any more than defending American airspace occurred to the USAF before 9/11.

It's not completely clear why Villa picked Columbus for his debut American raid. There are stories he'd been cheated by a local storekeeper, and it really may have been as simple as that. Villa took things personally; it's why he lost at Celaya. So he was capable of ordering a raid, risking his little force, just to punish a storekeeper for giving incorrect change.

But there's one clear reason any guerrilla commander will instantly understand: There was a U.S. Cavalry base, Camp Furlong, in town. Though they usually avoid conventional forces in pitched battles, guerrillas also need a constant resupply of guns and ammo, and what's a better place to get them than your local military base? It works especially well when the base is as sleepy, as Camp Furlong was. I think this must be where they sent the F Troop guys when the series was canceled. Villa's spies had told him the Thirteenth Cavalry, occupying Camp Furlong, wouldn't be a problem. And they were right. It seems the cav troopers had been partying pretty hard the night before, and they weren't in the mood to play John Wayne when Villa's pistoleros overran the base at four in the morning. Their commander, Colonel Slocum, wasn't even on base.

Villa's men quietly rode north, crossed the border by night, and rendezvoused a mile outside town, dismounting to go over the ground. Villa's officers were survivors of the Dorados, experienced guerrillas; they split into columns to overrun the town and the base from every direction at once. They galloped into the center of town, started looting, and dragged some civvies from the little hotel. One civvie actually managed to survive by figuring out what was going on and shouting, "Viva Mexico!" just as they were about to shoot her. Other locals were too sleepy to remember their high-school Spanish, so they were stood up in the street and shot. See, kids? Studying pays off (which is also the lesson of Celaya, by the way: The nerd Obregón beats the jock Villa).

Eventually the bad-luck Thirteenth Cav managed to get its coffee and aspirin and form up to fight off the invaders. They had help in the form of the huge fire that Villa's men had started in the center of town. With the flames for background, they picked off enough Villistas that the rest decided to advance southward, to the border, as fast as their loot-loaded ponies could carry them. The Villistas lost about a hundred men in the raid, according to the Americans. Could be true, could be an inflated body count to cover up the sheer embarrassment of being invaded by an army of only a thousand men.

President Wilson was not happy. He called up the National Guard for border duty—first, fifteen thousand men to patrol the

New Mexico sector of the border, though later he upped the number to seventy-five thousand. That's a huge commitment of American troops, especially when you consider that this was in the middle of World War I, when the army should have been busy training new recruits and gearing up for the European theater.

Wilson wasted very little time ordering a counterraid. On March 15, 1916, a week after the Columbus raid, an American punitive expedition led by General John J. "Black Jack" Pershing marched into Mexico to get Villa. Now this was not a popular move among our southern neighbors, even the Villa-haters among them. You think PC warfare started in the 1960s? Nope; Wilson gave Pershing a whole book full of rules, like, "No using Mexican railways," that tied at least one of Pershing's hands behind his back.

Pershing had ten thousand troops and some serious hi-tech matériel by 1916 standards, including a reconnaissance aircraft, the Curtiss JN-2. Because the Mexican government wouldn't let the American troops use the local railways, Pershing's resupply was a complicated mixture of trucks and trains: trains to the border or as close to it as they could get, then trucks down into Mexico to the troop concentrations.

That set the tone for the whole expedition: frustrating, bureaucratic, half-assed, and, in the end, a failure. Pershing never got the all-out confrontation with Villa he wanted. Maybe Villa had learned the lessons of Celaya after all, if a little late, and realized that his horsemen couldn't face modern armies in pitched battle. Or maybe, and this is my guess, Villa was more interested in reviving his legend with the locals, playing Robin Hood, than in losing more men against the Yanquis. Nothing delights a peasant like seeing the rich, heavily armed troops outwitted by the lightly armed locals. So that's the show that Villa, a showman at heart, gave them: He let the huge American force stumble around the canyons of northern Mexico asking people if they'd seen Pancho Villa in bad menu-Spanish, giving everybody a good laugh—and more importantly, a chance to make some real money off the foreign soldiers, who made more than the average Mexican peasant could dream of getting. Those American troops caught on fast that Mexican cantinas stayed open twenty-four hours a day—very handy when you only have a short leave—and they also noticed that the local bar girls were totally free of any anti-gringo sentiment. In fact, the girls welcomed the Yankee troops and their dollars enthusiastically. Since it was pretty clear that Villa wasn't going to show, it all turned into one big party.

All Pershing's hi-tech advantages were beaten by the guerrilla's usual allies, geography and treachery. Northern Mexico looks like Afghanistan, all gullies and ridges; all six of Pershing's aircraft crashed into those ridges within the first few months, and Indian scouts led the American men into blind gullies. Pershing was so pissed off he cabled the president: "Villa is nowhere and everywhere."

The only guy who came out of it looking good was young George Patton, who realized intelligence was the key to fighting irregulars. On his own initiative, he tracked down Julio Cardenas, one of Villa's top aides, and then led a raid in civilian cars and clothes, blasting Cardenas's hacienda and bringing Julio's corpse back tied to the hood of Patton's Packard.

After months of frustration, Pershing's men did what conventional armies always do in these situations: started firing blind. In June 1916, they shot up a unit of the Mexican Army, which was supposed to be an ally, at a town called Carrizal. That didn't help much with winning the hearts and minds of the Mexicans. Besides, there was this little thing called WW I going on, and Wilson finally realized his troops had better start gearing up for the kind of war they were good at, the kind that had been going on in France since 1914.

And there, of course, Black Jack Pershing became a legend. If his reputation had rested only on his exploits in Mexico, he'd be a punch line instead. That's the problem with counterinsurgency operations: They don't usually make generals look good. It's too easy for the guerrillas to make the occupiers look like fools. Villa's men played the American punitive expedition in a very interesting way, almost a twenty-first-century way: They weren't really interested in killing the gringo troops; they just wanted to embarrass them. Which wasn't that hard, since only Patton among the American officers took the trouble to get accurate intelligence, the real core of counterinsurgency warfare. Without that sort of intelligence, all the Villistas had to do to disguise themselves was take off their trademark bandito ammunition belts. Once they did that, they were invisible to the Americans. Supposedly, Villa's whole officer corps even attended a movie, incognito, with hundreds of Thirteenth Cav troopers.

Now that was the sort of thing you'd want to put in a United States vs. Mexico highlight film. In fact, most of the highlight film would come from that amazing year, 1916. Compared to that year, you have to admit that right now it's All Quiet on the Mexican Front.

WHEN IT COMES TO KIM
WE GOT NO DONG

AM I THE only American who doesn't understand why we didn't zap that North Korean ICBM designed to hit the United States on the launch pad back in 2007? Seems like everybody, liberals and right-wingers, agrees we don't need to worry about Kim's silly ol' ICBMs (intercontinental ballistic missiles). Kim's just acting up, trying to get attention.

Well, if Kim was trying to get my attention, it worked. I'm funny that way—every time somebody aims a nuke-capable ICBM at me, I overreact like you wouldn't believe.

And I don't care if the missile fell into the ocean. As far as I'm concerned, it's the thought that counts. Like if the psycho down the block starts cleaning his rifle and howling, "I'm comin' fer you, Brecher!" I wouldn't be too reassured if the cops told me, "Don't worry, he's a terrible shot!"

The name of the town where North Korea tests its missiles says it all about our reaction: No-Dong. That's what U.S. presidents have been showing for almost forty years, every time North Korea slaps us in the face: no dong whatsoever.

It's not like the North Koreans are shy about what they're doing. They've said over and over that their plan is to develop nuclear weapons and the ICBMs to send them toward U.S. cities. They hate us like poison, and they're not shy about announcing this, either.

I remember listening to the translation while a North Korean vet told what he thought was a very funny story about playing with the corpses of some U.S. soldiers his men had killed: "We grabbed some dirt and put it in their mouths, saying, 'Oh, are you hungry? Here, eat some dirt!'" Then he laughed for the camera, to show how funny it was. If you've ever seen an insane North Korean officer try to laugh . . . makes me gag just remembering his expression, the sounds that came out of his mouth.

The point is, the North Korean military threat is serious. Saddam never posed a threat to the American homeland; Mu'ammar Gadhafi was a paper tiger from the get-go; but North Korea is crazy enough, smart enough, and tough enough to press that nuclear trigger as soon as it's operational.

North Korea's missile-testing ground has been operational since 1990. We've been surveilling the site since the Koreans started building it in 1988. Just looking at where they put it, on the Sea of Japan, as far from the Chinese and Russian borders as you can get in their country, tells you what they're up to. They wanted a spot where their so-called allies, Russia and China, couldn't interfere without fighting their way across the entire peninsula, and as close to Japan as possible, because next to us, North Koreans hate Japan most. That's their style: real clear, no bullshit, in your face.

And they're serious about security, which is why we have to rely on satellite pix and a few defectors to find out what's going on up there. According to a North Korean defector named Im Young-Sun, the military ordered all civvies living within eighty kilometers of the No-Dong base to leave, find somewhere else to live, right now.

Nobody complained. North Korean complainers have the life expectancy of a Sunni door-to-door salesman working Sadr City.

Satellite pictures show that the No-Dong base is crude, simple stuff. And that leads a lot of peacenik bloggers to claim we don't have to take the North Korean ICBM launch program seriously. For one thing, the roads leading to No-Dong are just dirt tracks, and there are no winter quarters for the staff. That, along with spoiling our Independence Day, is why Kim decided to test his ICBM on July 5: because you can't test anything except thermal socks at No-Dong come winter.

But the peaceniks just don't get how serious and crazy North Korea's military is. It doesn't need winter housing or paved roads, because it doesn't pamper its soldiers, its physicists, or anyone except the Dear Leader, Kim Jong-Il, with his kidnapped South Korean actresses and porn DVDs. If it had to, the military would order a few villages to line up and carry the ICBM on their backs to the launch pad through the mud or snow, and if a few hundred peasants got squished along the way, well . . . it's all in the name of the People. Who's complaining?

Just to show he's a nice guy, Kim threw all those evicted peasants a bone: He named the ICBM that North Korea launched on July 5 the Taepodong-2 after one of the evacuated villages, Taepodong.

By the way—I can't resist those names. No-Dong is pretty good, but Taepodong is even funnier—sounds like an X-rated episode of *Dragnet*: "What type o'dong was it, Ma'am?" "Oh, nothing to worry about, only stayed up about forty-two seconds."

And it's true, the Taepodong-2 only stayed up forty-two seconds. That's supposed to cheer us up. It shouldn't, though. For one thing, how do you know the missile wasn't supposed to take that dive at the forty-two-second point?

Two key points here: First, developing a working ICBM takes a lot of tests, and not all of them are meant to test the full trajectory of the missile. U.S. ICBMs generally need about twenty test launches before they go into production. Smaller missiles get way more than that; the reason ICBMs only get twenty is that they're so damn expensive even the DoD (Department of Defense) has to economize. So maybe this was a typical first test in a series, designed to check out launch and first-stage components. Forty-two seconds may have been the programmed duration of flight.

Second point: Short flight means the test bed falls into the ocean near the North Korean coast, where our subs and recovery ships (like the *Glomar Explorer*, which retrieved half a Soviet sub from the deep ocean) can't grab the remains. After all, Kim doesn't have the whole of the South Pacific to test and recover ICBMs like we do, or all of Siberia like the Soviets did.

The test missile fell in two chunks (first and second stage), but both came down so close to the North Korea coast that nobody's going after them. See, North Korea never bought into that twelve-mile-limit rule. Its fast attack crafts patrol aggressively up to two hundred miles from the North Korea coastline. And the North Koreans will attack anything when they're in the mood. There're lots of reasons for that attitude, starting with (a) they're insane, and (b) North Korea makes most of its foreign exchange by exporting pure heroin, speed, and any other drug that decadent capitalist youth will buy, so it doesn't want anybody even looking at coastal freighter traffic out of Pyongyang.

The U.S. Navy learned about North Korea's coastal patrolling the hard way back in 1968, when North Korea grabbed a high-tech U.S. intel ship, the USS *Pueblo*, fifteen miles off its coast. North Korean marines boarded the ship, killed one crewman, and took the other eighty-two back to Pyongyang, where they were tortured for eleven months. The U.S. Navy had screwed up, as usual, dumping an old, slow vessel loaded with top secret listening gear to patrol right off the coast of the world's most dangerous enemy nation, with no escort whatsoever. The *Pueblo* was armed with two machine guns, but the crew, a bunch of tech geeks, never fired a shot. They were busy trying to feed top-secret documents into their hand-fed stove. Yup, that's all they had for destroying America's most secret recon records.

Then the North Korea boats fired a 57-mm shell into the *Pueblo*, killing one guy and wounding three others, and the *Pueblo* was taken—the biggest intelligence haul in history for the Soviets, and the Commies didn't lose a man getting it.

You'd think we'd have leveled Pyongyang in retaliation. But I'm telling you, we always wimp out against North Korea. The *Pueblo's* crew was tortured for nearly a year, humiliated, forced to make videos begging the North Koreans' pardon—and we did nothing.

The wuss-outs kept coming. In 1969, North Korea shot down a U.S. EC-121. All thirty-one crew were killed.

We did nothing.

In 1976, in one of the weirder, Viking-style attacks, a crew of North Korea soldiers who were pruning trees under the "supervision" of U.S. officers at the "truce village" of Panmunjom decided to prune their supervisors instead, and hacked two American officers to death.

We did nothing.

So fools like me, who thought we'd vaporize that ICBM on the launch pad, were the sort of suckers who pay the light bill for all those lit-up Vegas casinos. Should've known better.

One thing you'll notice, though, is that our worst wuss-outs came while we were wasting men and matériel on dumb wars: 'Nam in 1968–1969 and Iraq in 2006.

Actually, we had a better excuse for cowardice toward North Korea back in the 1960s: We didn't want to start a nuclear war with the USSR. That won't work today, but still, our best response is, "Ha-ha, Kim, ya missed!"

That's what everybody's saying, even Pat Buchanan, who I usually agree with.* So I went over to Free Republic, a good, reliable, hard-right Web site, thinking there'd be some rage from the wacky Freepers at the way Bush let the country down.** Nope. It made every insane excuse for Bush you could think up, like "I bet we knocked that missile out of the sky with some secret death-ray laser" and "Ha-ha, stupid gooks can't even build an ICBM that works!"

Look, a wimp-out is a wimp-out, whether it's the liberal LBJ who left our sailors to be tortured when the *Pueblo* was grabbed, or Bush letting North Korea test missiles designed to hit California. Face facts.

---

* See, for example, Patrick J. Buchanan, "Blowback from Moscow," Antiwar.com Web page, November 30, 2007, available at www.antiwar.com/pat/.
** Free Republic Web site, www.freerepublic.com/focus/f-news/browse.

And don't try to hide behind amateur theories about ICBMs and antiballistic missiles, like the Freepers' claim that we must've shot down the Taepodong-2 with an "electromagnetic ray" (that's a quote from some idiot's post). Even Pentagon R&D, the most optimistic people in the country, except for those smiley muscle girls who work at gyms and tell you how you can lose twenty-five pounds by July, isn't claiming we'll have a working laser ABM system by 2010. And I'll bet you that we won't have it ready by 2012 . . . or 2015, or 20-ever.

The concept is theoretically pretty cool: laser turrets on modified 747s, linked up to sensor nets on antimissile ship screens and land radar arrays. The plan is to have these laser-armed 747s flying patrol at intervals just big enough to allow us to cover the whole arc of the planet where an ICBM might launch.

But I've followed every DoD R&D initiative since I was in junior high, and I know a pipe dream when I see one. ABM is like Star Wars and the B-1 bomber: all about dividends to shareholders, not about war or weapons that actually work.

You have to realize that ICBMs are the most fearsome weapon ever made. Once they get rolling, their cruising speed is fifteen thousand miles per hour. To stop one in midflight, you need a missile or beam that will track and strike and stop a self-guiding missile the size of a farm silo that's moving through near-space six times faster than the fastest interceptor aircraft ever built.

Forget about killing it with beam weapons. They just don't exist. If they get built, I'd much rather have the job of building an ICBM that was hardened against them (reflective armor, warhead deep inside the fuselage, decoy missiles) than the impossible job of inventing some death ray that can break through those defenses in the very few seconds you've got between launch and detonation over an American city.

So that leaves ABMs. You've got two basic kinds: short-range ABMs to counter Scuds or SS-20 short- or midrange nuke-capable missiles, and anti-ICBM interceptors. Both, frankly, are pretty shaky tech. But the short-range models have some chance of working. The anti-ICBM type is, as far as I can tell, pure bullshit, like Star Wars.

Let's start with the short-range antimissile missile we're giving Japan, in the hope it'll save Japan from North Korea Scuds and SS-20s. This missile was a navy design—that's a warning sign number one—the SM-3, first fitted to Aegis cruisers. The land-based version, PAC-3, is designed to handle Scuds, not ICBMs. The navy has dropped the warhead used in smaller designs like the Patriot, because we figured out in Gulf War I that the Scud is too big and dumb to be knocked down with a small warhead.

By the way, that's not the Patriot's fault. Patriot is a damn good design and did exactly what it was supposed to do: get close to the target and detonate. Trouble was, it was designed to destroy Soviet jets—very fragile targets—not Scuds, which are just giant rocks.

It's the guidance systems, the electronics, that make a missile vulnerable to small warheads. No guidance, and it's like David trying to drop Goliath with a wad of tofu.

The Scud is as strong and dumb as a thrown boulder. To knock a boulder off course, you need another boulder—so the new anti-Scud missiles have no warhead. Instead, they use a plain old heavy weight where the warhead would be, like a lead-filled war club. It's called a "hit-to-kill kinetic warhead," or KW, but that's all it is, a big chunk of metal to whack a Scud off course. The new ABM motto is "Ramming speed!"

This makes it an even tougher job, because they don't just have to get close like a warhead does. They have to hit the Scud directly, and hard enough to deflect it.

Then there's the issue of saturation. Koreans . . . Dude, they may be crazy but they sure ain't stupid. Think back to your last math class. I bet the Koreans came tops, right? These people can figure. So, facing a gold-plated guided weapon like the SM-3, they'll figure it can maybe take out a Scud. Key word: *a* Scud. Not two hundred Scuds. Or two thousand. Scuds are unguided tubes of fuel, not that hard or expensive to make. You launch two thousand against a screen of Aegis cruisers; you lose the first ten . . . or twenty . . . or fifty . . . So what? If even one out of ten makes it, it destroys a ship worth billions. Who wins that exchange?

Now put nukes on, say, one out of every fifty Scuds, and send two thousand against Japan. I wouldn't want to be slurping my Soba in Tokyo while that real-world video game played out. That's why nobody's laughing in Japan. Koreans hate Japan already, even in the South. A nuke-tipped Scud would make Hiroshima look like an M-80 in a trash can.

That's the bad news (unless you're a Japanese anime fan, in which case it's a dream come true). Now for the way, way worse news: the anti-ICBM program. This missile is the Ground-Based Midcourse Interceptor (GBMI). Notice the word *midcourse*. That means this thing is supposed to hit an ICBM at its full speed, something like fifteen thousand miles per hour. Yeah, sure.

The development of the GBMI has been long and slow, even by Pentagon standards. And embarrassing. If you follow DoD tests, you know it's standard practice to rig them in the new weapons systems' favor. Like, if Defense is testing a new antitank missile, which the program engineers know is not ready, well . . . Dozens of times, they've been caught tagging the target tank with infrared or other beepers, so their lemon of a design can hit the target. The bigger the budget and the lousier the tech, the more chance they're faking it. And based on recent news about the GBMI, I'd bet the rent that this weapons system does not work, never will work, is only in place to siphon money to contractors.

I'm basing this on a weasel-worded press release issued on December 20, 2005, by the Missile Defense Agency: "Information regarding the operational status of missile defense assets, to include the number of operationally available ground and sea-based interceptor missiles, and the operational status of system sensors and radars has historically been and will remain classified."

Hard to read, isn't it? It's meant to be. Press releases like that are meant to bamboozle the civvies. They hope you'll just give up and leave it to them. Luckily, I've been reading this crap since age twelve, and I can translate for you. What the Missile Defense

Agency is telling you is that from now on, they ain't gonna tell you shit about the testing program for the GBMI. Their excuse is, naturally, "it's classified," but believe me, when a weapons system works, DoD is faster with the publicity than Madonna's agent. And in the early stages of testing the GBMI, it was in the press every week billing the system as America's savior. So when some bureaucratic slime starts feeding you this line of crap, it means just one thing: The damn weapon is a bust.

Another clue that the GBMI doesn't work is that . . . Well, guess how many are in the U.S. inventory? A grand total of eleven. That's right, we've got eleven of these ICBM-killers to protect our cities. So if a real nuke power like Russia attacked us, it's just barely possible that eleven American cities might be saved. Too bad for the other few hundred. They'd look like bonfires on a beach—a very dark, radioactive beach.

Of course, the real reason we only have eleven is that even the designers and their bought-off military bagmen know the thing just plain doesn't work. And never will.

That's not even to mention all the scary stuff an ICBM designer can invent to fool our stooge ABMs. Here are some examples: ICBMs that break into twelve minimissiles midflight, like early MIRVs (multiple independently targetable reentry vehicles). Or supercooled ICBMs launched along with a dozen uncooled decoy ICBMs, so our ABMs jump the fakes while the real thing, the ultimate coolster, har-har, glides down to erase Portland or San Diego without a scratch on it.

Or, if you want the ultimate nightmare scenario, how about nukes that don't even require a missile to reach their targets, because North Korean secret agents (the best in the world, by the way) have already deposited nukes at the bottom of Oakland harbor, or unloaded them in a sealed, lead-lined container at a rail depot in Chicago? What if Kim is making these noisy launches as the ultimate decoy, when he's already got nukes in place along the West Coast?

Maybe he does, maybe not. But the key point for a military planner is figuring out before the war starts whether the offense or defense will have the advantage. In 1914, everybody picked offense, but defense won. When 1939 rolls along, they all pick defense—and offense wins.

Apply that to ICBM vs. ABM technology right now. To me, it's real clear that the offense—the ICBM—will literally destroy the defense, ABM. Along with every city those pitiful ABMs are supposed to protect.

That's why I don't think it's so funny that North Korea's perfecting nuclear weapons and ICBMs at full speed while we waste our manpower in Iraq and our money on anti-ICBM cash siphons that have way, way less chance of working than the Maginot Line ever did.

AMERICAN NATIONALISM:
EXTINCT SINCE DESERT ONE

I'M ALWAYS GETTING flamed for daring to criticize Victor Davis Hanson, the ivory-tower darling of the neocons. That's not surprising. What's weird is that Hanson's defenders aren't so much angry as confused by my angle of attack. They're used to bashing liberals, and don't know what to make of a simple old American nationalist like me.

We're getting so rare, nobody even recognizes us nationalists when they come across one of us. We're like those damn ivory-billed woodpeckers flapping around the swamps, except nobody's looking for us. Hell, they'd send the exterminator out if they saw one of us. I can see it now: some van with a big, plastic war-nerd head glued on top, a recycled fat-guy mannequin from the old Bob's Big Boy painted up to look like me, and a slogan: "Kills War Nerds Dead!" They'd call the campaign "The War to End All War Nerds."

The whole political landscape these days—the whole swamp—is divided between peacenik leftists who think war is wrong because it hurts children and other living things, and neocons who back the Iraq disaster even though they know it means pouring American lives (though not their lives) and money into the sewer.

There's nobody speaking for simple pro-Americans like me, except maybe Pat Buchanan. (And he weirds me out, too, with his thing about Mexicans. What's wrong with Mexicans? They're the best soldiers we've got. Just check the casualty lists from Iraq: they read like the employee time sheet at your local burrito shack.) Us American nationalists used to be the majority, what they called the "silent majority." We went extinct faster than passenger pigeons, wiped out in only twenty-five years. That's because twenty-five years ago, something happened that was as disastrous for America as that asteroid for the dinosaurs: Jimmy Carter's big wimp-out in the Iran hostage crisis of 1979–1980. That's what drove America crazy.

Let me set the stage, but with the truth this time, not the crap the official sources give you. In 1978, Iran was the most powerful country in the Middle East, rapidly modernizing under the shah, Reza Pahlavi. You hear a lot of nonsense about his "repressive" policies, but the truth is way simpler: The shah's problem was that he actually *was* trying to make Iran a modern, powerful country. In 1963, the shah started his "White Revolution," a typical Kennedy-style reform plan, kind of out-commie-ing the commies.

He was trying to do for Iran exactly what Mustafa Kemal Atatürk did for Turkey in the 1920s. But the shah had two problems: His "dynasty" was new and unpopular—set up by his cavalry-officer dad's coup in 1921—and he was dealing with Shia Islam, which is way crazier and more self-destructive than Sunni. The Shia have a bigger martyr complex than Cindy Sheehan does, and they're always willing to do whatever it takes to mess themselves up. So Iran basically looked at the shah's reforms and said nope, it's too good, we'd rather go back to the Middle Ages.

Of course, that's not the official story. The leftist academics will tell you the Iranians overthrew the shah in revenge for persecution from his "feared and hated SAVAK secret police." The truth is, SAVAK was a small (fifteen thousand men), defensive counter-intelligence service. Unless you were actively involved in Islamist or Communist conspiracies, it would pretty much leave you alone, which was a lot more than you can say for the cops/spies of any other regime in the four thousand years of Persian or Iranian history, including the creeps running the country now.

The other lie you hear about the shah is that he was corrupt. He skimmed from the petro-dollars coming in, sure—but compared with any other Middle Eastern ruler, the shah was squeaky-clean. He actually put Iran's oil revenues to work changing the country, building roads, irrigation projects, and setting up an educational system (the first in the country's history).

But nobody felt grateful. The intelligentsia was full of fashionable commies; they wanted chaos. The successful entrepreneur types mostly emigrated before they could contribute to building a solid middle class, taking their free educations with them. And the Shiite mullahs were furious that they were losing power as people got more middle-class and more interested in progress. When the shah decided to stop paying off the mullahs, they called in their Frankenstein: Ayatollah Khomeini.

Khomeini—if you're old enough to remember 1979, you won't forget his face. He looked like a two-hundred-year-old Dracula in black robes. The faces said it all: the shah, with his expensive suits, or the man in black.

They went with Khomeini. The shah and his U.S. backers couldn't believe it. Suddenly, their expensive armed forces were useless, because the troops wouldn't fire on the crowds, a lethal mix of commie romantics and Shiite fanatics, who were screaming for the shah's blood. As the lefties say, "This is what democracy looks like," and it wasn't pretty: half a million people in the streets screaming for a return to the Dark Ages. Not much you can do about that, unless you find a way to slip Thorazine into the water supply.

On January 16, 1979, the shah flew out of Iran for a "vacation." By that time, the Iranians were so crazy that nobody much wanted to take the vacationer: Every Club Med from Tahiti to Timbuktu was suddenly overbooked. He was even denied entry to the United States and ended up in Egypt.

The Islamist "students" of Tehran blamed the United States, anyway, and grabbed seventy U.S. Embassy employees for a few hours. You'd think this would have been warning enough to evacuate the Tehran embassy. Nope. Back then, remember, nobody took Islam very seriously. We were still scared of the poor ol' pitiful commies, and fatally underestimated the power of the mullahs, just like the shah did.

Our diplomats thought they were safe because everybody knows foreign embassies are off limits, sovereign territory. Except Iranians don't have that tradition.

Our last chance to evacuate the embassy was October 22, 1979, when the United States finally admitted the dying shah for urgent gall-bladder surgery. Two weeks later—and for those two weeks, there were daily, giant protests with a million people screaming, *Marg bar Amrika!* ("Death to America!")—a crowd of radicals swarmed the embassy. The marine guards were ordered not to fire on the crowds, so we gave up without a fight, setting the pattern for this whole humiliating episode.

The "students" were amateurs, so some staff escaped and took refuge in the Canadian embassy. The occupiers released some hostages, mostly women, non-Americans, and blacks. The rest were blindfolded, handcuffed, and toyed around with. There were mock executions with unloaded rifles—that kind of sadistic crap.

The world was holding its breath waiting to see what America, the strongest power in the world, would do. Nobody, and I remember this well, could believe it as the weeks went by and we did nothing. Nothing.

We had the bad luck to have as president this freak, Jimmy Carter. What a piece of work he was. We knew he was a Christian, but we didn't know he was the kind of soft-headed Christian who actually believed in turning the other cheek when you're hit. All our presidents were churchgoers, but I don't think we've ever had a president who actually bought that nonsense, and I pray (or I would if I still believed in God) that we never do again. Richard Nixon, for example, was a Quaker—but he wasn't exactly what you'd call a pacifist.

I'd like to blame the Democrats for our current problems, but before Carter, our Democratic presidents had been damn fine war leaders. Wilson, FDR, Truman—when it was time to fight, they went in with both fists flying. Even LBJ can't be faulted for squeamishness. He may not have fought smart in Vietnam, but he was no peacenik, turn-the-other-cheek freak.

Carter was a whole different animal from those guys. He didn't threaten the hostage-takers, he "negotiated." Meaning, he begged. "Please, Mister Khomeini, can we have our hostages back?" It was the lowest point in American history. Every night on the news, there were scenes to make you sick, blindfolded hostages being shown off to giant rallies in Tehran.

And Carter settled for embargoing oil from Iran. Meaning my parents had to pay double for gas. Oh, and he froze some of the Iranians' assets. Which must've really hurt, because now that oil prices shot up, the mullahs were rolling in rials.

We didn't know it then, but Carter was some sort of sick Gandhi mutant version of a Southern Baptist. The most expensive armed forces in history were just dying to make those bearded bastards pay, and Carter sat back and tried talking to them nicely. We could have done things that would make our name feared throughout history. We could have made them forget Genghis Khan, who was responsible for turning eastern Iran into the moonscape it still is today.

I used to lie in my room after the news, dreaming of what the USAF could do if Carter took the leash off. Like announce that we were going to nuke Khomeini's "holy city," Qom, if the hostages weren't released. And do it. Then announce we were going to nuke another, bigger city—and do it. And keep doing it, going from smaller to bigger Iranian cities until Tehran was the only one left. Then, if the idiots didn't let the hostages go, sadly announce that all the hostages were brutally butchered, and seal Tehran underneath hot, radioactive glass.

I guarantee you, we wouldn't be having our current problems if we'd done that twenty-five years ago.

If you don't have the stomach for that level of violence, then do what one high-ranking air force officer suggested: using our jamming/e-warfare planes to wipe out all telecommunications across Iran. See if they're so eager for the Dark Ages, after all.

We did none of the above. Carter's brain trust started dreaming about rescue raids, like what the Israelis had pulled off in Entebbe. That's how Charlie Beckwith's pitiful Operation Eagle Claw was born. Carter wanted a plan that would snatch the hostages from safe houses scattered in an enemy city of four million people.

Stupid. American Special Forces missions have less than a 50 percent success rate, and the odds on this one were much, much worse than that. The only way to get the hostages out was to hurt Iran enough to make it *give* the hostages back, screaming, "Take them! Take them!" And Carter had ruled that out.

His secretary of state, Cyrus Vance, who looked like a Cub Scout leader, knew it wouldn't work. Even Beckwith, the mission commander, knew it was hopeless. He calculated the risk of failure at 99.9 percent, but the poor bastard followed his commander in chief's orders and devised a plan.

It was maybe the worst plan in history. Eight RH-53D Sea Stallion heavy-lift choppers—not the best ones we had, either, but so-called hangar queens, whose commanders weren't warned of the seriousness of the mission—would take off from the USS *Nimitz* and rendezvous with six C-130 transports at Desert One, a desert point near Iran's southern coast. After being refueled, the eight choppers would take Delta Force to Desert Two, fifty miles outside Tehran, where they were supposed to hide for a full day before being infiltrated into Tehran in trucks.

So that's two big, loud landing strips that we were supposed to manage inside Iran without getting spotted. Plus a full day of trying to hide out.

If you've read Andy McNab's *Bravo Two Zero* about what happened when his SAS (Special Air Service) team tried to hide out in rural Iraq during Gulf War I, you know how crazy that was. Before they even got unpacked, McNab's guys, the best soldiers in the world, were spotted by an old man herding goats.

If the Delta guys had somehow managed to go undiscovered and make it into Tehran in those trucks—another big if—and if they somehow found and rescued the hostages (an if the size of those Dodge pickups they sell by the pound) the plan was that they'd take the hostages by truck to a downtown Tehran soccer stadium. Choppers would fly them from there to Manzariyeh air base forty miles southeast of Tehran, where C-141s would land, pick up the Delta operators and hostages, and fly them home.

With some plans, you can find the flaw and say, "Aha! There's the problem!" But this plan was so hopeless, so complicated, with so many impossible stages open to so many obvious disasters, that you can't even isolate a single flaw. It was all flaws, and no logic.

On April 24, 1980, Operation Eagle Claw was launched. Soon after hitting the Iranian desert, the RH-53Ds flew into a haboob—a violent dust storm that makes the desert a Hell for pilots. The first chopper dropped with mechanical problems two hours from the *Nimitz.* Another had to turn around after trying to fly through the dust storm.

That left six choppers, the bare minimum, still working. They landed at the Desert One rendezvous an hour late. The C-130s were already waiting. The choppers were refueled and the Delta Force team was itching to go, when they found out that one of the choppers was inoperable—hydraulic failure. That was it: The plan wouldn't work with just five choppers.

Beckwith had no choice but to scrub the mission right there in the desert. All because Carter only authorized eight lousy choppers.

When Nixon heard about it, he had a great comment: "Eight? Why not a thousand? It's not like we don't have them!"

Carter should've listened to the Quaker Nixon. What's the world coming to when a Quaker ex-president has the right warlike attitude and a Southern Baptist, which Carter supposedly was, cringes like a pacifist?

But the worst was yet to come. Eight men—five air force crew and three marine chopper crew—died when one RH-53D tried to take off, got blown by the sandstorm into a taxiing C-130, and turned both aircraft into a huge fireball. We were very lucky a lot more men didn't die.

There were forty-four troops on that plane, and only a heroic effort by the load master got the jammed doors open so the men could escape. The survivors flew off on the five surviving C-130s. And when the Iranians noticed the columns of black smoke, they hopped on their camels and found the wreckage of Carter's rescue mission. Every newspaper in the world, every TV station, carried this picture that's burned into my eyes for life: some greasy, stupid mullah grinning at the camera as he holds up the charred arm of an American serviceman.

I can't describe the sick, terrible feeling I had watching that on TV, then seeing it again on the front page of the paper. Like watching your family get raped while you're strapped in a chair. From that moment, Reagan was in. His handlers made sure the hostages weren't released before the election. They timed it nicely: The hostages finally got out on Inauguration Day, 444 days after they were captured.

Carter was still trying to micromanage the negotiations. He brought a phone to Reagan's inauguration.

We took revenge, in a way, by arming Saddam in his war against Iran. His tanks crossed the border on September 22, 1980. The Iranians paid big-time, losing 500,000 dead and more than a million wounded. We fed Saddam intelligence and matériel to bleed the Iranians, and they bled, all right. But it wasn't a very satisfying kind of vengeance, doing it by proxy. It was sneaky and weak, the kind of thing the Venetians or Austrians would have done, not worthy of America.

And it was America that really suffered, thanks to Carter's insane pacifism. The old tradition of American nationalism, what they're now calling "paleoconservatism," was destroyed forever by that humiliation in the desert. Ever since then, America has been so scared of sounding weak that we keep falling for the chickenhawks who woof the loudest, even when it's obvious they don't have a clue about war or national power.

Just compare the two Bushes: Bush Senior engineered our greatest victory since 1945 in Gulf War I—and he was voted out. He was a real vet, a pilot who'd been shot down in WW II—but he didn't know how to strut, how to woof. People didn't take to him and didn't care that he brought us a glorious victory. He couldn't woof, so we got rid of him.

Whereas people still love his worthless son, even though that fool has led us into our most disastrous military failure in history. They'd rather have a noisy chickenhawk than a quiet hero—they'd rather have Dubya than his dad.

The trouble is that guys who are good at woofing generally believe their own noise. So Dubya actually believes all that "Bring it on!" crap. His dad, the real hero, warned him not to occupy Iraq. Dad was an old-style paleocon; he was thinking about keeping America strong and safe during and after the war. Dubya and his handlers don't give a damn about America, never did. They're in love with their own noise. And we're in love with it, too, following it right down the toilet.

It didn't have to be this way. If any other past president had been in the Oval Office when the Iran Hostage Crisis went down, we'd have had the mullahs begging us to take back our diplomats—and Khomeini's "holy city" of Qom would be a lake of molten glass. But we had Jimmy Carter, a man who once got mugged by a rabbit. And that's what drove us into the arms of sleazy neoconmen like Cheney and Dubya, who know too much about how to fool the suckers back home and not a damn thing about the big, bad world.

And who suckered them into invading Iraq? You guessed it: Iran, by sending double agents like Ahmed Chalabi to tell the neocons it was going to be a cakewalk. Meanwhile, our forces are so bogged down by an Iranian-influenced insurgency that we can't threaten Iran anymore. It's still fucking with America, and fucking us hard.

Now all Iran has to do is wait a couple years and stroll into the oil fields of Basra. Without firing a shot, Iran gets all of Shiite Iraq, 60 percent of the Iraqi population, and two-thirds of the oil reserves. And America will be stuck with even shriller chickenhawks pissing the nation's power and might away. The result: game, set, and match to the mullahs.

Part 2

AFRICA

LESS IS MAURITANIA:
YOU WANT ANARCHY?

ANYBODY CATCH THE latest coup in Mauritania? God, I feel like Jay Leno on a worse-than-usual night, just asking the question. "Anybody here from Mauritania? No? Nobody?" Too bad, because for some reason, coup stories from hellholes like this make me feel all warm inside, like a good vineyard arson.

Mauritania is one of those chunks of worthless African real estate that is a paradise for flies and scorpions—not so great for us mammals. The permanent skulking grounds of tribes that were kicked out of someplace better.

When the Berbers were pushed out of the good land in the more fertile valleys of Morocco, some fled south into the desert. When black African tribes got shoved away from the wetlands by the Senegal River, they fled north onto the sands.

And that's the Mauritanian population today: Moors from the north and black Africans from the south in about equal numbers, hating each other, wishing they were somewhere else. Just to make it more confusing, there are "white" Moors and "black" Moors. The black Moors used to be kept as slaves by the whites, but that only makes them even snobbier about their Moorishness. They have a real Moorier-than-thou attitude and go around sneering at the black non-Moors. Snobby slaves—there's a lot of that going around.

Nobody lives in Mauritania by choice, unless you count scorpions—which is why there were only 1.5 million people in this one-million-square-kilometer country (three times the size of Arizona) at independence in 1960. That population has doubled now to

3 million people, in spite of the fact that 90 percent of the arable land has turned into desert. Not to mention that all those busy Taiwanese fishing trawlers have scooped up every last sand eel from Mauritanian waters. Like that old America song says, the ocean is a desert, too—at least in Mauritania.

It's a typical African pattern: The less livable the place is, the faster the people breed. There's another pattern in Mauritania that's typical of Africa: The countryside has emptied, and the cities are overflowing with surplus people. Nobody lives the old nomad life here anymore. All the kids hang around the cities practicing their dance moves and watching old kung fu movies. They're one of the key ingredients for your classic African coups: lots of what Ali G. would call da yout', scuffing around, bored, just waiting for a couple of jeeps to roar past waving a revolutionary flag. A little action! Sure beats watching the termite mounds grow.

What I like about places like Mauritania is that Mauritania is what Fresno will look like a hundred years from now. I'll be safely dead—the good side of being fat with kidney problems—but all the jocks who messed with me in high school... Well, those poor, healthy suckers will have to watch the long slide down, watch their grandkids become the goatherds of the twenty-second century. I can see it now: tribes of sunburnt, feral Anglos wandering around the ruins of Fresno landmarks like Wild Water Adventures, begging Soylent Green packets from the Chinese do-gooders. They'll try hard not to pity you, try to be understanding when they visit your campground in the ruins of the giant waterslide park, but they'll hold their hi-tech handkerchiefs to their noses—there's nothing like the smell of goats in close quarters. They'll barely be able to keep from puking while they listen to your stories about how Fresno used to be a big deal, all lit up, swimming pools everywhere.

Mauritania is full of stories like that, about its glorious past. This was the home base of the Almoravids, the Taliban of the eleventh century. Real fun-loving fundamentalist Muslims, the kind who go crazy at the thought that somebody might be playing music, drawing pictures, drinking wine, or otherwise offending Allah. Allah's a funny guy: he's down with all kinds of rough stuff—torture, slavery—but he can't stand music.

Like the Taliban, the Almoravids came out of nowhere (the Mauritanian desert) and won it all: They rampaged against backsliders from Ghana to Morocco and even stomped the uppity Christians in Spain. When the Almoravids were through, no Spaniard could ever make music again—which explains the Iglesias family, father and son.

Of course, slavery is outlawed in Mauritania. In fact, according to one account I read, "Slavery has been outlawed several times." I guess you just can't outlaw slavery too often. It makes the Westerners happy, and of course, it never trickles down to the actual slaves.

You might as well try to bring back the 55-mph limit on I-5. Slaves are just about the only natural resource this landscape produces; outlaw them, and the Mauritanian economy would fall apart.

The real point of outlawing slavery early and often is that it keeps the Western aid flowing. Those guilt-ridden rich countries give every man, woman, and child in Mauritania about $170 per year. Not that it actually reaches those poor peasants. It stays in the pockets of the airport managers and government ministers, where it belongs.

So Mauritania is a perfect little laboratory of the Hell that is Africa. And that's how you have to understand the coup of August 2005—as a sample of what's happening across the Sahel in those half-Arab, half-black countries that have a surplus of births and locusts, and a shortage of everything else.

The French held Mauritania until 1960, but their attitude was nicely summed up in an order from their colonial administration: "Let us not hear from you."

That was all they asked of Mauritania. That was all anybody wanted from the place.

Mauritania stayed quiet until the 1970s, when Mokhtar Ould Daddah, its president for life, stupidly got involved in the war between Morocco and the Polisario guerrillas fighting for an independent Spanish Sahara. These guerrillas pioneered the use of the "technical"—a Toyota pickup with a bed-mounted heavy machine gun—as the MBT (main battle tank) of low-cost desert wars. They really scooted around the Sahara in those things. Thanks to safe havens and logistical support from Algeria, the guerrillas could hit outposts anywhere in the Western Sahara.

In fact, Polisario columns managed to attack Nouakchott, the capital of Mauritania. When you consider that Nouakchott is on the coast, more than two hundred miles from the border, you can see why the Mauritanian officer corps was embarrassed—embarrassed enough to stage a coup in 1977. One minute Mauritania was singing, "My Heart Belongs to Daddah," and the next, Daddah didn't even have visiting rights.

The coups kept coming. In 1984, Mauritania's officer corps decided it was time for a new face on the national currency and installed a guy named Maaouiya Ould Sid'Ahmed Taya, who did pretty well, slapping down a handful of countercoups and even winning a few elections. Then Taya did the one thing no ruler in a little backwater should ever do: He got involved in the big-boys' games. Though to be fair, it wasn't totally his fault. He just got caught in the gears as the big Islam vs. the West war started cranking up.

By the 1990s, Islamists were starting to act up even in a sleepy place like Mauritania. These guys are good at PR. They pass their tapes hand-to-hand, until even those unemployed surplus kids leaning on termite mounds in Nouakchott can hear some Saudi preacher tell them to get off their duffs and go start a jihad in the neighborhood. Next thing you know, your local goof-off is a Jihadi, getting props like crazy and calling himself Abu Semtex.

Taya, the president, was sick and tired of getting noise from these brats. After all, he'd proven his right to govern twice over: first with the traditional coup and then with one of those goddamn Western-style "elections." What more could they want?

So in the great Mauritanian tradition, he joined the wrong side of the big war, using that dumb old proverb, "The enemy of my enemy is my friend." You know, if there's a stupider saying in the world, I'd like to know what it is. The enemy of your enemy is *not*

usually your friend. The enemy of your enemy is usually also your enemy. Duh!

But Taya figured, if these local Islamists are my enemy, and if their enemy is Israel and the United States, then all I have to do is sign up with those guys, and together we'll squash the Jihadis.

What he didn't take into account is local advantage. Your gang may be ten times the size of the other gang, but if you're backed into an alley with a dozen of their guys coming at you, that advantage won't help you much.

By the time Taya figured this out, it was too late for him. In 1999, he made the mistake of formally opening diplomatic ties with Israel. Mauritania was one of only three Arab countries to do this, and by far the weakest of the three. It was suicide for his regime. Every muezzin in the country was on the air next morning denouncing him as a traitor to Allah. After 2001, he signed on to the War on Terror, admitting U.S. troops to Mauritania to help train local forces.

What he didn't get was that Mauritania was never going to be a priority for the United States. We were glad to get Mauritania's endorsement—it went right up there on the wall next to the pledges of alliance from Togo, Panama, and Kyrgyzstan—but there wasn't much we could do to prop up Taya's regime, short of sending in troops. And nobody's ever cared enough about the place to do that.

So Taya was in deep trouble, way out on a limb with the West but not getting any real help from it. And the coup attempts came faster than ever. In 2003, a military coup attempt ended with Taya still in power, but only after he committed all his loyal soldiers to heavy fighting in the capital. There were two more attempted coups in 2004. Taya stomped them, barely. He was hanging tough until . . .

Well, I'll let you guess. When does the smart, up-and-coming African officer stage a coup? If you're a real fan of the game, you know the answer: when the leader is out of the country. So in a way, it was the death of King Fahd of Saudi Arabia on August 1, 2005, that doomed Taya's regime. Taya owed the Saudis big-time for decades of foreign aid, and he had to go to the funeral. So Colonel Ely Ould Mohammed Vall, Mauritania's coup plotter number one, waited until he saw Taya's jet sailing off toward Riyadh and declared himself the new leader. It was easy; no casualties, no riots. By all accounts, the people were glad of it. They never did get why their country would be cozying up to the West, anyway. *"Allahu akbar!"* is about as advanced as politics gets in these parts of the world.

Taya did better than a lot of former dictators, in that he's still alive and in possession of his toenails and genitalia. He's relaxing in Qatar, a U.S. protectorate on the Persian Gulf. It's generally a safe place, though a dead Chechen leader named Zelimkhan Yandarbiyev might beg to differ—he was killed by Russian agents in Qatar in 2004.

But Taya doesn't really have to worry. The Chechnya war is high-stakes, high-risk. Mauritania isn't that important to anybody. Nobody's going to follow Taya to Qatar. Nobody in Mauritania could scare up the airfare.

The new regime has released twenty-one Islamic radicals jailed by Taya's government. They'll probably reward their benefactors in the usual way: by staging a coup of their own and hanging the guys who let them out of prison.

But what we're seeing now is a little feud between different factions of the so-called Moors, the Arab-Berber ethnic group. The real trouble for Mauritania is going to come from the blacks down south who are getting sick of the northern whiteys telling them what to do.

Then there's Niger, just to the east. Believe it or not, Niger makes Mauritania look like La Jolla. At least Mauritania's got coastal real estate, even if there ain't no more fish in the sea.

What you really see when you look hard at places like Mauritania is how unimportant these countries' borders really are. What's happening here is happening all across the Sahel: North vs. South, Arab vs. "black," Islam vs. Western. And all of it is bubbling up against a background of rapid desertification plus rising birthrate.

In other words, accelerated catastrophe from now until something really big comes along to make us forget all the little blips on the historical graph.

IT'S D-DAY IN ZALAMBESSA!

LET'S SEE HOW well you know your military history. Give the date and place of this communiqué:

```
Our Victorious Forces Liberate Zalambessa!!
```

Our victorious and heroic air and ground forces have liberated the town of Zalambessa after completely annihilating the enemy army which was on the verge of collapse yesterday. Our valiant forces raised the flag over Zalambessa town at midnight. Yesterday, the Irob and Egala areas were already liberated.

It sounds like something from the late nineteenth or early twentieth century, from the age of the great wars between nation-states. But the communiqué was actually issued by the Ethiopian Army on May 25, 2000. I guess nobody told the Ethiopians that the age of nationalism was over. In some parts of the world, the great days of nation-building are right now, the great wars are right now, and the whole age-of-heroes thing is going strong.

When you live in what they call the developed world—meaning Fresno, where only real-estate developers count—you forget there's places where life is still going strong. Like the Horn of Africa. The countries around the horn are like an honor roll for blood 'n' guts: Somalia, Eritrea, Djibouti—and right across the water, another crazy-house, Yemen.

The Horn gives you hope that the world isn't totally dulled-out yet. I may have to live like an ant in a suit, but in the Horn, people still live wild. Remember Somalia? Back when Uncle Sam tried to "help" the Sammies, they mugged a whole reinforced company of Rangers and D-boys (soldiers from our Delta Force). *Black Hawk Down*, the book and the movie, may tell it like a big triumph, but let's face some facts here: The Rangers went up against men, women, and kids, and barely got out alive. If it hadn't been for the gunships hosing down Mogadishu nonstop, every soldier we sent in would've been swarmed over, stripped, and dragged behind a Toyota like Achilles dragged Hector, with those crazy black skeletons screaming over them.

We shouldn't feel bad about the Mog street fight. For one thing, we killed a hundred Somalis for every one of us they got. Besides, getting angry with the Somalis would be like getting mad at a lion for mauling some liberal who tried to give it a bowl of granola. It's not the lion's fault; that's what lions do. Just admire the lion for what it is.

Keeping your cool when the odd battalion gets wiped out by the savages is part of what having an empire is all about. The Romans admired any Teutonic tribe that managed to wipe out a legion or two. The British felt the same way. Kipling even wrote a poem honoring the Somalis who wiped out a nineteenth-century British army.

And then, of course, the British went back in with a bigger army and killed every fucking one of those brave suckers at long range, with Maxim guns and heavy artillery. That's the other part of being a successful empire: You don't get mad, you get even. You take your time, assemble the right technology, and shred the fuckers—then help the survivors up and offer them a job as your native auxiliaries.

But the liberals already have us convinced that war is some kind of abnormality. Well, it didn't use to be, and in the Horn of Africa, it still isn't. In the Horn, war is normal and comes in all sizes from family stabbings, to clan-vs.-clan war like Somalia, to total war between nation-states.

Which is what the Eritrea-Ethiopia war is. This is definitely not your typical African bush war—the kind you see in Sierra Leone or

Liberia, with gangs sneaking around attacking villages, avoiding combat, carrying nothing bigger than your basic irregular-warfare kit of AK-47s and RPGs (rocket-propelled grenades), and specializing in rape and mutilation.

The Ethiopian-Eritrean war is more like the Franco-Prussian War, or even the Western Front in 1914. These are two countries fully supplied with the best of mid-twentieth-century Soviet weaponry and smart enough to keep it running. And use it. And boy, have they used it! They've had Verduns, Stalingrads, Marnes down there—and nobody even notices!

Eritrea is like the Prussia of Africa: a tiny state of hard people who'll take on anybody. The Eritreans rebuilt an entire railroad with their bare hands. Imagine what that must've looked like: hundreds of thousands of ordinary people, whole families, digging rock and hammering track for no pay, out there in some of the hottest, driest, nastiest landscape in the world. And it wasn't because the authorities terrorized them into it: It was for the good of the nation. Imagine what kind of soldiers those people must be! If there were a few more Eritreans, they'd probably march across the whole continent: Greater Eritrea (formerly known as "Africa").

But there are only 3.5 million Eritreans. Which means they can't afford to spend soldiers the way Ethiopia, with a population of 60 million, can. So the Eritreans specialize in defensive fighting, especially trench warfare. Ethiopia, with the big population, has a reputation for spending its soldiers' lives a little more recklessly. The Eritreans even accused Ethiopia of using "human-wave tactics" after the Ethiopians broke the supposedly impregnable Eritrean trench lines a couple of years ago.

The Ethiopians deny the human-wave charge and say they simply understand mobile warfare better than the Eritreans do. After their big breakthrough in 2000, one of the Ethiopian generals said, "The Eritreans only know how to fight in trenches!" The Ethiopians say they smashed the Eritrean trench network in classic manner: flanking the strongpoints on both sides, then attacking from front and rear at once.

If Eritrea is like an African Prussia, Ethiopia . . . well, Ethiopia is just plain weird. In a very cool way. The Amharic people who live in the highlands, and ran the place till recently, have their own version of racism. They consider themselves the only really white people in the world. The way they see it, "white" Europeans are really red, and other Africans, the ones they used to sell as slaves (slavery wasn't outlawed in Ethiopia till 1928), are black.

The Ethiopians picked up Coptic Christianity early, and they have a long and bloody history of fighting off jihads launched by a dozen of the Islamic kingdoms around them. When you start researching Ethiopian history, you come across these really cool wall murals of Ethiopian knights with eyes like eggs, stabbing Arabs and Bantu and Somalis at their feet.

The Ethiopians' greatest day came in 1896, at the battle of Adowa, where the Abyssinian emperor, Menelik II, slaughtered an Italian army. The news that Africans had beaten a European colonial army blew everybody away, Europeans and Africans both.

Adowa meant that Ethiopia avoided outright colonization—until 1935, when Mussolini, the Rodney Dangerfield of fascism, tried to avenge Italian honor, assuming there is such a thing. He sent in his Nazi-wannabe troops. It was tanks against spears, biplanes dispensing chlorine gas vs. cavalry. And the Italians *still* took a while to win.

You know, the Italians really deserve their reputation for being cowards—whereas, if you ask me, the French get a bad rap. The French fought like tigers in WW I, lost 1.5 million men, took the worst the Germans gave out, and held on to win. The Brits like to sneer at the French, but if England had shared a long land border with Germany in 1914 or 1939, how long do you think the war would've lasted? And the same thing holds for the nineteenth century: If Wellington had had to meet Napoleon one-on-one, without Russian or Prussian help, just British troops vs. French . . . are you kidding me? Wellington would've been the duke of some prison cell in Paris. The French deserve more respect than they get.

But the Italians don't. It took them years to beat the Ethiopians, and when Addis Ababa finally fell, Haile Selassie took off on a world tour that included Jamaica. You know how all that Rasta stuff got started? Because some Jamaicans were so excited by the idea of a black emperor that they decided he was God. So those Rasta images—that lion with a sword—that's an Ethiopian military insignia. Pretty cool, huh? Kinda funny, too, when you think of Selassie, who bought and sold black slaves, waving to the Jamaican crowds wondering what these people had to do with him.

Selassie came back to power in Ethiopia in 1945 and went back to his good old bloody ways. One of his dumber moves was trying to annex Eritrea in 1961. That turned into a long losing war—one of the dozens of wars, plagues, and famines going on around Ethiopia. The emperor finally fled in 1974, when the usual suspects—ambitious army officers mixed up with Marxist high-school teachers—decided he had to go. They figured they could do better at putting out the fires than some pint-sized, wrinkly king could.

They were wrong. They inherited all the rebellions and had no more luck putting them down—not even with the help of the fifteen thousand Cubans Fidel Castro sent to help out. The rebel group that finally took power in Ethiopia was the TPLF (Tigrayan People's Liberation Front). Their best friends were the EPLF (Eritrean People's Liberation Front), which took over Eritrea. These groups were bestest pals. They even helped each other against the old Marxist regime, sharing weapons, planning, and intelligence. In 1991, when the TPLF marched into Addis Ababa and the EPLF assumed power in Asmara, they showered each other with love notes and promises of eternal alliance.

But it's hard to stay friends when you're running African countries. The TPLF leaders got a lot of flak inside Ethiopia for being the EPLF's lapdogs. The EPLF was so high on its own victory speeches, it started picking fights with everybody—and when it stupidly picked a fight with Ethiopia over currency, the TPLF group running Ethiopia jumped at the chance to show the home folks they weren't no lapdogs to those snotty Eritreans. It was a bit like the way the Russian royal family rushed into a disastrous war against Germany in 1914 just to prove Tsarina Alexandra, a German by birth, wasn't no durn Kraut-lover.

The two countries decided to fight over the crummiest, most worthless land around: a little triangle of scrub around the town of Badme, where the border was hard to define. Both sides had plenty of manpower, even after fifteen years of border wars, because the Horn of Africa has some of the highest birthrates in the world. A whole new generation of kids was ready for call-up. The Eritrean leader Issaias Afwerki said he was glad that the new "Coca-Cola generation" of Eritreans were going to get the chance to see what his generation had gone through. (Afwerki has an AK round imbedded in his skull, which may explain this comment.)

While the United States fumbled around doing its usual "Now can't y'all shake hands and be friends?" routine, the Ethiopians went on a shopping spree: MiGs, antitank missiles, radar systems—if it was on sale and came in olive drab, they bought it. The Eritreans, with less capital, went for construction, making their "skyline trenches" even deeper, stronger, more impregnable.

In February 1998, the Ethiopians made their move, attacking the skyline trench at Badme, the crummy desert hamlet they were supposedly fighting over. The Ethiopians used tanks the way they're supposed to be used: as mobile weapons, not the boring dug-in artillery you see so often these days. The T-55s went slamming across the valley at full speed, right at the Eritrean lines. The Eritreans reacted with massed artillery barrages, emptying every tube they had into the attackers. It was a classic battle: one side fighting WW I trench-warfare style, the other using a classic WW II blitzkrieg approach.

And it developed in classic lines: pincer and counterpincer movement. The Eritreans made the fatal mistake of coming out of their trenches to surround Ethiopian penetrations and were enveloped in turn by the second and third waves of the Ethiopian advance. They were blown to pieces.

Another classic doctrine soon came into play: When discipline and morale are roughly equal, numbers will tell. And the Ethiopians had the numbers. The Eritreans couldn't go on trading casualties and fell back to their second lines. When the Ethiopians attacked those lines, the Eritreans were ready: Fifteen thousand Ethiopian troops were killed in less than one day. Even more impressive, the Eritreans knocked out forty to fifty Ethiopian tanks. That's not easy when both tanks and antitank weapons are Soviet, because the Soviets were better at tanks than antitank weapons.

By 2000, Ethiopia had made its point, pushed back the border, and forced Eritrea to back off. Both parties let it go to stalemate and brought in the United Nations, which is still yammering away uselessly about a permanent solution.

In a weird way, everybody won in this war. Eritrea is now the tightest-knit country in Africa, pretty impressive when you realize there wasn't really an Eritrea till recently. There's no such thing as an Eritrean ethnic group; it's just an old colonial border. But now, everybody inside that border is an Eritrean nationalist to the bone. And Ethiopia, a crazy, multiethnic African Bosnia, is suddenly full of national pride.

The Western press goes on and on about the dead and the suffering. But this war was a sign of life. It's like those tectonic plates they talk about: In some parts of the world, the planet's still young. Volcanoes are spouting, there are earthquakes all the time, whole continents are moving. In other places, the crust is already dead and cooled, and nothing ever happens. The Horn of Africa is like the tectonic hotspot of the whole damn planet. Part of that is that yeah, people die. But people die in Denmark and Fresno, too. They just die of boredom instead of bullets.

BIAFRA:
KILLER CESSNAS AND CRAZY SWEDES

THERE'S ONE OF those Crock-Pot, slow African bush wars just comin' to a boil in the bubbling crude of the Niger River delta in Nigeria. The locals are forming an army to make the Nigerian government give them a share of the income from all the oil they've found in the delta, but nobody seems to remember that this miserable maze of fever swamp was the focus of the biggest war in modern Africa—the Biafra War.

Nigeria's a typical West African mess of a country, only bigger and meaner. It's divided up the usual way: The coastal tribes are Christianized from sucking up to the European colonists. The further inland you go, the drier, hungrier, and more Islamic it gets.

The Brits grabbed the Nigerian coastline from the Portuguese when they realized there was money to be made, and turned the two big coastal tribes, the Ibo and Yoruba, into overseers on the Nigerian plantations. That left a lot of the inland Muslim tribes, the Hausa-Fulani people of the Sahel, permanently pissed off, sharpening their knives, and biding their time. The Hausa-Fulani got their chance in 1963, when the last Brit in Nigeria hopped a plane, yelling back to the natives, "Congratulations, chaps! You're independent!"

As soon as the Brits bugged out, the tribal massacres got going. Muslims in the north hacked to death every Ibo they could find. They hated these smartasses from the coast—and now the Redcoats weren't there to stop them from taking revenge. Thirty thousand Ibos were killed in a few days.

The massacres kind of soured the Ibo on the idea of Nigeria as one big, happy, intertribal family. In 1967, an Ibo general in the Nigerian Army declared that the Ibo region was now an independent country, Biafra. The Nigerian Army, a big, sleazy outfit, begged to differ and invaded the Ibo region in southeast Nigeria. The army had 250,000 men. The Biafran/Ibo army had maybe a tenth that many, but the troops were brave and smart—the Ibo had always been the brains of Nigeria.

Every time it was a question of real battle on anything like equal terms, the Biafran rebels won. They stopped the government troops cold, then grabbed tactical surprise by staging a long-range raid into western Nigeria. A risky advance like that by untrained civilian recruits (which is what most of the Ibo fighters were) is really impressive.

But sad to say, courage doesn't count for much in West African warfare. It's ruthlessness that wins these wars, and the Nigerian junta had it. Instead of facing the Ibo army man to man, the Nigerian troops grabbed the coastline around the Niger River delta, the supply route the Ibo needed. They stopped all food shipments heading for Ibo territory and sat back to let the Ibo starve.

The Biafrans were still winning every battle and losing the war like Robert E. Lee in 1865—starved out, strangled from behind. They realized they needed to open the supply route and decided to take back the Niger delta. And they got some help from outside. The best example, one of the few real heroes you'll get in this sleazy world, was a Swede, believe it or not. A Swedish count, no less. Carl Gustav von Rosen volunteered to do close-air support for the Biafran army, hosing down the government troops on low-level strafing runs—with tiny converted prop planes, like little Cessnas. Is that glorious, or what?

The mismatch in the air war was total. The Nigerian Air Force had MiG-17 fighters, Il-28 bombers, DC-3 transports (converted to bombers), and a few choppers.

Those Ilyushin and MiG designs were the high point of Soviet military aviation design. Don't kid yourself; the Soviets built some great planes. The Il-28 was a big, fast bomber with a bomb load of sixteen thousand pounds and a three-man crew, including a tail gunner manning twin 23-mm cannon. You wouldn't want to tailgate one of these.

The MiG-17 was even better. It might have been the best fighter in the world when it went into service in 1953, and even in the mid-1960s, it was good enough to win against our Phantom F-4s in air combat over North Vietnam. U.S. pilots were way more scared of the MiG-17 than the follow-on model, the MiG-21. The maneuverability and powerful cannon of the MiG-17 were a big reason the United States dropped all those Cold War notions about fighter craft as manned surface-to-air missiles, all speed and no close-in capability, and went back to nose cannon, maneuverability, and teaching air combat with Top Gun schools.

Up against all this great hardware, the Biafrans had . . . nothing. Then this crazy Swede von Rosen came up with the kind of idea that would only work in Africa. Since he couldn't get the Biafrans any jet aircraft, he'd just buy some prop-driven trainers and refit them for combat.

Von Rosen is such a great character, he almost makes me want to reconsider hating the Swedes. He was a throwback to the time when Swedish pikemen turned the tide in the Thirty Years War.

Von Rosen specialized in noble lost causes. Way back in 1938, when he was just a kid, he'd volunteered to fly for the Finns in their brilliant, hopeless fight against the Red Army. The Finns had no bombers, so von Rosen just grabbed a civilian airliner, loaded it up with bombs, and dropped them on the Reds.

Thirty years later, in August 1968, von Rosen was working as a civilian pilot, delivering aircraft to Africa. He ran into some priests who were trying to find somebody brave enough to fly medical supplies into Biafra. The mercenaries they'd hired called it off as too dangerous. Von Rosen volunteered to fly the DC-7 into Biafra with the supplies. The Biafrans were so grateful and were fighting so bravely against all the odds that von Rosen warmed to them as he had to the Finns.

The Biafrans needed somebody to help them deal with the Nigerian Air Force, which was fighting a nasty war even by African standards. In the whole course of the Biafra War, there's no record of a Nigerian Air Force plane attacking a military target. That would've been dangerous—and not nearly as much fun as bombing refugee camps, hospitals, and fleeing civilians. Those were the favorite targets—in fact, the air force's only targets.

Von Rosen tried to find the Ibo some modern jet aircraft, but nobody wanted to sell to the Biafrans for fear of upsetting the Nigerian government, a much bigger customer. So he started thinking about small, prop-driven aircraft. There's a long history of using slow prop planes in bush warfare. Even the USAF, which has a major hard-on for afterburners and chrome, was forced to adopt a slow, well-armored CAS (close air support) plane, the A-10. The air force hated it at first, but it proved itself in both Gulf wars, when other, more expensive, fancy CAS toys like the U.S. Army's lousy AH-64 Apache attack chopper left the field in disgrace.

In Vietnam, the classic jungle air war, the United States used two planes that were slow as molasses but did the job. One of the best, and ugliest, was the A-1 Skyraider, a chunky WW II–style plugger. The USAF hated it and was always trying to twist combat reports to make the Phantom look good and the Skyraider look bad, but pilots agreed: You were much better off going in low and slow in a Skyraider than zooming by in an F-4.

But the Skyraider was high-tech compared with the little putt-putt plane von Rosen decided to build his force around: the MFI-9, a tiny, prop-driven, Swedish-made trainer that looks like those ultralights people build in their garages. This plane could park in subcompact spaces at the mall. It had a maximum payload of five hundred pounds—that's me plus a couple of medium-sized dogs. Lucky thing Swedes are skinny.

Von Rosen bought five of these little "Fleas" down the coast in Gabon, slapped on a coat of green Volkswagen paint to make them look military, and installed wing pods for unguided 68-mm antiarmor rockets. Then he and his pilots (three Swedes, three Biafrans) flew them back to Biafra and into combat.

They blew the Hell out of the Nigerian Army. These little planes were impossible to bring down. Not a single one was knocked out of the sky, although they'd buzz home riddled with bullet holes. They could fly three missions a day, and their list of targets included Nigerian airfields, power plants, and troop concentrations.

The Fleas turned their weaknesses into advantages. They were so slow that they had to fly really low—which made them almost impossible to hit in the jungle, since you never saw them till they were on top of you. The low speed also made for better aim: Almost half of the four hundred rockets the little planes fired hit their targets, which is an amazing percentage for unguided air-to-surface munitions. (There used to be a joke in the USAF that if it wasn't for the law of gravity, unguided air-to-surface rockets couldn't even hit the ground.)

The Biafran air force managed to destroy three MiG-17s and an Il-28 on the ground. Killing planes on the ground may not be as glorious as shooting them out of the sky, but they're just as destroyed. The Fleas also took out a few helicopters, an airport tower, a British Canberra bomber, and a half-dozen trucks. And they blew away at least five hundred Nigerian troops. It was one of the few really glorious exploits you get in late-twentieth-century war.

But it wasn't enough to turn the tide of the war. The rest of the world turned its back on the Ibo and let the Nigerians starve them into submission. The USSR sold the Nigerian forces every plane, tank, and gun they could fit in their shopping cart, and the British let their own pilots fly as Nigerian Air Force mercenaries, bombing Biafran cities and blowing up convoys trying to bring food to the Ibo.

The famine in Biafra was the first time the world saw those pictures of African kids with skeleton arms and legs and big, swollen bellies looking up at the camera. It was easy to get shots like that in Biafra, because the whole country was starving.

A year into the war, the Ibo had nothing left. No food, no ammunition, not even any fuel, which is ironic considering they were sitting on the big Delta oilfields.

Even the bravest troops can't fight when they're dying of starvation. So in 1969, the Nigerian Army attacked with 120,000 men and pushed through the center of Biafra, dividing the Ibo zone in half. It was like Sherman's march to the sea: It broke the Biafrans' backs. Early in 1970, Biafra surrendered.

Nobody knows exactly how many people died. The lowest estimate is one million. Some say as many as three million. Almost all of them were Ibo civilians.

The Ibo were punished for their uppity behavior by being frozen out of the Nigerian government. For more than thirty years, they've been watching the oil pumped out of their land make a bunch of sleazy generals and politicians rich while they get nothing. They have every right to be pissed off. But the Biafra War showed the world that in Africa, right doesn't have much to do with it. As the greatest Swede of them all used to say, "God is on the side of the big battalions."

ONWARD CHRISTIAN SOLDIERS:
THE LORD'S RESISTANCE ARMY

CHRISTIANS ARE STONE killers. You put a Christian and a lion in an arena, and the Christian'll have the lion for lunch. Just look around you: Lions are just about extinct, but the whole world is full of Christians singin' about God's love, ready to disembowel anybody who won't join the chorus.

In this chapter, I'm honoring some great Christian killers: the Lord's Resistance Army of Uganda. These kids—and they are kids, mostly thirteen to sixteen years old—get my vote for the funniest army on the planet. And that's a pretty big award, when you consider that the Dutch armed forces are included in the competition.

The Lord's Resistance Army came out of one tough neighborhood: Uganda in the 1970s. You say "Uganda," and people think Idi Amin. But he was way overhyped as a killer, a big teddy bear compared to the "moderate" leader who overthrew him. This "moderate" was a former altar boy named—get this—Apollo Milton Obote.

It's always "ex-altar boys" who have a dozen bodies under the concrete. And when the former altar boy is also a "moderate," according to the Western press, then damn, get ready for a serious bloodbath. Nobody can kill like a moderate. Amin was a noisy killer, feeding people to the crocs, beating them to death, eating their flesh. Dictators like him and Bokassa never last. It's the moderates who do the really large-scale, efficient slaughtering.

That's the lesson of the twentieth century: If you want to kill a few people and get bad press, then go ahead, dress in black, drink blood, and talk about how you love torture. Like Amin, Bokassa, and Hitler. But if you're serious about wiping out whole populations, wear a dove of peace and talk about progress and love. That's what Stalin did, and he wiped out half the population of Ukraine without getting a single piece of bad publicity from the contemporary Western press.

Obote was smart; he knew he needed that "moderate" label if he was going to wipe out all his enemies. So he smiled a lot and wore suits and talked progress . . . and then went to work. When a densely populated Bantu zone called the Luwero Crescent gave him trouble, his soldiers went in and killed every goddamn human being in the place. Ever hear about it? No you didn't, because the respectable papers didn't want to know. Amin was evil; Obote was a "moderate."

The survivors of Luwero, mostly kids too young to be worth killing, formed up in a kind of bush army and kept fighting, even when their leader, Yoweri Museveni, said, "Fuck it," and flew to London. And to everybody's surprise (including Museveni), they won. Obote's soldiers fled north still picking people-meat from between their teeth. Museveni flew home in time to celebrate his victory and resume command. He is now the official ruler of the land. Ta-da!

A real Cinderella story, Central Africa style.

But Obote wasn't the only former altar boy in Uganda. There was another, way crazier and more fun: Joseph Kony, leader of the Lord's Resistance Army. Little Joseph came from a very devout Christian family: His Aunt Alice founded the LRA and passed it on to him when she died. Aunt Alice Lakwena started some of the great traditions of the LRA, like telling your troops that if they just wore her special amulets, bullets won't hurt them. Aunt Alice had everybody in the LRA believing God hisself would be their Kevlar vest. This turned out to be untrue, but there was a great escape clause: By the time the chumps found out the amulets didn't work as advertised, they were *dead*! Now that's the way to run a complaint department: thousands of satisfied customers and dissatisfied but uncomplaining corpses.

The LRA gets backing from Sudan, which uses it to massacre other Christians like the Dinka, who are rebelling against the

Arabs of the North. The North/South, Muslim/Christian war in Sudan is another of those meat-grinder wars that until recently just hasn't interested the Western press. It's inland, and the reporters don't like getting too far from the beach hotels. It's hot and malarial country; the victims are nobody's poster boys. I've had a soft spot for them, though, those Dinka, for quite a while, because I once saw a documentary that featured a yearly Dinka ritual where the young men compete to see who can get the fattest. You have to understand, these are the tallest and skinniest people on the planet. But every year, the cool guys of the tribe spend months doing nothing but sitting around drinking a mixture of blood and milk, trying to see how fat they can get. None of them gets all that fat—not by my standards, anyway—but it was nice just to see somebody appreciating fatness and all. There was a scene with the fattened-up contestants sitting in a little puddle pouring water over themselves, trying to cool off. God, I know the feeling! June now in Fresno, and it's already unbearable. Summer is the bad time for fat people, like winter used to be when people were poor and skinny.

The Dinka are being wiped out, village by village. The LRA is helping the Sudanese Muslims do it—but that's an old Christian game too, helping the heathens kill other Christians. Hell, it was the Crusaders who sacked Constantinople, broke its power, and set it up for the Turks to rape. Religion's nice, but rape and plunder are what it's all about.

People won't see this—won't see how simple and practical the African style of warfare really is. The LRA is at war with the Ugandan Army, but it's war Central Africa style. We're not talking Gettysburg or Verdun here. The idea isn't to have big battles, but to sneak up on an enemy village and kill all the civilians, take their livestock, and steal their stuff. Reporters like to call this "insane," which is crap. Which would you rather do, get sent off to another continent to fight heavily armed opponents (war Western-style) or kill the neighbors who wake you every damn morning with their stupid lawnmower (war African-style)? Especially if you can see they've got a nice DVD player in there? Personally, I'd much rather kill the neighbors and steal their stuff. And if they've got a daughter hitting prom age—well, that's just gravy.

And if they're Christians, so much the better. I'll tell you about my boss sometime—this little shit from suburban Atlanta whose first question in a job interview is "Where do you worship?" If I were going to sack and pillage any house in Fresno, it'd be his. Believe me, God would be On My Side. I'd shoot his livestock—two cats and a dog he brings to the office sometimes—and decide on the spot if his wife was saleable, African-style.

So I don't see what's so crazy about these African bush armies' way of making war. Verdun, Blenheim, Gallipoli—those were "insane." And if you still think tribal massacre is so weird, try remembering high-school PE. Now is it so hard to get? Life in an African bush army is just adolescent fantasy come to life. If I were a bit younger and in better shape…

ALGERIA:
THE PSYCHOS WILL INHERIT THE EARTH

SOME WARS MAKE it onto the TV news, and some don't. It's got nothing to do with how bloody or big they are. There are lots of pissant little "wars" that get more press than they deserve. Like Northern Ireland. In twenty-five years of fighting, you know how many people got killed? About 3,100. That works out to 125 people per year. Per *year!* That's not as much as a three-day weekend in Detroit. But just look at how much press those few Irish killings got. Every time a little bomb went off or one of the local drunks got popped on St. Patrick's Day, it was all over the news. So by now everybody thinks Northern Ireland is this big, bad trouble spot, when the truth is, you'd probably have to jump in front of a bus to get hurt there. Going into a Fresno 7-Eleven after midnight is about a thousand times more dangerous.

Then there are the big, bloody wars that never get on TV at all. Like Algeria. When was the last time you saw a live report from

Algeria on the news? Some 100,000 people got killed there in the last ten years. Maybe more, up to 170,000. Nobody's sure. And the killings were really sick, too: slit throats, people burned alive, mass rapes, and various farm tools used in nasty ways.

You'd think the TV news types would like that. But they never show anything from Algeria. I've been wondering why that is, and I've come up with three reasons.

First, it's too real. Too dangerous. TV reporters are chickenshit. You could see how scared they were during the Gulf War I, even though everybody with any sense knew Saddam's shitty army couldn't beat an egg, let alone America. So these CNN stars love going on location to places like Northern Ireland, where they can wear bulletproof vests and look brave without any real chance they'll get hurt. But they won't go anywhere near Algeria, because the war there is for real. The Algerian Islamic crazies kill every journalist they catch. Allah doesn't like reporters. Wolf Blitzer's not going to risk his overpaid hide in a place like that.

Second, the people getting killed in Algeria are Arabs. And the fact is, nobody likes Arabs. Yeah, Dubya has to go around saying we love the Arabs to death, but that's just politicians talking. Who really cares when they hear that another few Palestinians got blasted in some West Bank hellhole? And Westerners care even less when it's Arabs in Algeria.

The funny thing is, a lot of Algerians aren't Arabs at all. They're Berbers who have their own language and don't like Arabs, either. The Islamic throat-slitters hate the Berbers, because Berbers like to drink wine and make music and generally have a good time. The Berbers actually sound like pretty decent people who just picked the wrong place to live, like the Kurds did.

When you think about it, a lot of pretty interesting countries got swamped by the Arabs. Take the Egyptians, who had the coolest gods of anybody—the one with the jackal's head, the sun god, the sacred crocodiles, and so on. Or the Persians—the Greeks' best battles, like Marathon and Salamis, are always against the Persians. The Persian army was like this giant zoo of tribal fighters marching around on horses and camels, with every weapon in the world from slingers to heavy cavalry. Then the Arabs come screaming in out of the desert smashing up the statues of the gods, burning and outlawing everything they can think of, and what have the Egyptians and the Persians and the Berbers got now? No music, no statues, no booze, no women allowed out on the street. What a fucking waste. Sounds a lot like my life, in fact. No wonder it gets me depressed.

The third reason nobody hears about Algeria is that there's no moral to the story, and news types can't handle a story with no angle. Algeria is just a bloody mess with no good guys, no happy ending, no "lessons" for anybody, and so many different bad guys that it makes no sense to outsiders.

So Algeria is having a war nobody wants to know about. It's like that old hippie saying, "What if they held a war and nobody came?" Except it's more like "What if they held ten years of nonstop massacres and nobody cared?" Since nobody cares, nobody writes about it. So it's hard getting any decent info on Algeria, especially in English. The good stuff seems to be in French, and I'm proud to say I don't speak a word of that poodle-talk. Finding out about Algeria was tougher than any other war I've done, but I've got it taped now.

First thing to keep in mind is that Algeria has always been a bloody place, even before it was Algeria. Piracy was the main business on the North African coast. That's where we get that line about "the shores of Tripoli" in the Marine Corps hymn. Tripoli is in Libya, and it was the sort of place you had to send the marines into from time to time to rescue merchant ships that had got a little too close to the North African coast and been captured for ransom.

Violence is normal in Algeria. (It's normal all over the world; we just don't like to admit it.) Algeria also has a weird geography that makes it easier to understand why Algerians like to fight so much. It's a huge country, but nine-tenths of it is useless Sahara sand. Everybody lives on the Mediterranean coast or in the mountains near the coast. That means there's not really much land. And the birthrate is incredible. When Algeria kicked out the French in 1962, there were about ten million people. Now there are thirty million. Three-quarters of the population is under twenty-five. Too many kids plus Islam equals a lot of dumb boys who want to be Jihadis. Just think about it: a country where the whole "silent majority" is high-school age. I don't know about you, but for me, high school was the closest thing to Hell on earth. A whole country of high-school kids is bad enough, but Islamic high-school kids—it's like *Lord of the Flies* only with a bigger weapons budget.

So all the kids want to be Jihadis, but the old men running the country have other ideas. They're antireligious old commies who had their own war, a commie-led war for independence from the French, 1954–1962. The poor, sad French were trying to hang on to a little scrap of their empire, and Algeria, one of the few colonies they managed to settle in big numbers, was their last stand. There were a couple million French colonists living in Algeria, and the French put everything they had into holding on to it. If you ever run into a Frenchman who was born between 1930 and 1940, ask him if he was in Algeria. If he says no, he's probably lying.

The war was a bloody mess, maybe a million dead altogether, mostly Algerians. That's typical for guerrilla warfare: You expect to kill about ten natives for every soldier you lose. And even that doesn't mean you're going to stamp out the revolt. We killed maybe twelve Vietnamese for every GI who died, and we still lost. It was the same with Algeria: The French killed a whole lot of Algerians, but the Algerians just wanted it more than the French did. So the Algerians kept on coming, and the war ended with the French running for the docks. A million French settlers scrambled onto the boats just as the FLN (Front de libération nationale), the Algerian revolutionary commies, marched into Algiers.

The FLN did the usual thing for commie "national liberation" movements: they tortured all the "collaborators" to death, voted themselves into power for life, and started up a good secret police. And that was about all.

Algeria went into a socialist coma, the kind where there are lots of big posters and revolutionary slogans, but you can't buy a decent pair of shoes. The only thing that kept the place running was money from the oil and natural gas down in the Sahara. There was enough coming in from that to keep the ex-revolutionaries in caviar and Cadillacs, with enough left over to keep the rest of the population from actually starving.

But by 1990, things were bad. Oil revenues were down, and commies everywhere were in full retreat. The Algerian generals were getting nervous. The kids were into Islam, not Marx. Western pressure led to elections in 1991. The Islamists were leading and would've won. But the generals decided to cancel the elections. That's when it turned into all-out war between the Islamists and the army.

The biggest Islamic guerrilla force was the AIS (Armée islamique du salut), connected to the FIS (Front islamique du salut), the Islamic party that would've won the elections. But AIS looked like squeamish moderates compared with the GIA (Groupe islamique armé), another Islamic militia that does its killing south of Algiers. The GIA gets my vote for the sickest, craziest, bloodiest guerrilla group since the Khmer Rouge went out of business. The GIA conducts massacres that make Algeria the place you'd least like to spend your honeymoon.

Just killing isn't enough for these guys. Killing is for wimps. The GIA started coming up with new touches to keep the game interesting: burning people alive, bayoneting babies, raping and killing children in front of their parents. All in the name of God, you understand.

It got so bad that your run-of-the-mill Islamic lunatic in the street was getting sick of it. The GIA leaders, arguing about whether they might have been a little over the top, settled the argument in their usual way: by killing each other. The army was helping out, too, by killing any GIA leader it could find. What you ended up with was a bunch of little gangs of Islamic fanatics instead of one big group.

But the Algerian army never really tried to wipe out the GIA. The army shot a few of the GIA leaders, but there are a lot of reports about GIA crazies going into villages right next to army bases, killing and raping for hours, then strolling out with no re-action from the army. Supposedly, army helicopters even hovered over one of the worst massacres, where eight hundred villagers had their throats slashed, but never sent troops or did anything else to help. It takes a long time to kill eight hundred people with nothing but knives. Plenty long enough to send troops—if you want to.

One theory is that the Algerian army brass wanted to let the GIA make Islamic extremism look so sick that the voters would never go for it again. If that was the idea, it's worked, because the latest polls show Algerians turning against the Islamists. But there are other rumors that some of the Islamic loonies were actually army men in disguise, killing off villagers to settle private scores.

Even if there are some secret motives, you can't say the Algerian massacres are just the result of a few bad apples or part of some conspiracy theory. There are too many people doing the killings for that. Let's face up to a couple of depressing facts here.

First, Islam *does* glorify violence. When groups like the GIA say they're doing Allah's will by killing people who ain't following the right path, they've got the Quran on their side. The Quran is absolutely in favor of violence against everybody who's not already a Muslim. Anybody who tells you different is a liar. Speaking as a recovered Pentecostal, I'd say all religions are crap—but Islam is way, way the sickest and most violent of all. Dubya goes around sucking up to the Saudis with this crap about Islam being "a religion of peace." Islam is *not* a religion of peace and never has been. Face facts, damn it!

Second, the GIA is not just a few loonies. It'd be nice to believe that, but it's just not true. The GIA has at least fifteen thousand soldiers. You can't feed and supply that many men without cooperation from the civilian population. The newspeople like to tell you the GIA terrorizes the poor villagers, but that's bullshit. The GIA is recruited from those villagers, supported by them, fed and sheltered and hidden by them. If the GIA is sick, it's because a whole lot of Algerians like it that way.

The war got even sicker as it went on. My personal favorite for the coolest group of crazies is the Disciples of Satan, this GIA splinter group I read about. Sounds like a biker gang, but these guys make the Hell's Angels look like Oprah's book club. They started out as GIA fighters, but they got so messed up by what they'd seen and done that they decided there must not be a God at all. They turned into Islamic Satanists and went around trying to find newer and sicker ways to kill people as a way of making Satan happy. So they were doing the same sick shit as ever, but in Satan's name instead of Allah's.

Not everybody approved of the GIA. The Islamists who weren't completely out of their little minds started trying to isolate the group. Some formed a new group called the Salafist Group for Preaching and Combat (you gotta love that name!), which tried to be "good" guerrillas, sticking to military targets and not killing civilians unnecessarily. Meanwhile the AIS, the first and biggest Islamic guerrilla group, made a deal with the government in 1999. It got amnesty and agreed to help hunt down the crazies in the GIA.

It looked like things were looking up for Algeria—for a while. But lately, it all seems to be melting down. The GIA is still around. The Salafists are hunkered down in the mountains waiting to meet the army head-on. And the Berbers are getting sick of having their favorite musicians blown away for the crime of singing. (Apparently, Allah hates singers. Maybe we could pay the GIA to come over and whack Justin Timberlake.)

The poor Berbers. They're really the only people you can sympathize with in the whole sick country. It's like they're the only sane person in a family full of *Chainsaw Massacre* types. So they're the freaks, because they want to drink wine and sing and take it easy. They're the "evil" un-Islamic ones, because they're not as crazy as the Algerian Arabs. The sad thing is, they'll probably never be able to kill as well as the Islamists. You can't act as crazy as a really crazy person, no matter how hard you try. And the Berbers are just too sane for Algeria. They'll be stomped every time.

So whoever said that the meek are going to inherit the earth was dead wrong. You want an "angle" or a "moral" from Algeria? Here you go: The sick, the crazy, the psychos are going to inherit everything.

THE CONGO:
WAR WITHOUT BATTLES

WRITING ABOUT THE Congo is like dying: You have to deal with it sooner or later, but you're not looking forward to it.

I've tried every way I could to get out of talking about the Congo, but it's just too big and bloody a mess for an honest war-fan to ignore. Nobody knows exactly how many people have been slaughtered in the Congo over the past few years, but the BBC estimates 2.5 million. That's a lot of zeroes, a lot of bodies—especially for a war without battles. These people didn't die in the trenches. They died African-style: chopped to death with machetes, mowed down by squads of stoned twelve-year-olds, or just driven into the bush to die of hunger or malaria.

There's this term for what's going on in the Congo: *primitive warfare*. It doesn't mean simple weapons or illiterate soldiers. It means the way people fought before there were any nation-states. It's not pretty. It means avoiding combat, slinking around, looking for unguarded villages, and then going in and killing everybody in the place, except a few you think you can sell at the nearest slave market.

Ethnic cleansing is just a soft term for primitive warfare. It's always been the way people fight. I once took a first-year course in world literature at Stanislaus Community College—it was required—and I pissed off the professor good when he had us read a piece of *The Iliad*. It was about Achilles fighting with Agamemnon about a slave girl, and I just said, "Hey, that's just the way they fight in Africa right now!" He made me pay for that, the PC bastard. Naturally he was white, and naturally he made a big speech that had "racism" in it about a hundred times—you know, looking around at all the "people of color" in the room to make sure nobody was going to turn him in.

But I wasn't being racist at all; he was. And I still say if people thought about the Congo when they were reading the classics, they'd understand it better. Achilles raids a village, grabs the best-looking girl, moves on to ambush another village. In the meantime, one of Achilles' friends, some other ganja-smoking kid with an AK, decides he wants the girl instead. They settle it out in the bush somewhere. Boom: That's *The Iliad.* But damn it, the one thing people don't want to do is connect the classics with Congo-style "primitive warfare." First, there's the question of borders. In primitive warfare, there are no borders. You know, these spoiled "anarchy" kids, who like to draw a big *A* in a circle, they talk about "no borders" as if it's a good thing. You think so? Go to Africa. The Congo isn't really a country at all. It's lines on a map. The lines were drawn up by European colonizers at Berlin in 1884–1885. Most of the people at the table—the men chopping up Africa—had never even been there. They didn't know or care about tribal boundaries; they were just playing politics. The Congo borders got defined by where the colonies around it ended. The region wasn't worth much back then, so they let King Leopold of Belgium take it. I mean, for himself. Private property. The whole frickin' country.

A few years after they gave Leopold the country, rubber got big. Suddenly, Leopold's jungle was worth something, and he pushed his luck as far as he could—drafted every thug he could get in Europe or Africa to go in there and break heads to make sure the rubber quota was filled. Leopold was what you call a bottom-line guy. His goons had this habit of chopping off hands when people were slow getting their rubber. Maybe that sounds familiar? You may remember a lunatic named Foday Sankoh, up in Sierra Leone, who told his "soldiers" to chop off hands and feet to keep villagers in line. Maybe you think that's just the Africans being primitive, but it was the cute li'l Belgians who showed 'em how.

Look at Central Africa with the borders erased. Hundreds of tribes, overlapping districts like Bosnia. Worse still, some of the tribes have millions of people, and others amount to some schmo and his cousin and a dog. Not exactly nation-building material, even if the fucking Europeans had had the decency to leave them alone. The tribe that gave the Congo its name, the baKongo, don't even live in the Congo—most of them are down south in Angola, where they were one side of the big triangular U.S.-Soviet proxy war they had in the 1970s. There are at least 280 tribes in the Congo, and the dense rainforest means most are pretty small, isolated groups.

A lot of African countries got lucky when independence came in the 1960s. Either there was one dominant tribe covering most of the country, or there'd been a century or so of "civilization" that built some sort of educated class who were ready to take over. The Congo didn't have either. Leopold hadn't even bothered to teach the Congolese a thing. He just wanted the rubber—or the hands. Most of the country was thick jungle, with the river the only way to travel.

The biggest, strongest tribes in Central Africa were the Hutu and the Tutsi, both of whom were based in Rwanda and Burundi. They ended up in power over various parts of the Congo at the end of the twentieth century just because nobody in the Congo had the organization. The Hutu and the Tutsi are truly law-abiding, organized people. If you've only heard about them from the geno-cide news out of Rwanda, this might seem surprising. But to un-derstand this, you have to be willing to hear the bitter truth. And here it is: The people who do genocide best are law-abiding, decent, stand-up folks. Strange but true. Take the Germans: wouldn't hurt a fly . . . unless someone in uniform told them to. Then they would fry every fly on the planet.

The Tutsi and Hutu had been lucky—in a way. The European colonists liked hanging out in the Hutu and Tutsis' homelands, Rwanda and Burundi—cool mountain air, fertile volcanic soil. And they liked these two intelligent, obedient tribes. So the Europeans, um, "civilized" them. The Hutu and Tutsi turned into the most literate, Christian, tidy, hardworking people in Central Africa. Then the Europeans overseers left . . . and after a little while, these two tribes got that old itch to wipe each other out. It was all organized. The churches helped out. Two of the big war criminals were nuns. It's like *Invasion of the Body Snatchers*, imagining hundreds of thousands of neat, clean Hutus with machetes running around cheerfully hacking every Tutsi or Tutsi-lover they catch. The old line "I was just following orders" may seem pretty lame, but after you read about the Hutu killers, you end up kind of believing it. They did it because they were told to.

Rwanda and Burundi are two small, heavily populated countries due east of the Congo—so you could guess that their well-trained killers might be looking west and getting excited. Meanwhile, who was running the store in the Congo? Bad news: It was a corrupt, superstitious, stupid, dying old jerk-off named Joseph Mobutu—a guy only a CIA bagman could love. (We can really pick 'em, all right!) With Mobutu in charge (he later renamed himself Mobutu Sese Seko), the Congo wasn't a country, it was a racket. You always hear reporters jabbering about what a shame it is that "with all its mineral riches and natural wealth," the Congo is still a hellhole. Well, with leaders like Mobutu, heaven would be a hellhole in no time. He knew how to do two things: steal and play one tribe against another. That was all he needed to stay in power for life—meaning until 1997, when the bastard finally died.

Under Mobutu, the Congo was officially "at peace." Which meant it was small-scale stuff, murder and torture, instead of big armies. It'd be a lie to call this situation *peace*, but it kept the Congo out of the headlines. When war came, it was thanks to that dynamic duo, the Tutsis and the Hutus. The Congo was too fucked up to have a war by itself. To have a war, you need organization: soldiers who obey orders, lines of communication. The only people in the neighborhood who had what it took to make a war were . . . you guessed it! Those Hatfields 'n' McCoys of Central Africa: the Hutus and the Tutsis!

The bloodbath really got going in the early 1990s, after a suspicious plane crash that killed the leaders of Rwanda and Burundi.

The Rwandan Hutus polished up their machetes and started killing Tutsis. Maybe a million or so. Only then did the feud spill over into that big, stinking power vacuum to the west: the Congo.

One thing you notice about African bush wars: when one side is pushed to the edge of extinction, it can strike back against the enemy's soldiers, who aren't as willing to die. This happened in Uganda, in the Luwero Triangle, and it happened in Rwanda. With nothing left to lose, the Tutsis started retaking the country. The Hutus, who'd been so brave when it was a matter of chopping kids' heads open like coconuts, weren't so brave going up against real soldiers. They lit out for the jungle—for the Congo. The Tutsis' new army pursued and realized it had marched into the biggest power vacuum since Gerald Ford got sucked into Nixon's slipstream. There was just nobody to stop them. Mobutu had never wanted or allowed any power in the Congo other than him. Now that he was dead, there was nobody at all.

Mobutu had an old enemy, Laurent Kabila, who'd been hiding out in the bush preaching rebellion for decades, getting exactly nowhere. Kabila wasn't classic hero-rebel stuff. He was a fat man, for one thing. They always mention that in the wire stories, like getting fat is the biggest sin anybody could ever commit. Pisses me off. Us fat people have dreams too, you know. You know the saddest thing about being fat? Having some kind of heroic daydream, then suddenly seeing your reflection in a window or mirror. Suddenly you realize, whoa, I'm not entitled to dream about that stuff.

Well, to be fair, fat old Kabila wasn't very heroic by anybody's standards. Just another killer-thief with a taste for chorus girls and a history of ivory poaching and gem smuggling. But in the waste of the Congo, Kabila was the closest thing to new blood you could find. When Kabila saw how the Tutsi revenge strike just kept moving west toward the capital, Kinshasa, without meeting any armed opposition, he suddenly saw the light. After thirty years of preaching Maoism, Kabila started talking free enterprise. And even though he was from the Luba tribe, he became a born-again Tutsi for the duration.

Nobody, not even Kabila, expected this ragged little army to make it all the way to Kinshasa. But it did. Kabila was so shocked he had no idea what to do next. Then it came to him, the traditional Central African formula: Embezzle, lie, and murder your enemies! One of the fat man's bodyguards got sick of it and shot Kabila dead in January 2001.

Kabila's worthless son, Joseph, took over for his worthless dad. The Tutsis' brief period of clearheaded, soldierly discipline was over. Hell broke loose, on cue, back in the homelands of Rwanda and Burundi. Every cub scout pack in the Congo declared itself a liberation movement and declared its independence. In December 2002, the CIA dragged all the camo-wearing generals together, and all the crazy gangs in the Congo signed a peace pact.

Last time I checked, every party was accusing everybody else of violating the agreement. Now there's a surprise: a Congo peace deal breaking down. Who could have guessed? You wonder why the Foreign Service types even bother setting these conferences up. Who's kidding who?

Just figuring out who's who in this boneyard rumble is impossible. As near as I can tell, here are some of the factions:

The Mai-Mai: my personal faves. Hicks with bows and arrows. They believe charms make them immune to bullets. Funny how that notion hangs on.

The MLC (Mouvement de Libération du Congo): run by a big Congo businessman. Imagine if Ross Perot had his own army. They're backed by Uganda and call the shots in most of northern Congo.

The RCD-Goma (Rally for Congolese Democracy–Goma): This group is based, not so surprisingly, in Goma. They're Rwandan, originally, and run a big swath of Eastern Congo.

There it is, friends. Not a pretty picture. Remember what I said about borders? At the moment, there is no Congo. Uganda runs the north, Rwanda the east, Angola the south, and a bunch of stone-age loonies stalk around the backwoods bushwhacking anybody they think they can overpower. Meanwhile, a few thugs in Mercedes tool around Kinshasa running over stray corpses.

PLEASE DON'T EAT
THE PYGMIES

FANS OF MY column love sending me hot tips on the kind of little stories that make war interesting. Here's one a reader sent in from the Congo: "Army, rebel and tribal fighters, some believing the Pygmies are less than human or that eating their flesh would give them magic power, have been pursuing the Pygmies in forests, killing them and eating their flesh, activists said."

You can always count on the Congo to come through when the rest of the world is getting all dull and practical. You have to wonder what kind of arguments they have around the barbecue, munching away on a nice Pygmy drumstick. Do the ones chomping the little fella to get magic powers get flak from the ones who just like the taste? "Hey, magic man, let's see you fly now that you've had your Pygmy meat!"

The story didn't say who the "activists" were, but I like the idea of a bunch of Europeans fanning out in the jungle with little "Don't Eat a Pygmy" kits—you know, armbands with a little Pygmy in a red circle, trying to be sensitive to the local culture—then losing it when they walk into a village and see the local bigwigs just finishing a teeny arm or leg: "You savages! Oh no, did I say that?" I guess your typical activist would have to go off into the jungle and shoot himself if he got caught saying something incorrect like that. But hey, that wouldn't end his problems, not if the locals really had a taste for long-pig. You might be cremated the long, slow way: in a crock-pot with some yams.

The thing is, picking on Pygmies is pure discrimination—heightism. Maybe you could get Dustin Hoffman to do a charity visit. Those Hollywood liberals like to talk about "all the little people"—see how they like it when Dustin, who's short enough to play a pygmy, is suddenly one of the appetizers.

If there's one country that can give the Congo a run for its money in the crazy sweepstakes, it's Liberia. A reader sent me an update on one of my favorite military figures, General Butt Naked of Liberia.

Liberia's right next door to Sierra Leone and has a history similar to Sierra Leone's. Both countries were started up as places to settle freed slaves. Sierra Leone was a British project, and Liberia was American, but otherwise, it's the same story: Freed slaves set up little towns on the coast, make the inland tribes into slaves, and then the whole thing dissolves into massacres, with "armies" of thirteen-year-old boys in dresses carrying M-16s and killing and fucking, in that order, anybody they can catch.

General Butt Naked was like the Patton of these guys, the Robert E. Lee of Liberia. Instead of wearing wigs and high heels like most Liberian "army" kids, he started a wild new fashion: He—you guessed it!—wore nothing at all. Here's the item, just the way the reader sent it:

LIBERIA: Joshua Blahyi—formerly known as General Butt Naked and leader of the Butt Naked Battalion in Liberia's recent civil war—says that he now regrets the drunken murderous rampages he led his troops on, and says that he was a "slave to Satan". Speaking to the press from his new Soul-Winning Evangelical Ministry in Monrovia, General Butt Naked told reporters that at the age of 11 he had a telephone call from the Devil who demanded nudity on the battlefield, acts of indecency and regular human sacrifices to ensure his protection. "So, before leading my troops into battle, we would get drunk and drugged up, sacrifice a local teenager, drink their blood, then strip down to our shoes and go into battle wearing colourful wigs and carrying dainty purses we'd looted from civilians. We'd slaughter anyone we saw, chop their heads off and use them as soccer balls. We were nude, fearless, drunk and homicidal. We killed hundreds of people—so many I lost count. But in June last year God telephoned me and told me that I was not the hero I considered myself to be, so I stopped and became a preacher.

Just try imagining one of the general's military campaigns. It makes you realize how tame movies really are, even the ones that say they're all "dark" and daring. I've seen a lot of war movies, but none of them ever even tried to show anything this crazy.

Picture General Butt's "army" hitting a village. They grab a kid off a trail to the village, rip him up, drink his blood, and then get naked. They're already high on who knows what mix of drugs and booze, probably screeching like parrots. Oh, wait—I forgot about the purses and wigs. So they're in drag, naked, dripping blood from their mouths, and boom! they're sprinting into your village. The killing isn't even the fun part for them. That's just a day at the office for these guys. It's the big soccer game they're up for. So they get their pangas out and chop off a few dozen heads and start kicking them around.

Compared with that, *Apocalypse Now* is about as dark as *SpongeBob SquarePants*.

Of course, the general's a Christian now. The sad part is, I can imagine my folks going to see the bastard preach and getting all sentimental when he starts talking about how the Devil captured him at age eleven. Pentecostals are about the most easy-to-fool people in the world. All you have to do is say you found Jesus. Hugs and money and dinner invites. The Bible verse I hated the most, and that's saying something, was the one that says, "There is more joy in heaven over one sinner who repents than ninety-nine of the righteous." God loves people like General Naked. What that meant to me was God is crazy or stupid. General Naked may be preaching the Gospel now, but that's the kind of job-change psychos like him can do without breaking a sweat. And they can go back to the old psycho-killer job just as quick when the time's right.

And the time can be just about any time. One of the biggest, craziest killers in the history of Liberia, the exiled Charles Taylor, came back from Sierra Leone in June 2003. Anyplace else in the world, Taylor would've come home like Hannibal Lecter, complete with that little grille over the mouth. But Liberia's different. The locals were so happy to have Taylor back that they lined the road all the way from the airport to his house just for the chance to wave hello to the Homecoming King.

Taylor had gone to Sierra Leone a few years before and joined up with the one man in Africa who's maybe crazier than him: Foday Sankoh, leader of the RUF (Revolutionary United Front). You might not know the initials, but you've probably heard of the RUF's unique way of doing business: The soldiers used to go into a village in Sierra Leone and cut off arms and legs and pile them up in the middle of town. It was Sankoh's idea of a joke. He'd tell the villagers who were rolling around in agony, "Go ask the government for your arms and legs."

Taylor just naturally wound up working for a guy like that when he moved next door to Sierra Leone. Taylor's on trial now for "human rights violations" in the Hague—a clear case of Eurocentric, foreign moral imperialism, EU rules being imposed on Africa. Just a new way of forcibly Christianizing the poor bastards, although don't expect anybody like Bono to say so. Do-gooders like him are too ignorant to realize that human-rights crusaders are just missionaries in a new disguise, like *Terminator 2*. Taylor's boycotting his own trial, and he's right. He should borrow Martin Sheen's line from *Apocalypse Now*: arresting people for murder in Liberia is like handing out speeding tickets at the Indy 500.

As for General Butt Naked, he's doing what Pentecostal bad boys always do: selling his sinful past. In January 2008, he appeared before some "reconciliation commission," claiming that he killed twenty thousand people. Sad to see such a great character lowering himself to the ultimate military disgrace: inflated body counts.

GADHAFI:
BUCKLES, SIZE XXXL

SOME PARTS OF the world should be declared Zones of Total Bullshit. Take Libya. It seems like everybody who even tries to talk about the place starts lying. The latest lie is that "Libya has renounced terrorism and weapons of mass destruction (WMDs)" because Gadhafi, the little colonel who runs the place, saw what happened to Saddam and surrendered to the forces of good. Here's a typical headline from 2003–2004: "Gadhafi Buckles After Eyeing Saddam in His Spider Hole."

Saying that Gadhafi buckled just now is like saying that a sixty-year-old prostitute just lost her virginity. Gadhafi's done more buckles than the Bangladeshi sweatshops that make my XL belts. For more than thirty years, Gadhafi has specialized in giving in to any pressure—then taking revenge, backstabbing-style.

And saying Gadhafi has renounced weapons of mass destruction is more crap. Officially, what he did was announce that he's giving up any plans for missiles with a range of more than 186 kilometers and weapons with a payload of more than 1,000 pounds. Sounds nice, but it means absolutely nothing. Gadhafi's history shows two things: First, he'll say anything, sign anything, to save his skin; second, he'll find a sneaky, bushwhacker's way to get even. Not with missiles or air-dropped bombs, but by funneling oil money to somebody who's already got a grudge against whoever's bothering him. Getting him to renounce WMDs is like getting the Mafia to sign a pledge that they won't conduct air raids. That's not how they do things in the first place, so they'll be happy to sign. Then they'll take revenge with a knife, or a silenced .22, or a car bomb.

Gadhafi's army and air force never were worth a damn. The only Libyan organization that ever worked efficiently was the secret police, and it does its business mafia-style, in the dark, on the sly. If you want to see how Gadhafi works, take a look at two classic cases: the U.S. air raids in 1986, and the civil war in Chad.

If anybody deserves credit for scaring Libya straight, it's those F-111s that Reagan sent hunting for Gadhafi's presidential tents so they could leave him a few thousand-pound calling cards. George W. Bush and Dick Cheney's taking credit for it now is ridiculous. Next, they'll be claiming they led the charge up San Juan Hill.

For you kids who are too young to remember the raids, here's a little background. First thing to realize is that Reagan was a closet peacenik, a real disappointment to guys like me who thought he'd release the dogs of war that Carter had been keeping penned up. Most of the reason people voted for Reagan in 1980 was they thought he'd stop appeasing every anti-American terrorist bum. I remember drooling thinking about the way our fighter-bombers were going to level Tehran once Reagan got in.

But Reagan seemed afraid to hit any place bigger than Rhode Island. Instead of vaporizing Khomeini's hometown, he thanked the Iranians all nice when they handed back the hostages. I couldn't believe it. He wouldn't even send Stingers to the Afghan mujahedeen till the Soviet's Mi-24 helicopters had practically wiped them out. And the only countries he attacked were basket cases you needed an electron microscope to find. Anybody remember the heroic invasion of Grenada? Reagan's PR flacks were strutting because our invasion force managed to overwhelm a brigade of Cuban construction workers "after a fierce firefight." It was a hard time to be an American war fan. Like Johnny Cash says, "I hung my head."

Then Reagan found an enemy that was just his style: a drama queen named Mu'ammar Gadhafi who was all talk and no guts. Gadhafi took power in Libya way back in 1969—it was your classic coup by "idealistic young officers"—and ever since, he's used Libya as a private video shoot, where he imitates whatever's cool in Third World attitudes at the time. Back in the 1970s, naturally, he was a "socialist" and a "Pan-Arabist." Gadhafi had himself named head of the Revolution Command Council and the only legal political party, which he naturally called the Arab Socialist Union. He took over Libyan TV for speeches so long and boring they made Castro look like the Five-Minute Manager. He pranced around in nomadic robes, got himself an all-girl bodyguard unit, and wrote one of those all-knowing little books that dictators like to put on their résumés. Mao had the "little red book," so Gadhafi came out with his "little green book," and made it a felony for anybody not to be carrying one around at all times.

If there was anybody who was just begging to be slapped down, it was Gadhafi. He declared an official Line of Death around the Gulf of Sidra, halfway out into the Mediterranean, and swore that anybody who crossed that line was finito. So we sent a couple of fighters over it, and blew the Libyan MiGs that came to meet them right into the water. It was sweet. We did it again, and this time, we blasted two of Libya's destroyers away when they steamed at us.

By this time, even a sunshine soldier like Reagan was feeling pretty good about slapping Gadhafi around. It was as safe as mouthing off to your own reflection in the mirror, *Taxi Driver* style. So in April 1986, after the Libyans bombed a GI disco in West Berlin, Reagan sent the planes at last.

The raid was officially called Operation Eldorado Canyon. Don't ask me where they got that name. Sounds more like one of those subdivisions they're building on the dry riverbed outside Fresno. The goal was to kill or at least scare the Hell out of Gadhafi.

There was one complication: the Europeans, who were chickenshit as usual. Nobody but Margaret Thatcher would let their territory be used for bases or even overflight. The one leader with balls on the whole continent, and it was a woman. How do you Europeans live with yourselves? You used to *be* somebody. Now look at you. Can't breed, can't fight, won't stand up for yourselves ... makes me sick.

Anyway, no overflight meant our planes had to take off from England, fly over the Atlantic, through the Straits of Gibraltar, and then turn right to hit Libya—a 6,400-mile trip. The only plane we had that could handle a trip that long and deliver any significant ordnance in a night attack was the old F-111 Aardvark. This was already an old, old aircraft. A big, fast, smooth piece of Detroit iron that flew, kind of like a 1961 Caddy with wings. Plenty of front-seat legroom, with pilot and copilot sitting side by side as if they were cruising Main Street.

The Aardvark, I hate to say it, didn't exactly cover itself with glory in the raid. Out of eighteen F-111s that fanned out over Libya to hit terrorist training camps, ministries, and Gadhafi's royal tent, only four actually dropped their bomb load. Eight planes had technical problems, and six couldn't be sure of their targets. To sum it up, the raid was a tactical failure.

But like a lot of tactical failures, it turned into something like a strategic success—thanks to Gadhafi, who instead of manning the barricades and daring the Yankees to try it again, bitched out totally and begged us not to hurt him anymore. He made us look good and proved in the process what a total pussy he was, is, and always will be. So when Gadhafi crawls around kissing our feet and begs us not to hurt him, it's just him doing what comes naturally.

Gadhafi is such a wimp that he didn't just buckle to the United States and Britain way back in the 1980s, but he even buckled to Chad, the lowliest, most messed-up country in the world. What the Hell does Libya have to do with Chad, you're wondering? Well, it was like the only date Gadhafi could get to the prom—the only country even more messed up than Libya. Gadhafi started out looking east, to Egypt and Israel. He tried to unite Libya with Egypt in one big, happy Israel-fighting family. The Egyptians had a good line about that merger: "It is an excellent plan. Libya has the money and we have the brains." Libya had the money because it's got oil. That's the only reason Gadhafi can afford to run around embracing causes and printing his book.

The money was the only thing Egypt wanted from Libya. Sadat was way too smart to let a big-mouth flake like Gadhafi in on his real plans. When the Egyptians attacked in Sinai in 1973, they made a point of not telling their Libyan pals about it. Gadhafi was so offended he stomped off in his high heels and sulked. If his fellow Arabs were going to be all mean to him like that, he'd find new friends. So he decided Libya wasn't so much Arab as African. Instead of Pan-Arabism, he took up Pan-Africanism, started wearing those funky dashikis and playing those little hand-harp things, talking about his "brothers" down south, across the Sahara.

This had the black Africans laughing so hard they turned blue, because the coast of Libya used to be the world's biggest Wal-Mart in the trade in black Africans. Introduce a Libyan to a black man, and instead of shaking hands, the Libyan'll pry the guy's mouth open, check out his teeth, and say, "Seventy-five dinars, not a shekel more!"

The rest of Africa was happy to take the crazy Arab's money, but they didn't really want much to do with him. So Gadhafi decided to get his own little imperialist game going. The only African country close enough and weak enough for Libya to mess with was Chad.

I love that name. A country named Chad. Sounds like somebody who lived next door to the Brady Bunch. But if Chad actually lived next to the Bradys, Greg would be roasting over a slow fire and Marcia would be standing naked on an auction block, because Chad is one of the hungriest, craziest, most desperate places on the planet. Chad has every possible birth defect you could give a country if you wanted to make sure it was going to be screwed up forever. It's in Africa, for starters. It's landlocked. It's mostly desert, with one small, fertile zone down in the south to make all the desert nomads jealous. It's got the classic Sahel division between Muslim north and Christian south. It had the French in charge for most of the twentieth century (I said the French were good soldiers; I never said they were good colonizers). And maybe worst of all, it was stuck due south of Libya just when Gadhafi started turning his greedy little eyes in that direction.

There were so many little wars going on in Chad in the late 1970s that Gadhafi could pick which ones he wanted to fund. And boy, was he fickle. He started out doing the obvious thing, backing Muslims in the north rebelling against Christians in the south.

You have to feel sorry for the poor black people down south. For hundreds of years, they were nothing but livestock on the hoof for the Muslim slave traders who would raid south and capture whole villages to sell. Then the French come along and show the blacks the benefits of civilization by drafting them into the French army. Next thing you know, black guys who'd never been out of the village end up in the trenches at the Marne. Not many of them ever came home from that European vacation.

Then finally, the southern blacks in Chad get the one piece of good luck in history: The French pull out, and since the south had the only fertile land and the only real city, they get to be on top for once. No more slave traders carrying off your kids. No more recruiting officers humming the Marseillaise while they help your son trace his name on the enlistment papers. For once, the Africans could look forward to minding their own business and dealing with ordinary misery like drought, locusts, and every kind of tropical disease known to man. Paradise!

Well, it didn't happen, thanks to good old Gadhafi. With the money and arms the Libyan secret service sent him, the Muslim leader Hissène Habré made his move and captured the capital, a mud-brick hellhole called N'Djamena.

This was strictly by the book, according to African warfare rules, which state "The worse the hellhole, the harder they fight for it."

The rest of the civil war went by the book, too. The black Christian southerners fled the city, headed south to stay with relatives, and started killing any Arabs or Muslims they could find. They found about ten thousand, by all accounts, chopped them up, and felt better about losing their city gig. Then—and again, this is strictly old-school, by-the-book stuff—the winners started getting ready to turn on each other, without even bothering to thank the foreigners who'd bankrolled them. Once he'd taken the capital, Habré wouldn't even return Gadhafi's calls. In his classic drama-queen style, Gadhafi flounced around his tent, sulked, and did what he always does: gave money to his ex-best-friend's worst enemy. Habre's worst enemy happened to be Wadal Abdelkader Kamougué, a black Christian colonel from southern Chad. So much for Islamic unity.

Then Gadhafi switched his backing again, to a group of Chadian rebels who had migrated south from Libya. The idea was to lead up to annexing the northern half of Libya. So much for African unity. When that failed, Gadhafi decided to withdraw from most of Chad, but he gave himself a little going-away present, annexing a piece of northern Chad called the Aozou Strip.

Then came the ultimate humiliation: Gadhafi's army and air force couldn't even hold on to that. Habré's rebels took it from the Libyans in a battle that might've been the debut of a major new weapons system of the late twentieth century, the *technical*. If you've read up on Somalia, you know that a technical is just a Toyota four-wheel-drive pickup with a big machine gun or grenade launcher welded onto the bed. The Chad rebels used technicals to zoom into town, blast up the Libyan garrison, and zoom out. It had Gadhafi's sorry-assed soldiers pissing their pants. They brought in the Libyan Air Force, took back the town—and then got even more faced when the Chadians sent a convoy of technicals right into Libya to shoot up an airbase a hundred miles north of the border.

That was it for Gadhafi. He did what he always does when somebody fronts up to him: He caved. Since then, he's been very, very polite to the Chadians.

You get the picture? This is a man who has no guts and no shame. Getting him to buckle is nothing new and nothing to brag about. You want to do something impressive? Get Kim Jong-Il to sing "Give Peace a Chance." Yeah—big televised duet with Yoko. That's when I'll be impressed.

BURUNDI:
HEIGHTISM REARS ITS UGLY HEAD

WE ALL KNOW peace treaties don't matter. You see a headline "Peace Treaty in the Congo" or "Accord Signed on Rwanda," and you go on to the next story, because you know it doesn't mean a thing. Even the words they use sound fake, like *accord*. It's one of those words they only use in the papers. They could sign an accord a day in Central Africa—in fact, it seems as if they do—and the only difference it would make would be on some bureaucrat's résumé.

Maybe that's what these deals are about, when you come down to it—getting it on your résumé, so you can go back to the State Department and say, "I'm the guy who brokered Peace Treaty Number 3,549 in Rwanda/Burundi/Congo/Uganda/Tanzania. It was a great treaty, too—lasted almost two weeks!"

All those countries, jammed up against each other—that's part of the problem. The more countries you have on your borders, the more enemies you've got. If you've ever played Risk (and if you haven't played Risk, what the Hell are you doing reading this book?), you know that the worst continent to have is Europe, because it can be attacked from about half the countries on the board. The best one to have is Australia, because even if it's worth just two armies, you can only attack it from one country, so all you have to do is pile armies up on New Guinea and you just rake in your two armies every turn.

Burundi would be the worst country on the board in Risk, because it's tiny, not worth much, and open to attack from just about anywhere south of the Sahara. All these countries are like an Alcoholics Anonymous chapter in reverse. They're like war junkies who keep each other from quitting. If peace breaks out in Uganda, there's always a war next door in Tanzania or the Congo ready to "spill over" (that's the word the newspapers always use) and start things up again. Then when Tanzania goes quiet, there's always some handy little bush war in Uganda ready to return the favor. The regional motto should be "Hey, buddy, got a light?"

When you look hard at a place like Burundi, you start to realize that war is normal in most of the world. Tribes move around and try to grab the good land just over the next hill, and when they do, the locals try to push them back. Boom, you've got a war.

Europe used to be like that. People don't remember that the Hungarians only got to Europe a thousand years ago. They came straight off the steppes and cut through Eastern Europe like a small-time Mongol horde, and when they came to a nice piece of grazing land, they said, "We're staying." In those days, it was tribes, not land, that counted. So a king wasn't king of any particular piece of land; he was king of his tribe of people: King of the Franks, or King of the Magyars. The big battles come when one tribe decides to make the move on another tribe. That's what the Battle of Hastings was, for one example: Normans vs. Saxons in a classic gang turf war, South Central LA with chain-mail hauberks instead of Raiders jackets.

Central Africa is like how Europe used to be: People are still moving around, trying to elbow themselves some room. A thousand years ago, the only people in Burundi or Rwanda were the Pygmies. It's too bad they didn't get to keep the place. It'd be a blast, nothing but gorillas and Pygmies. But it was too good to last. Bantu people, taller, darker tribes who raised cattle and farmed crops, came down from the north and started killing off or enslaving the Pygmies, chopping down the forests, and multiplying. Most of the time, farmer tribes end up defeating hunter tribes, because farms make more food, so the farmers outnumber the hunters in a generation or so. So the Bantu farmers outnumbered the Pygmy hunters in a few generations.

The first Bantu tribe to elbow its way into Rwanda-Burundi was the Hutu, the famous "short people" in the tall-short war in Rwanda. The most recent arrival, the Tutsi, showed up around the time Cortés was taking down the Aztecs. The Tutsis were even taller than the Hutus, who were already way taller than the Pygmies.

In fact, what happened is a clear case of heightism, a new prejudice the liberals haven't caught on to yet. First, the really short Pygmies get killed by the pretty tall Hutus, and then, the really, really tall Tutsis charge down out of the north and start killing off the Hutus. Heightism rears its ugly head! Call Hillary! I bet those heightist Tutsis play that old Randy Newman song, "Short People Got No Reason to Live," before they head out on a Hutu-hacking mission. (The only other time the Wa-Tutsi get into the history of music was back in the 1960s, when their name turned up in a dance hit from Motown, "Do the Watusi," but that's another story.)

The Tutsis weren't just tall; they were serious badasses, the Vikings of East Africa. They killed the Hutu kings, made the Hutu peasants into slaves, and settled down to a nice, happy life raising cattle to buy wives or raising wives to buy cattle, depending on which was in short supply on a given day. The Tutsis claimed all the land, on the legal basis that if you objected, they'd kill you. So if you were a Hutu peasant and wanted to raise crops or graze cattle, you had to ask your Tutsi overlord to let you take some land as a sharecropper. If he agreed, you gave him half of your crop, or more if he had a hangover or just didn't like your looks.

If you know anything about medieval Europe, this lifestyle should sound familiar. It's good old feudalism, where a lot of little barons in small castles line up behind a few big barons in big castles, who line up either with or against a king in the biggest castle of all. These barons were black and didn't joust, but otherwise, it was pretty much pure feudalism. Lots of fun for the Tutsi overlords, not that much fun for the Hutu peasants, and not too bad for the cattle. Probably not that much fun for the wives, but nobody worried about their opinion back then.

Around the time we were having the Civil War, the Europeans started poking around the whole East African lakes region, sniffing out the Nile headwaters, but the palefaces were slow in making it all the way inland to Burundi. A German count showed up in 1894–I bet he felt right at home with all those Tutsi barons–and Germany got a "protectorate" over Rwanda-Burundi in 1899. In 1915, when the Germans were busy back in Europe, the Belgians snuck east from the Congo, made sure no Germans were around, and then proudly claimed all of Rwanda-Burundi. They kept it until 1945 and then agreed to give the UN formal control till independence in 1962.

But these dates don't matter much. When you say Burundi became independent, you're not talking about George Washington and James Monroe debating the rights of man. You're talking about a little medieval kingdom with a small, warlike aristocracy and a big, sullen peasant population getting jerked around by the dumbest of all the European colonizers, the Belgians. These guys were bad news wherever they went. They turned the Congo into one big killing zone and had enough energy left over to play tribe-vs.-tribe games with the Tutsis and Hutus, stirring up old tribal hatreds and then losing control of them.

Meanwhile, the whole phony newspaper-talk about "democratic elections" and "representative democracy" was installed by the UN like one of those compulsory Microsoft upgrades that's so damn efficient it destroys all your documents. Nobody asked if the "democratic" upgrade made sense on the ground in Burundi. They just knew that the whole world was supposed to be run like some stupid high-school student-body election. So the Burundians started parties with big names like "Front for Democracy in Burundi" and "Union for National Progress." And underneath, the same old feudal games were going on. The parties were just new names for tribes. Front for Democracy meant Hutu, and Union for National Progress meant Tutsi. The only difference was that the Europeans wouldn't let the Tutsi barons get too medieval on the Hutus' asses any more. That meant that the Hutus could start using their advantage in numbers.

Pretty soon, the basic Burundi pattern was clear: Hutus rise up, start killing Tutsis; Tutsi army units and militias return the favor, only more so. A classic example was the Hutu rebellion in 1970: The Hutus chopped up 10,000 Tutsis, and the Tutsis upped the ante by killing 150,000 Hutus.

Once these massacres start, everybody in the killing zone who's not already dead flees into one of the next-door countries. And naturally, all those scared, starving, pissed-off refugees start trouble across the border, in whatever hellhole they've run to: Uganda, the Congo, Tanzania. That's why you can count on East Africa to keep the party going for a long, long time.

This is pretty much the same pattern you see in Rwanda, which makes sense because the two so-called countries are part of the same volcanic highland, with the same tribal mix. And when "democracy" gets in the way, one tribe or the other goes back to the good old way of settling things: Kill the bastard. So when a Hutu was elected president of Burundi in 1991, the Tutsis were so offended that they took the un-democratic step of blowing him away.

That's when the current war cycle started. It turned into a classic tribal guerrilla war. The Hutu militias took to the forest and started recruiting peasants as informers, food suppliers, or part-time guerrillas. The Tutsis, who run the Burundi Army, did what every counterinsurgency army does: burn down rebel villages, kill peasants in reprisal after guerrilla ambushes, and resettle the peasants in army-run concentration camps. In Vietnam, we called these things new-life hamlets; in Burundi, the Tutsi army brass call them resettlement villages. These resettlement places don't stop the insurgency, but they punish the peasants real well, which means there'll always be another generation of Hutus, pissed off and starving, ready for payback the next time they can jump a few unguarded Tutsi villages.

Amnesty International has officially declared that both sides in the Burundi war were committing "human rights violations." The whole point of guerrilla war is to commit human-rights violations. There are no battles in this kind of war, just massacres and ambushes. As I keep saying, that's what war is, most of the time, for most of the people in the world—and who's to say that Gettysburg and Verdun are good wars and tribal chop-fests are bad wars?

If there was any justice in all this mess, it'd mean giving the place back to the gorillas (no pun intended) and the Pygmies. But since that's not going to happen, you may as well get used to seeing headlines like "New Accord in Burundi" and then, about two weeks later, the other kind of headline: "Massacres Threaten Burundi Peace." I always like they way they say peace is "threatened." Yeah, right. Just like there's a "threat" that Alabama might go Republican.

DARFUR:
A WHOLE NEW HELL

THIS CHAPTER IS dedicated to a War Nerd fan named Jon Dickey, who sent in an article on the war in Darfur, in Western Sudan, with a note: "Dude you should check out this sick shit." Dude, I did! And you were right, it's sick. And like a lot of sick shit, it's funny. So sick it got me thinking about God, even. And for me, that's pretty sick.

The story comes out of the *Guardian*, a Brit paper—the Brits generally do a better job of telling the horrible truth than we do. It's about the Janjaweed militia I once described as the "camel-mounted mobile rape squad" that's working overtime terrorizing the black people who farm Darfur in Sudan.

Well, the *Guardian* came up with what you might call a human-interest story about the Janjaweed: It has its own cheerleading squad. That's right: While the men of the Janjaweed are burning a village, killing the men and raping the women, the Janjaweed Women's Auxiliary stands there on the sidelines singing songs about how great it is to see their black neighbors getting raped and killed.

Like one analyst said, these women "appear to be the communicators during the attacks." That's them—great communicators, just like Reagan. Always ready to put a positive spin on rape and pillage and all that stuff—because let's face it, without a few communicators around to help the viewer understand what they're seeing, it could look bad for the Janja-boys. And girls.

I was thinking of making fun of these girls by making up some cheers for them, high-school style. You know: "Whadda we want? RAPE! When do we want it? NOW!" or when they send in their version of Johnny Wadd, "Abdul, Abdul, he's our man, if he can't rape 'em, no one can!"

Like I said, I was thinking about doing that . . . until I read what these Janjaweed girls actually do sing. That's when I realized there's no point trying to improve on perfection. These so-called Arabs hate the locals for being black, in spite of the fact that most Sudanese "Arabs" could pass for black at a Louis Farrakhan benefit and must do some serious denial when they look in a mirror. I'm telling you—every racial joke from *Blazing Saddles* is happening for real out there in Darfur.

Anyway, turns out most of the songs these "Arab" women sing are about how ugly the black locals are. And the lyrics! Here's a sample, a classic from Sudanese cheerleader camp: While the village is burning and the women are being gang-raped, the girls grab their pom-poms and chant, "You are gorillas, you are black, and you are badly dressed."

You get that last bit? "You are badly dressed"? When I was in high school, there was an old joke, "You're ugly and your mom dresses you funny." I guess it wouldn't play that well in Sudan. They must be real fashion slaves over there. You wouldn't think it from the pictures, but that's the ultimate insult. I mean picture it to yourself: Your husband's lying there bleeding out, you and your daughters are being gang-raped, and these Dallas Cowgirls from Hell are singing, "You are badly dressed"! Oh, that's a low blow, ladies. Killing, burning, and raping, sure, that's normal—but don't make fun of somebody's wardrobe!

Like all great communicators, these chicks are versatile. Some of their cheers go for what you might call a global picture of the operation, like this one:

The blood of the blacks runs like water,
We take their goods and we chase them from our area and our
cattle will be on their land,
The power of [Sudanese President Omar Hassan]
al-Bashir belongs to the Arabs,
And we will kill you until the end, you blacks,
We have killed your god.

It finishes up with a nice little dance routine whereby the head cheerleader somersaults over a mound of dead farmers.

Like I said, you couldn't make this up. One of my favorite kill-lines was in *Hot Shots Part Deux* (one of the all-time great movies), where Saddam says to Lloyd Bridges, "I will kill you until you die from it." I thought that was just kidding around, but after reading that bit from the cheerleaders, "We will kill you until the end, you blacks," I'm not so sure. Maybe it was like a direct translation from the Arabic. I figure some of the lines suffer in translation, though, because some are a little wordy. Try saying that line, "We take their goods, . . . " et cetera, while doing the splits on a slippery gym floor—or a slippery black village knee-deep in blood, for that matter.

The usual schoolmarm reaction to this kind of joking is the old line, "That's not funny; it's sick." I never got that line. Why can't it be both? I mean, obviously it's sick, and the sickest bits are the funniest, like the idea of a bunch of 99 percent black "Arab" women clapping along while their husbands rape other women, making fun of the rape victims' clothes. Since when did *sick* and *funny* stop hanging out together?

The schoolmarm idea is that if you laugh at something sick, it proves there's nothing but *sick* in your head. I don't know about you, but I can hold a lot of things in my head at once. The test, I guess, would be what would happen if you happened to be commanding a unit that interrupted one of those mass rapes. I'm not sure what I'd do. Everything I've read so far makes me lean toward the blacks here, against the Arabs. But not for any big Christian reason. More because of the old underdog-backing instinct and the chance to play big, chivalrous hero. Along with the fact that it pisses me off, people who lie to themselves so badly they won't admit they're black themselves. And since when are Arabs better-looking than blacks? Every picture I've seen shows black Sudanese looking like how I wish I looked, incredibly tall and skinny and wiry.

But that's not denying that I get off on rape and pillage, too. Hell yes. That's always been one of the big attractions of going to war: Anything goes. When the Russians reached East Prussia on their push to Berlin, they started raping every woman they could catch. To death, sometimes. Yeah, you can say the Germans had it coming, but admit it, that's not what you liked about it. The fun part is the idea that in wartime, if it was a big enough, rough enough war, you could do anything you want to the conquered people. Remember, *The Iliad* starts off with a fight about who gets rape rights to that slave girl, name starts with a *B*.

By tradition, a commander gave his army three days to play with the people of a conquered city. Sometimes it dragged on a little long, if the troops were excited or if they'd commandeered a lot of liquor. When the Turks took Constantinople, they had the best three days of their lives, playing with those Greek girls after lopping their dads' heads off. And I admit it, I used to spend a lot of time imagining the sack of Constantinople, taking your pick of the survivors.

You know what really makes me laugh? When the Christians say that I think this way because I don't have God in my life and, if I did, I wouldn't think all this bad stuff. It's incredible how damn dumb people can be. Has anybody out there actually read the Bible? Because I did, and it says one thing, over and over: Kill *all* the conquered people. That's right, the Bible is way more hard-core, way meaner than those Janjaweed guys, *or* the Turks, *or* Achilles. Those guys had the sort of casual, have-a-little-fun attitude to dealing with a captured city.

Not the Bible. God can't stand the idea that his guys might be tempted by the captured women. And it's not because he cares about those gentile ladies. Nope, it's because if his Israelites start getting turned on by these infidels, they might start worshipping "strange gods." That's right: God is like a jealous bitch when it comes to conquered women. And his take is real simple: Kill 'em all!

I really wonder how anybody can read the Bible and not see it. It's not like this is a hidden message or something. It's right out there, again and again, nice and simple. It used to weird me out no end in Sunday School, the way people could recite those verses from Joshua and Judges and not have a clue what they were saying.

Here's a nice example. Weirds me out even now, picking up that Bible—never had the heart to get rid of it, I put so much effort into memorizing all that stuff. And now it pays off, because I can find you chapter and verse, as they say, to show how God feels about handling conquered people. The Israelites have taken Jericho, right? All that cute old gospel-music crap about "the walls come tumblin' down"—but what they don't usually quote is the aftermath. Here we go—Joshua 6:21: "They devoted the city to the Lord and destroyed with the sword every living thing in it—men and women, young and old, cattle, sheep and donkeys."*

---

* Compare this run-in in Darfur in July 2006, described in "The Horrors of Darfur's Ground Zero," *Australian*, May 28, 2007, available at www.theaustralian.news.com.au/story/0,20867,21803054-2703,00.html: "Seven women who had pooled money last July to rent a donkey and cart ventured out of the refugee camp to gather firewood, hoping to sell it for cash to feed their families. They told AP they were gang-raped, beaten and robbed. The women say the men's camels and their uniforms marked them as Janjaweed.

I used to feel all sick and excited at once when I heard that expression, "They devoted the city to the Lord." It sounded so nice, and it meant they killed everyone—babies, children, grandmas. That's devotion, I guess. I like the way God includes the livestock, too: "cattle, sheep and donkeys." That's right, don't want any heathen cattle spreading their sick cattle-cults among the children of Israel.

God's not just being mean here. He's dealing with the fact that the Middle East was one of those multiethnic, multireligion parts of the world. And God wasn't having any of it. He says about a million times that if the Israelites leave any of the captured women alive, they'll start fornicating with the conquerors—God doesn't have a very high opinion of his people, you'll notice—and next thing you know, there'll be all these mongrel brats worshipping Baal. Can't have that . . . so kill 'em all.

I'm not picking weird, unusual verses here. It's all over Deuteronomy, Numbers—I used to win prizes for this stuff, so you really don't want to get in a Bible-quoting contest with me. God worries mainly about wiping out the tribes occupying the land he's set out for his people—the losers have got to go, down to the last baby. "In the towns your Lord has given to you, do not leave anything that breathes alive." That's Deuteronomy. I don't recall the verse, and to be honest, just picking up the damn book is making my heart start pounding and my face turn even redder than usual. Like the saying

---

The women said 10 Arabs on camels surrounded them, shouting insults and shooting rifles in the air.

"The women first attempted to flee. 'But I didn't even try, because I couldn't run,' being seven months pregnant, said Aisha, a petite 18-year-old whose raspy voice sounds more like that of an old woman. She said four men stayed behind to flay her with sticks, while the others chased down the rest of her group.

"Once rounded up, the women said, they were beaten and their rented donkey killed. Zahya, 30, had brought her 18-year-old daughter, Fatmya, and her baby. The baby was thrown to the ground and both women were raped. The baby survived.

"Zahya said the women were lined up and assaulted side by side, and she saw four men taking turns raping Aisha.

"The women said the attackers then stripped them naked and jeered at them as they fled. A camp leader said: 'Ever since, I've made sure that women living on the outskirts of the camp have spare sets of clothes to give out.'"

goes, don't get me started. Oh, it's all there, all right, all the kill lists. Somewhere, God names all the tribes to be killed, starting with the Hittites—which always blew me away because, frankly, the Israelites didn't seem like such great warriors, I couldn't believe they could take the Hittites.

But then they had Yahweh himself as cheerleader—the greatest communicator of them all, and a real sweetheart.*

TRADING PLACES:
LIBERIA'S POMPOUS SLAVES

I'VE ALREADY DISCUSSED some of the great military figures Liberia has given the world, like General Butt Naked and his platinum-blonde, drag queen psycho killers. But I've never told the hilarious, totally sick story of how Liberia got the way it is.

Liberian history is supposedly tragic, which is newspaper code for "funny as Hell." I can't help it; it is. It's not like I don't sympathize. I do. I mean, which slum did your grandparents come from? Probably some starved village where the coal mine's been closed since it ate a whole shift of locals. How'd you like it if everybody in your neighborhood took up a collection to send you back there,

---

* The BBC ("Darfur War Crimes Suspect Defiant," BBC News, February 28, 2007; available at http://news.bbc.co.uk/2/hi/africa/6404467.stm) reported on these guys' total lack of guilt:
"Sudan's humanitarian affairs minister, accused of war crimes in Darfur by the International Criminal Court (ICC), has said the move against him is political.
"Ahmed Haroun said he 'did not feel guilty,' his conscience was clear and that he was ready to defend himself.
"The ICC accuses Mr Haroun and a Janjaweed militia leader, known as Ali Kushayb, of 51 counts of war crimes and crimes against humanity.
"Some 200,000 people have died in the four-year conflict in Darfur.
"'I am not worried at all and I do not feel guilty because I acted within the legal framework and in accordance with the general interest,' Mr Haroun told AFP news agency.
"Mr Haroun was the former interior minister in charge of Darfur and according to the ICC was responsible for organising and funding the Arab militia known as the Janjaweed.
"Ali Kushayb is accused of ordering the murder, torture and mass rape against innocent civilians during attacks on villages near Kodoom, Bindisi Mukjar and Arawala in west Darfur."

even if you didn't speak a word of the language? "We feel you don't fit in here in Santa Barbara and you'll never be truly happy until you're back in Lower Slobovia."

That's how Liberia started. It was white people's idea from the start. They were worried about free blacks, who made up about a tenth of the two million black people in the United States. The two extremes of the slavery issue, abolitionists and crazy slave owners, agreed that something had to be done about all those free blacks.

The abolitionists loved black people so much they wanted them to go far, far away. So did the slave owners, who announced with no evidence at all that free blacks were "promoters of mischief." (I don't know what "mischief" means—maybe they TP'd those *Gone with the Wind* plantation houses.)

A group of rich white do-gooders including Francis Scott Key, who wrote "The Star Spangled Banner," got together to raise the money to send free blacks back to Africa. For them, Key had a special version of the national anthem: "Oh say, can you see / the home of the brave? If so, you're standing too close / Go about four thousand miles southeast, to West Africaaaa."

Congress came through with a big grant, and in 1819, a ship with eighty-eight freed blacks and three white chaperons landed in that other success-story for replanting blacks, Sierra Leone. After gassing up at Freetown, they headed down the coast to the promised land, Liberia.

Within three weeks of arriving at their new home, all three whites and twenty-two of the blacks died of fever. That's barely time to start naming things Free This and Free That.

Instead, they named the place Perseverance. A little truth in advertising. The rich whites sitting home safe in the United States were determined to persevere in Liberia, even if it meant shipping every black they could catch straight into the most disease-ridden, lethal climate in the world. They worked a deal with the U.S. Navy that any slave ships intercepted on the high seas would be detoured to Liberia and would have to dump their cargo there, which meant that no matter how many colonists died, more were always on the way.

It was like a do-gooder version of Darwin, only sped up. Most of the newcomers died so fast they barely had time to thank their benefactors. But a few survived. And they were the ones who married and had kids, so eventually, you got a population that had some degree of resistance to all the tropical diseases.

Once they realized they weren't all going to die in the next week, the settlers went to work on the most fundamental thing in any society: setting up cliques. There were three big ones in Liberia: the freed slaves who were "black"; the ones who were "mulatto"; and way back there in the bush, the natives. Naturally, none of these cliques liked each other.

The next step, naturally, was sucking up to the people who abused you. Is this starting to remind you of high school? That's because high school is a totally typical example of how people act when they have to start a society from scratch.

So instead of making peace with the natives, the Liberians spent the 1840s trying to get officially recognized by the whites. The funny bit is that the European states didn't have too much problem with recognition, but the United States—the country that started Liberia with a huge grant from Congress—refused to recognize Liberia until 1862. Guess why. Yup: because the U.S. South might object to having a black ambassador in Washington, D.C.

It makes you wonder how the United States finally agreed to recognize Liberia. I mean, it's 1862, the Confederacy's at war with the United States, and some bureaucrat's still sweating over the decision: "Well, Mr. Lincoln, our focus groups show there might be a negative reaction in some of the border districts."

By this time, however, Liberia was a full-grown country, doing what West African coastal enclaves are supposed to do: getting ripped off in "development" loans from the West, having ridiculous border disputes over some fever-ridden chunk of bush, and making the inland natives feel like dirt. British banks ripped the Liberians off so badly that one Liberian president—"the Liberian Lincoln," no less—had to swim for his life to a British ship in the harbor of Monrovia, the new Liberian capital city.

Monrovia was named after James Monroe, one of the supporters of the Liberian colonization plan. His famous comment on Liberia was, "Love you guys, wish you could stay longer, here's your hat."

My favorite border dispute was between Liberia and that other outpost of freedom, Sierra Leone. In 1883, Sierra Leone claimed territory that Liberia held. The British backed up the Sierra Leoneans, Uncle Sam decided to stay out of it, and the Liberians had to back down. Next, it was the French, in the Ivory Coast next door, grabbing another chunk of territory. Through it all, Uncle Sam kept his distance from his black nephews in Liberia. It was like he was a little embarrassed by them.

One reason the United States might've been embarrassed by the Liberians is that they kept trying to look white. And they succeeded. Take a look at the pictures of Liberian leaders from the 1800s and they look like Confederate generals with a tan—a lot of white blood in there. The Liberians were proud of that; the United States wasn't.

These American-born Liberians were never more than 5 percent of the population, but they ran the coast, had the money, understood more about the outside world—so they considered themselves the elite. They felt even whiter when they compared themselves with the natives, who were pure West African—some of the darkest people in the world. To remind everybody of the difference, the settlers called themselves Americo-Liberians and put on a lot of airs, with stiff collars and muttonchop sideburns, not to mention that other mark of higher civilization, land grabs.

Nobody was really sure how far inland Liberia's borders went. Basically, it was as much as it wanted or could grab. Nobody worried much about the natives; they were black and uncivilized. The Americo-Liberians were as racist as the slave owners their ancestors had returned to Africa to get away from. These settlers sent their kids to school in the United States to make sure they didn't get too African and, until the 1860s, didn't even try to find out who lived in the jungle they'd claimed.

By the 1890s, you had the ultimate in, uh, black comedy: Liberian gunboats sailing upriver to bombard savage native tribes who were resisting civilization. In fact, they were resisting it too well: When the Americo-Liberian army marched inland to teach the Gola tribe a lesson, the soldiers got their café-au-lait asses kicked.

Liberian military history recovered its former glory in 1917, when Liberia formally joined the Allies against the Germans in WW I. There was panic among the General Staff in Berlin when the news arrived. But there was rejoicing in Monrovia, because it meant all German assets in Liberia could be seized and handed out to deserving Americo-Liberian pals.

But then unrest flared up inland, in darkest Liberia. The Americo-Liberian government sent a party to investigate. It turned out the tribes back there had heard a rumor that slavery was going to be abolished, and they were outraged. The government explained it was just PR, a decree to impress the foreigners. But the natives were still restless, so the government had to send a big force to convince the Kru, the biggest tribe, to be peaceful. The civilized Americo-Liberians accomplished this by sacking the Krus' towns and killing off their warriors.

World War II was Liberia's golden age—by Liberian standards, that is. Once again, the country took its stand for liberty, enlisting on the Allied side. But now, this actually meant something, because whereas WW I was basically a European war, WW II was truly a worldwide deal. So the United States set up some bases on the Liberian coast, with plenty of trickle-down for the locals. All kinds of fancy Western ideas started percolating through Monrovia. Women got the vote, and in the early 1960s, the Peace Corps did some of its earliest do-gooding in Liberia.

What did those kids actually do in the corps, anyway? As far as I know, they just hugged a lot of dark-skinned people and meant well. It's kind of fun to think of these white American hippies' welcoming party in Monrovia, with all the snooty mulattoes in town sipping cocktails and warning them about those terribly, terribly primitive blacks one meets inland.

Liberia's biggest break ever came when some genius realized that since Liberia was officially a country—recognized since 1862, remember!—it had the right to sell ship registrations. Which it started doing, cut-rate, to every tramp steamer that didn't want to bother with lifeboats or safety inspections.

Which is why, every time an oil tanker goes aground while the captain's dead drunk, or comes apart midocean, the papers call it "a Liberian-registered vessel." Your assurance of quality on the high seas.

That one is still a big money spinner for Liberia. Actually, Liberia was doing OK, by African standards, right up to the 1970s. It had had the same president from 1944 to 1971, an upstanding old guy with the great name of William Vacanarach Shadrach Tubman. With his suit and horn-rimmed glasses, he looks a little like Papa Doc Duvalier, the scary little dude who ruled Haiti at about the same time. But Tubman was a much more peaceful guy, who actually tried to include the inland tribes in the party. Investment picked up, schools got built, peace almost looked ready to break out. Almost.

When Tubman died, another fairly decent guy, William Tolbert, was elected president. Tolbert tried to move with the times, dressing up in those African clothes—little white cap, white leisure suit—that make you look like a hospital orderly on break, and carrying one of those sticks of office like Mobutu had in the Congo.

But he didn't move fast enough. In 1980, he and a dozen of his officials were killed in a coup. This is the moment when Liberia starts its big, long fall.

Turned out the coup was run by Master Sergeant Samuel K. Doe. Doe was the first of the monsters. Since him, it's been one long string of monsters calling the shots in Liberia.

Doe started the tradition of killing anybody who objected to his decisions and stealing everything he could grab. But compared with the next generation of Liberian wackos, he was a weak-kneed moderate. You get this pattern a lot in the Third World: The first army officer to stage a coup is just an ordinary murderer, but somehow, when he overthrows the old-style civilian politicians, all bets are off, and the contenders just get crazier and more violent all the time.

In 1989, an Americo-Liberian named Charles Taylor showed up in charge of a guerrilla army calling itself the National Patriotic

Front of Liberia. The NPFL announced it was going to overthrow Sergeant Doe.

Taylor and Doe went way back. In fact, Taylor had been in charge of the money during Doe's regime—until Doe accused Taylor of stealing government funds. Of course, that was like accusing him of breathing; it went without saying. But the charge meant that Doe and Taylor had had a fight. Taylor had to run off to the United States. He was comfortable there, because like most Americo-Liberian kids, he'd been sent to school there.

Then, to his own surprise, Taylor ended up in a Massachusetts prison on a Liberian extradition warrant. He was never extradited, though. Instead, he showed up in Liberia as leader of the NPFL. The question is, how did Taylor get out of jail in Massachusetts? Nobody's sure. His story is that he sawed through the bars, Count of Monte Christo style. Other people, cynical types, say he cut a deal with the CIA.

Everybody was sick of Doe, who was destroying Liberia in record time. He was shot, to everybody's satisfaction, in 1990. Taylor got the blame for that killing, along with a lot of other killings his guys had done back in the bush on their way to the capital. Charles had one of the all-time great answers for these nay-sayers: "Jesus Christ was accused of being a murderer in his time."

I'm still scratching my head on that one. From what I remember of Sunday School, they called Jesus a lot of stuff, but "murderer"? I must've missed that Sunday.

Still, Taylor should know; he's an ordained Baptist minister. And if there's one thing those rock-head Baptists can do, it's quote Scripture at you till you're ready to sign over your house and die.

After Doe was shot, Liberia just sort of rotted. Taylor's NPFL ran most of the country, but the young guys back in the bush had gotten a taste for carrying guns, killing people, and stealing their stuff. For the first time, they were starting to feel included in the Liberian political process, and they weren't in a hurry to have things go back to the dull old ways, with some pompous old man in a suit running things from the coast.

And the rest, as they say, is recent history.

EUROPE

THE FRENCH

THE BIG THING on the Web after the start of Gulf War II was all these sites with names like "I Hate France," with datelines of French military history, allegedly proving how the French are total cowards. If you want to see a sample of this dumb-ass Frog bashing, try this one: www.albinoblacksheep.com/text/france.htm. Well, I'm going to tell you guys something you probably don't want to hear: These sites are total bullshit, the notion that the French are cowards is total bullshit, and anybody who knows anything about European military history knows damn well that over the past thousand years, the French have the most glorious military history in Europe, maybe the world.

Before you send me more of those death threats, let me finish. I hated Jacques Chirac, too, and his disco foreign minister with the blow-dried 'do and the snotty smile. But there are two things I hate more than I hate the French: ignorant, fake war buffs and people who are ungrateful. And when an American mouths off about French military history, he's not just being ignorant, he's being ungrateful. I was raised to think ungrateful people were trash.

When I say ungrateful, I'm talking about the American Revolution. If you're a true American patriot, then this is the war that matters. Hell, most of you probably couldn't name three major battles from it, but try going back to when you read *Johnny Tremain* in fourth grade, and you might recall a little place called Yorktown, Virginia, where we bottled up Cornwallis's army, forced the Brits' surrender, and pretty much won the war. Well, news flash: "We" didn't win that battle, any more than the Northern Alliance conquered the Taliban.

The French army and navy won Yorktown for us. Americans didn't have the matériel or the training to mount a combined operation like that, with naval blockade and land siege. It was the French artillery forces and military engineers who ran the siege, and at sea, it was a French admiral, de Grasse, who kicked the shit out of the British navy when it tried to break the siege.

Long before that, in fact as soon as we showed at Saratoga that we could win once in a while, the French started pouring in huge shipments of everything, from cannon to uniforms. We'd never have got near Yorktown if it hadn't been for massive French aid.

So how come you bastards don't mention Yorktown on your cheap Web pages? I'll tell you why: because you're too ignorant to know about it and too dishonest to mention it if you did.

The thing that gets to me is why Americans hate the French so much when they only did us good and never did us any harm. Like, why not hate the Brits? They killed thousands of Americans in the Revolution, and thirty years later, the English came back and attacked us again. That time around, they managed to burn Washington, D.C., to the ground while they were at it. How come you web jerks never mention that?

Sure, the easy answer is because the Brits were with us on the Iraq invasion, and the French weren't. But being a war buff means knowing your history and respecting it. Besides, can you honestly say we were right and the Frogs were wrong about Iraq?

Well, so much for ungrateful. Now let's talk about ignorant. And that's what you are if you think the French can't fight: just plain ignorant. Appreciation of the French martial spirit is just about the most basic way you can distinguish real war nerds from fake little teachers' pets.

Let's take the toughest case first: the German invasion, 1940, when the French army supposedly disgraced itself against the Wehrmacht. This is the only real evidence you'll find to call the French cowards, and the more you know about it, the less it proves.

Yeah, the French were scared of Hitler. Who wasn't? Neville Chamberlain, the British prime minister, all but licked the führer's goose-steppers, basically let him have all of Central Europe, because

Britain was terrified of war with Germany. Hell, Stalin signed a sweetheart deal with Hitler out of sheer terror, and Stalin wasn't a man who scared easy.

The French were scared, all right. But they had reason to be. For starters, they'd barely begun to recover from their last little scrap with the Germans: a little squabble you might've heard of, called WW I.

WW I was the worst war in history to be a soldier in. WW II was worse if you were a civilian, but the trenches of WW I were five years of Hell like General Sherman never dreamed of. At the end of it a big chunk of northern France looked like the surface of the moon, only bloodier, nothing but craters and rats and entrails. Verdun. Just that name was enough to make Frenchmen and Germans, the few who survived it, wake up yelling for years afterward.

Out of a total population of 40 million fighting the Germans from 1914 to 1918, the French lost 1.5 million men. A lot of those guys died charging German machine-gun nests with bayonets. I'd really like to see one of you office smartasses joke about "surrender monkeys" with a French soldier, 1914 vintage. You'd piss your Dockers. Shit, we strut around like we're so tough, but we can't even handle a few uppity Iraqi villages. These guys faced the Germans head-on for five years, and we call them cowards?

And in the end, it was the Germans, not the French, who said calf-rope.

When the sequel war came, the French relied on their frontier fortifications and used their tanks (which, one on one, were better than the Germans' tanks) defensively. The Germans had a newer, better offensive strategy. So they won. And the French surrendered.

Which was damn sensible of them. This was the Wehrmacht. In two years, this German war machine conquered all of Western Europe and lost only thirty thousand troops in the process. That's less than the casualties of Gettysburg. You get the picture? Nobody, no army on earth, could've held off the Germans under the conditions that the French faced them.

The French lost because they had a long land border with Germany. The English survived because they had the English Channel between them and the Wehrmacht. When the English army faced the Wehrmacht at Dunkirk, well, thanks to spin, the tuck-tail-and-flee result got turned into some heroic tale of a brilliant British retreat. The fact is, even the Brits behaved like cowards in the face of the Wehrmacht, abandoning the French. It's that simple.

Here's a quick sampler of some of my favorite French victories, like an antidote to those ignorant Web sites. We'll start way back and move up to the twentieth century.

Tours, 732 A.D.

The Muslims had already taken Spain and were well on their way to taking the rest of Europe. The only power with a chance of stopping them was the French army under Charles "the Hammer" Martel, king of the Franks (French), who answered to the really cool nickname "the Hammer of God." It was the French who saved the continent's ass. All the smart money was on the Muslims: There were sixty thousand of them, crazy Jihadis whose cavalry was faster and deadlier than any in Europe. The French army was heavily outnumbered and had no cavalry. Fighting in phalanxes, they held against dozens of cavalry charges and, after at least two days of hand-to-hand combat, finally managed to hack their way to the Muslim center and kill their commander. The Muslims retreated to Spain, and Europe developed as an independent civilization.

Orleans, May 1429

Joan of Arc: Is she the most insanely cool military commander in history, or what? This French peasant girl gets instructions from her favorite saints to help out the French against the English invaders. She goes to the king (well, the dauphin, but close enough) and tells him to give her the army and she'll take it from there. And somehow she convinces him. She takes the army, which has lost every battle it's been in lately, to Orleans, which is under English siege. Now, Joan is a nice girl, so she tries to settle things peaceably.

She explains in a letter to the enemy commanders that everything can still be cool, "provided you give up France . . . and go back to your own countries, for God's sake. And if you do not, wait for the Maid, who will visit you briefly to your great sorrow."

The next day, she put on armor, mounted a charger, and prepared to lead the attack on the besiegers' fortifications. She ordered the gates opened, but the mayor refused until Joan explained that she, personally, would cut off his head. The gates went up, the French sallied out, and Joan led the first successful attack they'd made in years. The English strongpoints were taken, the siege was broken, and Joan's career in the cow-milking trade was over.

Braddock's Defeat (aka the Battle of Monongahela), July 1755

Next time you're driving through the Ohio Valley, remember you're passing near the site of a great French victory over an Anglo-American force twice the size of the French force. General Edward Braddock marched west from Virginia with 1,500 men—a very large army in eighteenth-century America. His orders were to seize French land and forts in the valley—your basic undeclared land-grab invasion. The French joined the local tribes to resist and then set up a classic ambush. It was a slaughter. More than half of Braddock's force—880 men—were killed or wounded. The only Anglo officer to escape unhurt was this guy called George Washington, and even he had two horses shot out from under him. After a few minutes of nonstop fire from French and Indians hidden in the woods, Braddock's command came apart like something out of Vietnam, post-Tet. Braddock was hit and wounded, but none of his troops would risk getting shot to rescue him.

Austerlitz, December 1805

You always hear about Austerlitz as "Napoleon's Greatest Victory," as if the little guy personally went out and wiped out the combined Russian and Austrian armies. The fact is, ever since the Revolution in 1789, French armies had been kicking ass against everybody. They were free citizens fighting against scared peasants and degenerate mercenaries, and it was no contest. At Austerlitz, sixty-five thousand French troops took on ninety thousand Russians and Austrians and destroyed them. Absolutely annihilated them. The French lost only eight thousand, compared with twenty-nine thousand of the enemy. The tactics Bonaparte used were very risky and would only have worked with superb troops: He encouraged the enemy to attack a weak line, then brought up reinforcements who'd been held out of sight. That kind of tactical plan takes iron discipline and perfect timing—and the French had it.

Jena, October 1806

Jena is just a quick reminder for anybody who thinks the Germans always beat the French. Napoleon takes on the Prussian army and destroys it. Twenty-seven thousand Prussian casualties vs. five thousand French. Prussian army routed, pursued for miles by French cavalry.

You might want to remember that the French under Napoleon are still the only army ever to have taken all of continental Europe, from Moscow to Madrid. I could keep listing French victories till I have another book. In fact, it's not a bad idea. A nice, big hardback this time, so you could take it to the assholes running all the anti-French-military sites and bash their heads in with it.

SPAIN VS. MOROCCO:
THE MUPPETS DO IWO JIMA

THE OSCAR FOR best military comedy of 2002 has to go to the island-claiming "war" between those great military powers, Spain and Morocco. It was a side-splitter from beginning to end.

Just imagine the battle of Iwo Jima turned into a Muppet movie, or the Bill Murray character in *Caddyshack* hitting Omaha Beach.

The Spanish and Moroccans had to overcome some tough competition for this award, especially from the U.S. Air Force. First the boys in blue decided to drop a fifteen-hundred-pound, laser-guided wedding present right on the bride and groom at a Pushtun wedding in Tora Bora. "Here comes the bride, there goes the neighborhood"—in little tiny pieces.

Maybe it was a mercy killing—compared with forty years as an Afghan wife, instant death probably looked good to the blushing bride.

The funniest bit was that the shredded guests turned out to be relatives of Hamid Karzai. He was so upset he publicly scolded the USAF: "Be more careful which weddings you obliterate, for goodness sake! Those people were my cousins!"

The USAF apologized, sort of. It said some wedding guests had fired on one of its planes. Turned out this was just the Pushtun way of celebrating: firing an AK-47 into the air. The Pushtun way always involves firing an AK. How do Pushtuns cook soup? Fire hot tracers into the pot. How do Pushtuns clean house? Trick question: They don't. But if they did, it'd be by blasting the floor with an AK on full automatic. How do Pushtuns vote? Put a 7.62-mm round through the candidate of their choice. Not the ballot, the candidate.

So if you're going to start killing Pushtuns every time they fire an AK, you may as well wipe out the whole tribe. Which, come to think of it . . .

The USAF had another hit comedy when a small plane crossed the no-fly zone over the White House. Bush and Cheney dived under their desks and called for a fighter intercept, but by the time the USAF got a single F-16 up, the Cessna was long gone. When Bush's handlers asked what the Hell took them so long, the USAF said, and I quote, "We hadn't thought about protecting the White House."

Your tax dollars at work.

But funny as the USAF can be, it couldn't match the laugh riot put on by Spain and Morocco in their fight over the Isle of Parsley. In case you weren't following the story, Spain and Morocco both claim this tiny island off the Moroccan coast. They even have different names for it: the Spanish call it *Perejil*, which means "parsley," and the Moroccans call it *Leila*, which supposedly means "night" in Arabic. (Personally, I thought "Leila" was the name of that Eric Clapton song about stealing George Harrison's wife, but if the Moroccans say it means "night," I guess they know what they're talking about. They're the Arabs, not me. Thank God.)

This island is worthless scrub. No water, no houses, nobody living there except a herd of goats. As far as I know, nobody did a referendum with the goats whether they wanted to go with Spain or Morocco. They were just grazing the chaparral as usual on July 11, 2002, when out of nowhere, a couple dozen Moroccan "gendarmes" occupy the island and run up the Moroccan flag.

In the Muppet-movie version, this is where Gonzo in a big turban and his belly-dancing chickens sail in, with Dom DeLuise as the admiral waving a plywood scimitar.

From a military standpoint, the interesting question is, why did the Moroccans just send a few gendarmes? Why not land real troops with shoulder-fired SAMs (surface-to-air missiles), a few antiship missiles? That stuff is light enough now that infantry can carry enough to defend itself pretty well against air and sea attack.

But that would be real war. Most countries can't do real war. It's too expensive. And now that everybody's got a video camera, real war looks bad—too gory, too messy. If they'd had video cameras at Gettysburg, the North would've elected a peace-at-any-price candidate like McClellan by the biggest landslide in history.

So armies are just big theater groups now. They're used to make "gestures"—sitcom war, Muppet war.

The Moroccans could never handle a real war, even against a spineless theme park like Spain. The Moroccan Royal Air Force (FARM) flew F-5s—the Plymouth Valiant of fighters—till 2002, when their rich friends the Saudis donated twenty used F-16s. But having the planes is one thing; getting decent pilots, radar techs, and maintenance crews is another. If it was just a matter of buying hardware, the Saudis would be a military power in the Middle East.

The people who really run Morocco—the usual clique of army officers plus corrupt royal family—know from bitter experience that their army is worthless. From 1976 to 1989 (or 1991, depending on whose story you believe), the Moroccan army tried to wipe out a guerrilla movement called Polisario, from the Spanish Sahara independence movement. The army failed so badly it had to build a giant sand wall on Morocco's southern border because the Polisario guys in their Toyota pickups (the true weapon of the early twenty-first century) were not only holding on to Spanish Sahara but actually starting to attack Moroccan towns. Polisario even occupied Lebueirat, a big military base in southern Morocco, in 1979. The Moroccan defense minister was dumped, and the king ordered the sandcastle barrier—not exactly a vote of confidence in his royal army.

And if all that wasn't enough to convince the Moroccans to stick to fake/comedy war, there's the fact that Spain's been in NATO since 1982, so if you fuck with Spain, you're basically fucking with the United States. It's true that the United States has a lot of sleazy little arms deals and quasi-alliances with Morocco, too, but remember the Falklands War. In that war between the United Kingdom and Argentina—both countries with close links to the United States—the Americans showed pretty clearly they'll always side with the NATO white folk. The United States was openly pro-British. Hell, we even passed on satellite intelligence that helped the Brits find and kill a harmless old Argentine "battleship," the *General Belgrano*. This poor old hulk was about as dangerous as a floating log, but thanks to U.S. data, a Brit nuke sub found it and blew it to bits, killing two thousand poor Argentine draftee sailors.

So the Moroccans knew they couldn't win a real war with Spain. That's why they purposely sent the weakest possible force—a dozen cops: because it's less embarrassing when cops get expelled than it is when your whole army gets butt-fucked and sent home in a cargo hold. Just ask the Argentineans. After the Brits kicked their asses in the Falklands, the junta fell. The fat-cat colonels running Morocco wouldn't risk such a thing happening to them.

The gendarmes didn't last long on the island. They'd probably been ordered not to resist, so when the Spanish choppered in seventy-five special forces to boot them off, the Moroccans surrendered without a fight. They were handcuffed and taken off the island. Not exactly Iwo Jima II. A gated retirement community on bingo night gets rowdier than this.

In the Muppet version, this would be Miss Piggy in a bullfighting uniform, shouting "*Olé! Ándale, ándale!*" while she rounds up Gonzo and his Muslim chickens, karate-chopping anybody who dawdles. Dom DeLuise, the Moroccan admiral, falls head-over-heels in love with her, and they sail home doing a comedy duet—a nice, peaceful ending, you'd think.

But you can always count on hometown media to promote war, as long as it's not going to happen to them. So back in Spain and Morocco, the papers and TV were busy stirring up the civilians.

This is when the nutcases come out to play: when their homeland has been insulted. So naturally, after Moroccan TV showed the gendarmes being led off by the Spanish infidels, a twenty-seven-year-old Moroccan civilian decided to take things into his own hands.

This guy—I have to say, he was a one-man jihad, comedy style.

This Moroccan Rambo steals a rowboat and paddles over to the island, armed with a Moroccan flag and a bottle of pills. That's all. No gun, no scimitar—just the flag and the pills. If this were a Muppet film, the lone Moroccan would be played by Kermit, natch. Little Kermie, in a rowboat, singing about peace and love and all that crap, sweeping Señorita Piggy off her feet. They'd agree to share the island, and the movie would end with a big show number, with Gonzo's belly-dancing chickens arm-in-arm with Señorita Piggy's flamenco-stompin' Spanish Special Forces.

It didn't go that well when the real Moroccan loony got to the island. He planted the Moroccan flag on the island—so far, so good—but when the Spanish troops came over to arrest him, he gulped down the pills. I guess his plan was to OD right there on the Isle of Parsley and go down in history as one of Morocco's great martyrs. Or maybe the pills were Ex-lax, and he wanted to explode, you know, kill the Spanish with shit-shrapnel.

But he didn't even manage to OD. Pretty lame.

I don't want to brag or anything, but I went to high school with people who could find a way to OD on every single thing you have in your bathroom. Including tap water. This one guy we called "Med fly" actually drank a bottle of malathion. And lived, sort of. And this pansy-ass Moroccan can't even manage to OD with a bottle of pills?

It's a sad commentary. The human race is going to Hell in a Honda.

Sadder for the Spanish, because they used to be the meanest fucking soldiers on the planet. Four hundred years ago, the thought of facing Spanish infantry would send most European armies running. Cortés and Pizarro stomped whole empires with a few dozen men. But they brought back so much booty the country just got lazy and weak. And now Spain can't do much but run beach hotels for soccer hooligans.

It must be sad to be a Spaniard now, when your best days are long gone. I've always wondered about that with Europeans—if you're a German or French guy living now, do you feel bitter because your country used to kick ass all over the world, but now it can't do anything? Like Spain can't even kill a Moroccan in a rowboat? If it was me, I'd be depressed. Maybe that's like an America-centric idea or something, but I'm not trying to be snotty about it. I just wonder.

But to be fair, the rest of the world isn't much better. War these days is mostly bluff. It's all woofing, cheap propaganda, PR stuff.

The fight over this stupid island was just a sideshow. The real fight is over a couple of pieces of Moroccan coastline that the Spanish still hold, thanks to some old colonial treaties (the same way the United States claims Guantanamo). The Moroccans were sending a message to the Spanish: Suppose we march a few thousand Moroccan civilians into those colonial holdovers? Do you squeamish Spaniards really have the balls to machine-gun ten thousand Moroccan civilians right there in front of the TV cameras?

The Moroccans have already tried this kind of "civilian invasion" technique—and it worked. They took the whole of the Spanish Sahara by sending 350,000 Moroccan civilians marching over the border. Totally unarmed, daring the guards to kill them. And not a shot was fired. The Moroccans had won a huge chunk of territory without firing a shot.

The story of the Spanish Sahara is very weird and still not settled. The Spanish got it as a consolation prize at the Berlin Conference of 1884, where the Europeans divided up Africa. Nobody else wanted this chunk of desert (average rainfall, zero), so they let poor old Spain have it. Although the desert population was tiny and disorganized, the Spanish still needed help from the French to keep the locals under control. After WW II, when the European powers started getting out of Africa, the Moroccans, seeing that the Spanish were too weak to hold the place, started moving in themselves.

There was a lot of fancy talk at the UN about a referendum—about letting the nomads decide their own fate—but the Moroccans weren't buying. They weren't squeamish Europeans. They've got all the ingredients for expansion: a big birthrate, a greedy army clique running the country, a strong religion. The Moroccans decided to grab the whole territory before the UN could organize a referendum.

On November 6, 1975, the Moroccans assembled 350,000 civilians at their southern border and marched into Spanish Sahara. Men, women, children, all waving green flags, yelling the usual "God is great" cheerleader routine. The UN just let them through. Like the Bosnians found out at Srebrenica, UN troops are about as much protection as a toilet-paper condom.

The funny thing is, the unarmed Moroccan civilians did a much better job of taking Spanish Sahara than the Moroccan army did of holding on to it. Polisario started a guerrilla war with Algerian backing and weapons, and it ran rings around the Moroccan army. Until the Moroccans built their sand wall, Polisario units in their Toyotas were hitting anywhere they wanted, then fading into the dunes. Right now, it looks as if the Moroccans won't be able to hold the place much longer. The Spanish are pushing the UN to get that referendum going (jeez, it's only a few decades late—why all the rush?), and apparently, they might finally succeed. In fact, one reason the Moroccans decided to push the Spanish up north is that the Moroccans want them to back off down south.

So the whole Spain-Morocco mess turns out to be a pretty good sample of war in the twenty-first century.

Which is a real downer. The lessons are all pretty depressing. For example: Actual military capability doesn't mean much. Armies are for making gestures, not fighting. The best way of invading a territory you want is the way the Moroccans did it in their "Green March" into Spanish Sahara: Assemble a big crowd of civilians, and send 'em across the border, daring your enemy to wipe them out on-camera, live.

Not many people in the United States noticed the Green March, but a lot of land-hungry juntas and oligarchies in the Third World paid close attention. Morocco had invented a new way of invading and seizing another country—and the coolest, funniest part is that it's a way invented by the one and only Gandhi himself! I predict you'll see a lot more Green Marches, with floods of unarmed "helpless civilians" walking over borders and daring troops to shoot them.

It's a weird thought, that the wars of the twenty-first century will use a war plan developed by Gandhi. But it seems pretty likely. Of course, there'll be countermeasures developed over time. Countermobs, maybe: your mob of unarmed civilians vs. our mob of unarmed civilians. It won't be pretty, but it'll work. It'll come down to camera work—like, can our people die sadder than yours? Can our shot-up children look sadder than yours? They better start teaching "How to Make Home Videos" at West Point.

THE BRECHER CURVE
GOES TO CORSICA

NOW THAT WE'VE got everything running so smooth in Iraq, I thought I'd talk about something a little lighter, to take our minds off all that peace and law and order that's busting out all over Saddamland. If Iraq gets any more peaceful, there won't be anybody left alive to enjoy all that expensive imported democracy we brought to the party.

This chapter has two parts. The first is educational, scientific—all that. I thought it up myself, too. The second part is what you might call the light comedy part of the chapter: I announce the winner of my competition to find the very fakest, wimpiest, no-contact "war" on the planet. But first, a war-nerd science lesson.

You know how Newton was sitting there picking his nose when he got hit by that apple obeying the law of gravity? Well, the same thing happened to me while I was watching the Najaf bombing reports. Not the apple—I was indoors—but the sudden, blinding flash of genius: It hit me like a diamond bullet that these casualty counts always go through the same three stages. First there's a ridiculously low number, then a high one, and then, about three days after the place went boom, a third count pretty close to accurate.

I'm calling it the Brecher Casualty Curve, just in case there's money in it. Like maybe I can get a DoD grant to do further study on all the mathematical wrinkles of my curve ... sit on my ass at home all day surfing war sites, writing off my pizza bills as business expenses. Sweet. And listen, compared to most DoD expenditures, my pizza bills are a great investment. Take the B-1 bomber ... please.

Let's watch the magical Brecher Curve in action, using the Najaf bombing as sort of a story-problem: "If 20,000 Shiites coming out of a mosque meet 2,000 kilograms of high explosive expanding at a zillion feet per second, how many Shiites will be missing from the next group hug?" We simply apply the curve and stand back to watch it work.

Stage 1: The local cops and PR boys invent a ridiculously low casualty figure, approximately one-fifth to one-third the real total. As in, "Sure, half of Najaf just vanished in a cloud of burning fertilizer, but that doesn't mean people *died!*" Remember the first figure they gave for the Najaf bomb? Seventeen dead, that's what they said. If you've watched as many of these things as I have, you knew that was a lie. What gets me is why all the wire-service and TV mouthpieces pass this shit on like they believe it. Do these guys actually look at ten square blocks of blood and rubble and believe it when the cops tell them only seventeen people bought it? Well, not for very long. That's how you get to the next stage.

Stage 2: The official story breaks down and the death toll zooms out of control. In the Najaf bomb, the figure went from 17 to 125 in a few hours. What happens is that after a few reporters wade around the local hospital getting their argyles dyed hemoglobin red and counting all the people lying in the hallways with blankets over their faces, the count boomerangs. You get a hysterical overcount. So just remember next time: This stage will *always* turn out to be too high, usually by about 20 percent. So get out that calculator you use once a year, around midnight on April 14, and do the math. That way, while the TV geeks are still stuck at Stage 2, you will be already at . . .

Stage 3: the actual death toll. This usually starts to come out about forty-eight hours after the truck goes boom. And it's almost always expressible in simple math:

Stage 3 = Stage 2 – 20%.

So in the Najaf bomb, Stage 3 was equal to Stage 2 (125 people) minus 20 percent of 125, or 25. Which would be, uh . . . 100 people. Yup, according to my all knowing, all-seeing Brecher Curve, the final death toll in Najaf would be 100. If your office was having a pool, you could have gotten a bet down on 100 before everybody tried to get in on it. In fact, it would have been smart to put a few bucks down on everything from 95 to 105. This thing has a margin of error, like us scientists always say.

Update: Well, the curve didn't work as promised in Najaf. The death toll stayed around 125. What I forgot to factor in was that the whole Pentagon PR stuff was working to damp down the corpse count, keeping it to a minimum. Well, that just proves the Department of Defense should fund my vital research into the Brecher Curve. It has the one thing Defense can't resist: It doesn't work.

On to something a little lighter, as I promised. Iraq was getting me down, so I decided to find the most harmless little no-contact, flag-football war in the world and write it up. I figured it had to be one of the little boutique wars in Europe, so I looked them all up. It blew me away how many of them there are over there. Like the Basques. When's the last time you heard about the Basque war of liberation? Hell, when's the last time you thought about Basques, period? The last I heard, they were all herding sheep in Nevada, poor bastards.

Turns out the Basques claim a chunk of land in southern France and northern Spain, and a few of them are willing to kill for it. But kill in a squeamish Eurotrash way. The Basque rebel "army," ETA, has been officially at war with Spain for twenty-odd years. Every year, the rebels set off a couple of lame little bombs and kill some poor Spanish cop or mayor on his way to work. The idea with this kind of war isn't to win battles. There are no battles. It's just to make the papers and the TV news a couple of times a year. Just to keep ETA's name out there. It's war the way a Hollywood agent would do it. The whole thing is unreal, because the Spanish Guardia Civil (sort of a cross between the Mounties and the FBI) knows the name of every last member of ETA. There's only a few hundred members, anyway. The Spanish could kill every last one in a few hours. But they're too "nice." Which means too pathetic, too weak, too just plain cowardly. So they let these guys plant a few bombs and kill a few cops, and the Guardia arrests one every now and then. Try that shit in a real country, like anyplace in East Asia, and your relatives will be insisting on a closed coffin at your funeral next week, because the cops won't kill you fast and easy. They frown on amateur terrorism out there.

But in Europe, you can get away with this crap for decades. It just proves what I'm always saying: The world is goin' Fag Planet faster than the leading man in your high-school drama class.

But it gets worse. Reading up on all the fake liberation armies in Europe, I realized that the Basques are the goddamn Wehrmacht compared with some of the other backyard rebels they've got over there. There are bowling teams scarier than these armies. They're what my grandpa used to call "brush-poppers," cowards who popped up behind a hedge and shot you in the back.

It was a tough call picking the dumbest and fakest one of all. There were some real beauties, like the Scottish Something-or-other army, and the Catalonian People's Something . . . I'm still not sure where Catalan is on the map, never mind why these guys think it should have its own anthem and license plates. You read up on all this stupid shit from America, and you think, why don't the fuckers just move if they don't like the neighbors? All this crap about "countries" smaller than Kern County. And uglier, if that's physically possible.

And who's the fakest of them all? The envelope, please . . .

Ladies and gentlemen, our winner is the FLNC!

Never heard of it? I don't blame you. Well, for starters, FLNC stands for "Fronte di Liberazione Naziunale di a Corsica."

Now if you know anything about war, you should have recognized one word, "Corsica." Corsica is just a little island between France and Italy, but it did produce one guy who was pretty good at war. Short guy, funny hat, name of Bonaparte. Yeah, him.

Unfortunately, Corsican military glory began and ended with the Little Corporal. But it does have this "war" for independence (from the French), run by the FLNC. This pitiful excuse for a war officially started in 1976, when the FLNC made a big announcement and ran up the Corsican flag. The FLNC supposedly has six hundred soldiers, but they never shoot anybody except each other. That's why they won the title of lamest army in the world: They never, ever try to kill the French troops in Corsica, but they're savage murderers when it comes to each other.

Real prizes, these guys. Take the way they carry out their bombings. They plant a lot of bombs, at least nine thousand since the 1970s—but the bombs are purposely weak, like about as strong as an M-80. The FLNC only puts its itsy bitsy bombies where nobody'll get hurt, see. They're "symbolic" bombs, meaning all they're designed to do is make a hole in something so it gets shown on the evening news and the FLNC gets its name on TV.

The FLNC is not exactly the people's choice, anyway. The pro-independence party gets less than 20 percent of the Corsican vote.

In fact, the French just arranged a referendum for independence. The whole island got to vote on whether to stick with those big, fat welfare checks from Paris or go it alone: *Vive le Corse*, poor but free!

It was no contest: Welfare and subsidized baguettes won hands down. This pisses the FLNC rebels off no end, but they won't listen to the voters and quit their phony war. Why should they? Why be another French wage slave when you can strut around being whispered about as a brave Corsican rebel? Especially when the lame Frog authorities won't even do anything to you. All the macho with none of the risk, damn! If I could find a Corsican great-grandma in the family tree, I'd head over and give it a try myself. It's gotta beat Fresno—those lucky bastards have a thirty-five-hour work week, and you can bet the brave Corsicans aren't revolting against *that* French law.

Here's a typical FLNC "military" operation. On September 18, 1999, the FLNC set off five bombs simultaneously, all over Corsica. At 2:30 A.M., when they were sure all the buildings would be empty. I mean, you wouldn't want your bombs to hurt any of your oppressors or anything.

Results of the big blitz: Total damage to buildings, none. Total casualties, zero. Total bullshit: total, dude.

You can go as far back in history as you want, and you won't find an army that specialized in not hurting its enemies. Like Bart Simpson says to the mall dojo-sensei when the guy starts preaching peace-through-karate, "Dude, I already know how *not* to hit a guy."

It makes you wonder what goes on in these people's heads. If they really want the French out, they'd do what the Algerians did and start seriously terrorizing them into running for the boats. The Algerians killed anybody who ate croissants or thought Jerry Lewis was funny. And it worked. Algeria may be a mess, but it's an independent mess.

The Corsicans with their toy army and Nerf bombings—it's like they know themselves they're fakes. This may sound like a harsh thing to say, but the way you can tell what people take seriously is what they'll kill for, like money, or pride, or country, or family honor, or whatever. The FLNC may sit around singing Corsican songs, but it doesn't have the guts to kill for the place.

But don't go thinking it's because they're nice guys. They're killers, but the only people they kill are . . . you guessed it: other Corsican nationalists. Not the French cops or soldiers, not the rich vacationers from Paris who've bought up most of the decent land in Corsica. Just each other.

They killed one of their own on August 25, 2003. A Corsican "militant" who'd done time for planting bombs was shot in a French-style drive-by: two guys on a motor scooter. That's what they really care about—who's top dog in the local pack. And that's all they care about.

Well damn, this was supposed to be all lighthearted and all. But I can't lie, this world is getting me down. You've got this "peace" in Iraq that costs more than the space shuttle and works about as well as the O-rings . . . then you've got these phony Euro-midget wars where the brave rebels are just my grandpa's "brush-poppers" on scooters. I mean, that's the worst of it, scooters. A drive-by on a scooter.

We're just no damn good, that's all.

WHY CAN'T I ENJOY THE EASTERN FRONT?

THE EASTERN FRONT, WW II. Two huge empires fighting to the death on a battle line stretching from the Arctic Ocean to the Black Sea. The stats alone are awesome, the sheer scale of everything that happened.

Take the battle of Kursk: 1.3 million Soviet troops with twenty thousand cannon, 3,500 tanks, and 2,400 planes facing 900,000 of the Wehrmacht's finest—that is, the finest divisions of the finest land army since the Mongols went out of business. The Wehrmacht brought a pretty fair arsenal of their own: 2,700 panzers and 2,000 aircraft. In one day of the Kursk campaign (July 12, 1943), thousands of Soviet and German tanks faced off and blasted each other point-blank, with each side losing over 300 tanks, while the air forces dueled in the skies.

This ought to be the ultimate in war. So why don't I enjoy it like I should?

There are a couple of reasons. One you can get from another key stat, civilian losses. Out of the 29 million Soviet citizens who died, 17 million were civilians. I'm no bleeding heart, but it's no fun imagining 17 million civilians getting shot, starved, or frozen to death. Maybe it's because I keep imagining those Russian tennis babes getting killed. What kind of idiot would massacre girls who look like Maria Sharapova? That's what I call a war crime.

Like I've said before, WW I was a horrible war to be in if you were a soldier, but not too bad if you were a civilian. Ninety-five percent of the dead in WW I were soldiers. WW II was bad enough for soldiers, especially Soviet and German soldiers, but it was sheer Hell for any civilians who lived anywhere between Warsaw and Moscow.

Mobility—that was the key difference between the civilian casualty rates in WW I and WW II. The more mobile a war, the harder it is on civilians. You can see that, even in wars where both armies make a real effort to spare civvies.

Take our own Civil War. In the eastern theater, with the Armies of the Potomac and Northern Virginia working each other over in a fairly small area west of Chesapeake Bay, civilians didn't get murdered in big numbers. When crops and farms were burned in the eastern theater (for example, in the Shenandoah Valley), it was out of hard military necessity. But out in the western theater, where war was a hit-and-run business, towns like Lawrence, Kansas, were wiped out in an afternoon, with no man, woman, or child spared. When you're only in town for a few hours, you have to win hearts and minds the fast way: by shooting them in the heart, or blowing their minds out the back of their heads.

WW I was an insanely static war, especially on the Western Front, with the armies locked into a face-off in huge trench lines, away from civilian populations. Except for a few families unlucky enough to live in the battle zones of northern France, it was easy for civilians to survive.

WW II on the Eastern Front was the opposite, the most mobile warfare since the Mongols, and just about as lethal for any civvies in the armies' path. If you lived in Poland or Belorussia, someone was going to kill you and your family; you just couldn't be sure who it would be. If those poor bastards had been able to see in 1941 what the next four years were going to be like, they'd have begged Dad to kill them all with a hatchet, then throw himself down the well, just to avoid the horrible suspense and get it over with.

Maybe it would be the Soviet commissars who killed you; they had a policy of killing all politically suspect civvies in regions that were about to fall to the Nazis. And to the NKVD (the Soviet secret police organization), "politically suspect" could mean nearly anything: Your hut was too solid, you owned one too many pigs, you didn't name your first child after Stalin. Weirdly enough, in 1941, it was the Nazis who were uncovering—literally—"human rights violations" in Eastern Europe; as the Germans advanced, they kept digging up fresh mass graves where the NKVD had dumped its prisoners as the Soviet army retreated.

On the other hand, the Nazis would kill you if you were a Jew—or if the ignorant *Obergefreiter* whose squad just rumbled into your village thought you looked like one. If you were a pretty Polish or Russian girl, you were likely to die, too, after the German or Rumanian or Hungarian soldiers had raped you. The Wehrmacht also had a policy of summary execution for communists, and a pretty flexible definition of what one was. And when in doubt, they killed.

The Germans killed for another Mongol-type reason: land clearance. The Mongols tended to kill people who were using up good grazing land and who were getting it all cluttered with houses and fences. The Germans thought the same way about Slavs, treating them like gophers or some other varmint that was spoiling the land they planned on turning into thousands of blond, blue-eyed little clock-tower towns. Why not get the varmints out of the way while you had the ordnance on the spot? You'd be doing a favor for the planners from Berlin who were supposed to follow the armies, laying out the new towns. So the army blasted the Belorussians and Ukrainians, even when the peasants came out on the roads with flowers, cheering the Wehrmacht columns.

That's what gets me down: those poor suckers thinking their saviors had arrived. You can't blame them. After Stalin, anybody else must have looked good. Especially to the Ukrainians, who'd been purposely starved to death by the millions in the early 1930s, when Stalin collectivized their farms.

It's weird how nobody remembers those millions of dead Ukrainians. It's like they just don't count. Everybody remembers all the poor Londoners killed in the Blitz. You know how many English civvies died in WW II? Less than sixty thousand! According to my calculator, that means that almost three hundred Soviets died for every Brit who got bombed. But all my life, I've been reading about the English "cowering" in the subway stations as the bombs fell. I never heard a word about the millions of Ukrainians who died in Stalin's famine, and I sure as Hell never realized that twenty-nine million Soviets died in WW II. Until I got serious about learning war on my own, all I ever heard was the Battle of Britain and D-Day, which were sideshows to the real war, back there in the snow in Russia.

Mobile warfare creates its own famine as it moves. It's a matter of logistics. If your army is in the trenches a few miles from Paris, the way the Franco-British army was in WW II, you can set up stable supply lines so your soldiers don't have to forage. The French *poilu* (grunt) in WW I lived on endless tin cans of tuna and beans, carted out from Paris by tired old horses and even tireder old trucks.

But when the armies are fighting on a front hundreds of miles wide and thousands of miles long, with huge chunks of land changing hands every day, that sort of resupply is impossible. So the armies go back to the old ways, "living off the land." Which means, basically, getting food from the peasants at bayonet point. It's standard military practice, but it's not pretty: A squad breaks down your farmhouse door, grabs your baby son, and starts sawing at his throat with a knife, screaming at you to tell them where your hoarded food is. Since those few sacks of grain and maybe a ham or two is all you've got to survive the winter, you don't much want to tell them. But then they start really cutting deep into Junior's throat, he's screaming, and you tell.

They dig up the hoard, and as likely as not, they shoot you all, anyway, for making them go through all that trouble. If they don't, you have to figure out a way to survive the Russian winter with no food.

To go back to America's Civil War again, Sherman's sweep through the Georgia breadbasket turned the war mobile in a big way and introduced living off the land, and the "freebooter" to American warfare. The further his army moved into enemy territory, the less the rules of war seemed to apply. Looting was taken for granted; if you had a pig or a chicken, consider it gone when his men showed. Burning was a real possibility; the army burned all the "big houses" (plantation mansions) in Georgia, and when it reached South Carolina, the state that started the whole mess, the soldiers burned everything, from shack to mansion.

And I've always wondered if that other rule of war, the one against rape, sort of got forgotten on the way to Columbia, South Carolina, too. That scene in *Gone with the Wind*, where what's-hername shoots the grinning freebooter coming up the stairs—I wonder how often that happened and the belle upstairs didn't have a pistol handy. They wouldn't have talked about it—the United States in the 1860s had to be the most tight-assed, straight-laced place in the history of the world. But I suspect it was more than hams and chickens those blue-bellies were grabbing on their way to the sea.

Another complication of mobile warfare for civvies is that your home town might change hands several times. This happened to thousands of towns and villages in Eastern Europe in WW II. If you got along too well with the Wehrmacht, you weren't going to have an easy time when the Soviet army rolled into town. If you lived in a strategic city like Kharkov (taken by the Wehrmacht in the autumn of 1941, recaptured by the Soviets in the winter of 1943, retaken by the Wehrmacht in the spring of 1943, and re-recaptured for good by the Soviets in the summer of 1943), you were going to have a difficult time explaining to one side or the other why you were still alive and hadn't done the patriotic thing by dying under enemy occupation. We're talking about millions of civilians dragged into the Gulag for the crime of surviving the Nazis. It just sort of gets me down to think of.

The other reason the Eastern Front depresses me is simpler: the results. All it did was bleed the two coolest armies in Europe, the only really interesting armies on the continent. The USSR won, but left its best people dead on the field. The Germans lost for all time, vanished from history forever. And by massacring all those civilians, that asshole Hitler ruined the whole idea that there was a heroic life in war. I don't even understand what that moron thought he was doing. All these neo-Nazi idiots, losers who wouldn't even have been let into the Wehrmacht, talk about "the white race"—well, wasn't every single person Hitler killed white? Talk about black-on-black crime! The Nazis were the ultimate in white-on-white massacre.

All it did was give war a bad name. All that was left when the Germans and Russians had bled each other to death was the Anglos: us and the Brits. All that was left to believe in after 1945 was business, making money—that whole stupid, boring, white-bread way of life. My life.

NERF WAR AND REAL WAR:
IRA VS. AL QAEDA

THE 2005 LONDON suicide bombs. Not your idea of making war? Well, I agree. We'd all rather see tank battles or dogfights. But we have to face facts: That kind of war only happens now on

PlayStation. Out in the world, it's dirty urban guerrilla warfare that counts.

So let's talk urban-war hardware for a second. That ought to thrill you metal-heads. Only in this case, we're talking plastic, as in plastic explosives. The London bombs were made with military plastic explosive.

Ah, Semtex, a bus-bomber's best friend. The Czechs made thousands of tons of it back in the day. They were mighty proud, too—the name *Semtex* comes from a suburb of Prague. It was like their beer: They wanted you to think of them when you, er, consumed it.

"This death has been brought to you by the Czech People's Republic!" The Czechs are still proud: There's actually an energy drink called Semtex. A big seller in Prague, I hear. I really want to know what their advertising slogan is: "For a *burst* of flavor!" It puts a new meaning on the Red Bull slogan: "Semtex Gives You Wings." Yeah, and seventy-two virgins, if you're lucky.

Until 2002, they were making Semtex without chemical taggers, the smelly chemicals added to plastic explosive to make it easier for dogs to sniff them out. The Czechs sold hundreds of tons of Unscented Semtex ("Hypoallergenic, for the sensitive terrorist!") to Gadhafi. And he gave them to the IRA.

Just so we're clear, I'm not implying the IRA had anything to do with these bombs. No way. They've pretty much stuck to 1997's ceasefire. This Semtex was probably sold to an Al Qaeda buyer by a middleman in Eastern Europe. But it's worth remembering the IRA's bombing campaigns, because you can see how they evolved away from targeting civilians to something more like giant pranks, or instant arson—destroying buildings without killing people.

The IRA has been around for a long time, but by the late 1960s, when British troops reoccupied Northern Ireland, the leadership in Dublin had turned into a typical Western communist party: all talk, no action. The guys on the street up North wanted to go back into action, but the Dublin committees said that wouldn't be cool with Marx. The hotheads up in Belfast told them to stick *Das Kapital* up Das Arse, dug up the guns they'd buried, and started potting

Tommies. They called themselves the Provisional IRA (Provos), as opposed to the so-called Official wing, aka the "Stickies." And to formalize the split, the Provos had a nice little blood feud with the Officials, with dozens of assassinations on both sides. After a couple of years, the Officials were dead or intimidated, and the Provos ruled the Catholic ghettoes of Belfast and Londonderry.

It took the Provos a while to realize that bombings and shootings in Ulster didn't accomplish anything. Finally, after years of blasting their own neighborhoods, the Micks started to understand that the British government didn't care what happened up there. Northern Ireland is a hellhole—one big welfare slum. The English hate the Northern Irish Protestants almost as much as they hate the Catholics and wouldn't mind if Ulster was wiped out by a meteor.

Eventually, the Provos realized that there was only one target the Brits really cared about: London. London is England. Almost a third of the country's population lives in Greater London. Hit London, and you cripple the whole UK. Imagine if New York had a population of 100 million and our next biggest city was someplace like Milwaukee. That's how important London is to Britain.

Even after it focused on London, it took the IRA twenty years to perfect a way of attacking London without drawing too much bad publicity. Because that's what the IRA's war was about: publicity, hearts-'n'-minds, not real military advantage. In its first London campaigns, the IRA used Gadhafi's Semtex to attack military targets. Some of the results were pretty funny, like when they killed seven cavalry horses bombing a military parade in Hyde Park in 1982.

It was a successful attack, with eight soldiers killed—but killing those horses drove the British papers into a frenzy. The Limeys are more horse-crazy than a sexually frustrated fourteen-year-old girl. They were ready to hang anybody with red hair or freckles after the pictures of dying horses hit the front page. You can slaughter all the people you want, but touch a pony, and those English ladies will pull your spleen out and squeeze it to pulp right before your eyes.

So the IRA went back to the drawing board, with a note-to-self: "No more dead animals, lads." It tried to think what would hurt the rich folks and had a flash: shopping! On December 17, 1983, an IRA bomb blew up Harrods Department Store (if you've seen Ali G.'s interview with the Arab who owns it, you might know it better as 'Arrods.)

Five shoppers got splatted, and the tabloids went wild. I mean, napalm is one thing, but messing with the retail season—talk about war crimes!

The IRA was slowly starting to understand that the more casualties it inflicted, the worse things went. The British media just splattered the pictures of bloody civilians all over the papers and TV, and the IRA was in bigger trouble than ever. It stuck to the idea of paralyzing London, but it started trying to think of ways to do it without hurting anyone.

Q: How can you blow up London without casualties?

A: Phone in lots of warnings, hours before the bombs are due to go off.

That's what the IRA started doing in the late 1980s. To cause maximum property damage, it started using trucks packed with fertilizer-based explosives and equipped with booby traps, so any attempt to defuse the bomb would set it off and vaporize the bomb experts working on it. It's hard to get ammonium nitrate to blow up on its own, so they used detonators fueled with Tovax, a commercial gel explosive. In the late 1980s, you could always tell an IRA man: He was the customer who ordered ten tons of fertilizer, even though he lived in a London high-rise.

The IRA's new London cadre was English-raised, so they didn't have that giveaway Belfast accent. They were classic urban guerrilla material: disciplined, young guys who held day jobs and didn't talk.

Their first success with this kind of bomb came on April 10, 1992. An IRA man drove a truck packed with more than a ton of fertilizer bomb mix to the London financial district, parked it, and walked away. No worries about parking tickets, and any tow-truck driver who messed with it would be real, real sorry.

Then IRA operatives began calling in warnings about the bomb, starting hours before it was set to go off. They even called radio and TV stations because these guys were afraid that if they only called Scotland Yard's Special Branch, the spooks there might not pass on the warning, since any casualties hurt the IRA and helped the Brits.

The warnings were passed on, the financial district was evacuated, and the bomb went off on schedule. Some of the most expensive corporate real estate in Central London turned into crushed glass and confetti. The financial cost to the UK was huge. The claims for bomb damage helped put Lloyd's of London in financial trouble for the first time in history. And there were other costs, like the slowdown in British economic performance when every package and car has to be searched and the thousands of nonproducing security jobs that had to be created.

Next year, they did it again, with the same MO: huge truck bomb, financial district of London, lots of warnings. And it worked. Only one death, and that was a photographer who went back into the danger zone without permission. It was total victory for the IRA: a deadly blow for the UK economy with no bloody-civilian photos in the papers to ruin it.

The IRA leadership figured it had made a point and tried something even more radical: It declared a ceasefire. IRA leaders like Gerry Adams were arguing that propaganda was the way to go—butter up Clinton, get Slick Willie to force the Brits out. They said bombs were a bad look and figured they could come across as peaceniks if they quit.

But the Brits were in no mood to make a deal. Prime Minister John Major didn't want to be the man who lost Ulster, so he ignored the ceasefire. After seventeen months of boring ol' peace, the IRA decided to send a little reminder that it hadn't gone totally soft. It started a new bombing campaign, this time with no attacks in Ulster at all. Its networks in England were so strong the IRA could make life in London unbearable without fouling its own neighborhoods in Ulster—an urban guerrilla's dream situation.

In February 1996, a truck packed with a half-ton of fertilizer exploded in London, near the offices of some of the most anti-IRA tabloid papers. Once the echoes of the blast faded, all you could hear were car alarms, sirens, and the sound of insurance agents sobbing.

The follow-up act came fast: In June 1996, the IRA decided to do a little road trip. It set off its biggest bomb ever, more than three thousand pounds of ammonium nitrate, in central Manchester. Same tactics: lots of warnings, no dead, huge damage.

There was a silver lining to this one: The center of Manchester was a disgusting slum, and the bomb cleared it right out. Urban planners were the only demographic that jumped up and down for joy when the evening news came on, and downtown Manchester is now, from what I've read, the cutest little yuppie paradise in the UK.

IRA cells were operating in every big English city, and the Special Branch just wasn't catching them. As long as the supply of fertilizer held out, the IRA was sitting pretty. If it had wanted to, the IRA could have put no-warning bombs all over the London transit system and killed tens, maybe hundreds of thousands, of commuters. But that wasn't the idea. They were taking it slow and soft, annoying the Brits to death instead.

The cost to the Brits in money, embarrassment, and nerves was just getting out of hand. When Tony Blair was elected in early 1997, he went to Belfast and met with the IRA leadership. A few months later, after months of schmoozing from Clinton, the IRA declared a second ceasefire. And this one took.

Now you can see the total contrast between the little fancy-schmancy Nerf warfare the IRA was doing and the total war that Al Qaeda practices. Al Qaeda isn't courting the Western press the way the IRA leaders are. Al Qaeda members don't want us to like them. They aim to kill as many civilians as they can. They don't want to sweet-talk us out of the Middle East; they want to smash our fingers until we let go and drop. For them, shots of bloody commuters stumbling out of the Tube stations are *good* publicity.

And it works, sometimes. In Spain: 200 dead on Madrid commuter trains, the government falls, and Spanish troops flee Iraq: *Mision cumplida!*

In fact, that's how I knew instantly it wasn't the Basques who set those bombs back then, like the Spanish government tried to claim: because the Basque "army," ETA, runs by the same wimpy rules that the IRA follows, and tries to blow stuff up without hurting anybody.

Al Qaeda plays by the good old rules: Kill as many as you can, and eventually, there'll be nothing left but brave corpses and live cowards.

Will it work on the Brits? I doubt it, in the short term, anyway. They're tough, tougher than most Americans realize. They've stuck with us even though they knew how lame the whole Iraq invasion was. It was like the polite English sidekick telling Dubya, "Er, I wouldn't disband the Iraqi Army just yet, old boy—ah well, too late!" "Um, ah, perhaps you shouldn't shoot all those demonstrators in Fallujah—whoops! Ah well, mistakes happen!"

ARISE, YE DANES!

By now, every unemployed Muslim on the planet has demanded that Denmark be beheaded. For a while there, every damn night, you saw on the news more of those Islamic demonstrations, with hordes of hairy guys raising their fists and chanting some crap.

Made me wish for a dive-bomber, or better yet a crop duster—if only I could have passed a pilot's physical.

Every time I see one of those crowds, I can't help but think of the smell there. That would be the worst thing about getting caught in an angry Muslim demonstration, worse even than getting attacked and beaten. It's the smell I fear. All those unwashed armpits right over your head, bashing you and chanting about their Allah. You'd beg for death, you'd be moaning, "O believers, in the name of Allah the Great, the Unshowered, the Never-Heard-of-Speedstick, Whose Armpits Stink Like Anchovies in a Broken Fridge, will one of you find a rock or a sharp object to finish me off, already?"

For the most part, the biggest action was in Lebanon and Syria, where Danish embassies were burned down. As soon as I heard that, I knew the burnings had been ordered by Bashar al-Assad's intel service, because *nothing* happens with *Islamic* on it in Beirut, never mind Damascus, unless the Syrian colonels in sunglasses OK it. Assad didn't give a damn about Danish cartoons—in fact, his Alawite clan doesn't even count as Muslim by most Imams' standards. He just wants to remind Bush every so often that taking down Syria may be a cakewalk in stage one, just like Iraq was, but stage two, the occupation, will be way worse than Iraq is now, because Assad's spies are smarter and tougher than Saddam's goons ever were.

So in a way I'm kind of glad those Danish embassies burned, because maybe Bush will take the hint and not land us in another tar swamp. One's plenty. But let's be realistic. Bush's last contact with reality was his senior-year report card at Yale. He didn't enjoy it and hasn't been back since. He'll jump into Syria unless one of the Joint Chiefs draws a pistol and changes the C-in-C's mind.

I saw the Danish cartoons online, and they're as tame and lame as you'd expect from twenty-first-century Denmark, a whole country working 24/7 to make sure it doesn't offend anybody, terrified it might be accused of being pro-Danish. God, we can't have that! Scandinavians are so worried they might offend some Third Worlder that they make perfect prey for any murderer or rapist lucky enough not to be blond and tall.

But I wonder, do you Danes ever feel pride in who you once were? I sure hope so. Because you truly were great, the most mobile and greedy (I mean that in a good way) of all the Vikings. You had the best of all worlds; you'd happily farm your little Danish pastures half the year, and then when summer came, Dad would kiss the wife and kids (and cow) good-bye and sail off to slaughter any settlement his and his buddies' longboats could reach. And thanks to their shallow draft, the longboats could sail far upriver, so even inlanders so far from the ocean that the whole village had goiters were nevertheless within range of the Danes.

"The Danes!" If somebody called out, "The Danes!" in Northern Europe a thousand years ago, he didn't mean that some scraggy, gloomy hippies were arriving at the backpacker hostel. Back then, the Danes weren't ashamed of being a warrior tribe, hacking lesser breeds from Ireland to Russia without mercy. It was a classic example of how you can combine socialism and entrepreneurship: All the men from a peaceful Danish village would polish up their axes—most Vikings used axes, because axes were cheaper than swords and more useful around the farm—and row off together.

Nobody could stop them. The sea was the only way to travel fast in those days, so the Vikings could burn, rape, and rob any town long before the local lord could muster his garrison, never mind reach the town under attack. And then, like the good little social democrats they were, the Vikings would head home to cuddle the kids, pamper the livestock, and spend the long nights making sure the wife produced another generation of raiders. If there's a better life, I can't imagine what it is.

Historians these days always emphasize how "the Vikings were essentially traders, not mere plunderers." Yeah, right. What that means is (a) professors hate to admit there was ever anything as glorious as the Vikings and (b) if you met the Vikings' longboats with a huge army and looked ready to fight, the Danes were smart enough to switch to sales mode: "Hi there! We're peaceful visitors here to, uh, what's the word? 'Trade'—yes, 'trade' with you wonderful people!" But let your guard down for a second, and they'd cut out the middleman—literally. It was just good business. Nothing makes your accountant happier than hearing you got your stock at the ultimate wholesale price.

Like all good raiders, the Danes thrived on tricks. If feeding the enemy a flattering line of bullshit would bring an advantage, the Vikings could spread the verbal cow-pies better than a DoD official spokesperson.

There's a famous case, the Battle of Maldon, 991 A.D. For once, the locals—in this case, the English—had the advantage. A Viking raiding party was stuck on a little offshore island. The only way ashore was a causeway so narrow three men could hold it. The Vikings tried the John Madden approach first, bulldogging the causeway. But the Anglo-Saxons had put their best men there, and the Vikings limped back to the island, where some Dark Ages PR whiz came up with a great idea: appeal to the Anglo-Saxons' notion of a fair fight.

The Vikings flattered the old Earl of Maldon and reminded him of the noble Anglo-Saxon tradition of fair combat, and the old idiot finally agreed to let the Vikings march unopposed to shore so the two sides could stage the first, last, and only Maldon Bowl. The game ended when the Vikings showed their gratitude to the old nobleman by hacking his head off and showing it to his men-at-arms. Which just shows that while amateurs think about fair play, pros go with Al Davis's rule: "Just win, baby."

The Vikings showed the same practical attitude when one of their own leaders got killed. Most Dark Ages European armies fought for a particular guy, and if he was killed, they broke and ran, like the Earl of Maldon's men did. Not the Vikings. If Sven, the raid leader, got his head lopped off, the Danes shrugged and kept fighting. In fact, Sven's head probably mouthed the change in lineup as the enemy held it up: "Olaf, you take over, I think I've got a medical problem!"

That practical attitude freaked those superstitious villagers so much they broke and ran as if their own leader were dead.

Eventually, coastal defenses improved enough to make Viking raids an unprofitable way to spend your summers. But the Danes still had plenty of fighting spirit left, so they applied it to wars closer to home. Medieval Scandinavia was almost always at war, with either Denmark or Sweden trying to unite the three kingdoms—including Norway, which was kind of the retarded little brother of the three—into one big, blond war machine. Too bad they didn't manage it. A mighty kingdom of the tall blonds could have gone on a worldwide pillage tour, filling the world up with their tall, blond genes, which could have made me a bit more appealing.

Instead, it was the Mongols who raped their way from Manchuria to Bavaria, leaving little Genghises to grow up getting some very funny looks from their surviving neighbors.

I'm serious about these Mongol genes. DNA studies show that in Central Asia, one out of every two hundred men has a gene linking him to Genghis Khan. Not his army, but Genghis personally. Which means he got to know this person's great-great-great (etc.) grandmothers real well in those long evenings after a day's massacring. Every war nerd in the world likes to quote Genghis's famous line about how great it is to kill your enemies "and clasp their women to your chest," but now we know he wasn't just giving pep talks. He was one of those player-coach guys, never asked anything of his men he wasn't willing to do himself.

While Genghis was spreading himself around, the Danes were busy fighting other blonds, especially Sweden. Like I've said before, Sweden used to be a real military power, a beautiful force—those amazing pikemen who walked into one of Peter the Great's fortress at Narva in the middle of a blizzard, vastly outnumbered, and astonished the Russian garrison so much the Russians just surrendered out of sheer admiration. Yeah, those blue-and-yellow cross stickers used to fly proudly, not just signal "I'm a Swede, please don't hurt me!" on a hippie's backpack.

And the Danes used to whack those tough Swedes around pretty regularly in their nonstop family fights. Take the Sweden-Denmark war of the 1560s. Just to show you how much esprit de corps these countries used to have, the war was fought over Denmark's right to use three crowns on its flag! The Danes kicked the Swedes' "numerically superior" asses on land and sea, in a major naval engagement (1564) and land battle (1565). The war didn't settle anything; when countries are young and strong, wars are for their own sake, a matter of pride, staying in shape, keeping limber.

That's how it should be, and still is in the few decent places (like the Horn of Africa). But little by little, the Danes got depressed and progressive—those two things are the same, if you ask me.

But I was surprised how late it happened. As recently as 1864, Denmark took on Prussia and Austria—pretty much all of Germany. Denmark lost, naturally, but there's no shame in that. With only forty thousand men, the Danish army fought pretty well in a series of holding actions that made the Prussians pay for every inch they pushed up the peninsula.

They sure made a better fight of it than the French did six years later, even though Denmark was in a hopeless position with none of the French army's money, manpower, or strategic depth. The Danes were just overpowered by a much bigger opponent; the French were humiliated by a smaller one. (Sorry, French people. You know I'm not one of these fools who call you cowards, but facts are facts, and you know yourselves the Franco-Prussian War wasn't exactly your finest hour.)

Once the twentieth century arrived, Denmark pretty much melted into liberal mush. I blame the Nazis, because they made militarism look bad. They ruined it for all of us except the jocks and business jerks who own the world now.

The one really interesting thing I read about recent Danish history is that one of the most important men in subatomic physics, Nils Bohr, was Danish. Hey, does that give any physics majors up there in Copenhagen any ideas? How hard can it be to cook a few nukes, especially when that Scandinavian welfare state will let you take a year or two off to surf the net looking for info? Just remember, make up a Web identity before you hit those sites. Just pick the name of the most famous Imam in Denmark, and use it as your avatar. Your pissant government won't take the hint, but the U.S. National Security Agency will quickly take note. You get the info you need to make your nuke, and the Imam gets an all-expenses-paid vacation in sunny Guantanamo, and everyone comes out ahead.

Somebody up there must have the guts to do it. You can't all be hippie ghosts. Just think how amazingly cool it would be to put your homemade nuke into one of those disgusting Eurotrash backpacks. Doesn't your axe hand itch sometimes, Danes? Honor this Nils Bohr, and do it the way the Vikings would. Vikings with nukes. Dream of that as you fall asleep to the sound of the foreigners you've welcomed and coddled smashing your cities—and maybe you'll wake up sane again, to a dream of nuclear-powered longboats heading south to turn the Holy Land into a glowing wasteland, like God intended. And by God, I mean Odin, not that Palestinian smooth-talker whose armpits are stinking up on the cross. When you had gods fit for Vikings, you were feared and respected; now you're just fucked.

THE
MIDDLE
EAST

MONSTER TRUCKS IN RAMALLAH

EVER SEE A monster truck show? They're big in Fresno, what with the white trash and *cholos*. The thrill is watching civilian cars get crushed by giant four-by-fours. But it's nothing compared to the monster truck show the Israelis put on in Ramallah in 2005. For some weird reason, I can't get enough of those car-crushing shots. You know, this sixty-one-ton Merkava 3 MBT grinds down Arafat Avenue in Ramallah or Jenin, accidentally on purpose scrunching a whole row of cars.

There's something so sweet about seeing a tank grind over little peace-type cars. Maybe it's a parking thing. Today I get home from work—and it's already hot as Hell in Fresno—so I get through the traffic out to my duplex on the edge of the desert, and I can't get a damn parking space! It's scrubland, it's the middle of nowhere, the coyotes howl out there on the golf course—and I still can't get a parking space! I'd understand if it was Manhattan—but Fresno?

I'd like to crush every damn Subaru Legacy on the block. So I was watching the mass car death on the West Bank real, real happy. I noticed something, too. Some cars go easy, like they're made of cardboard. But if you watch carefully, you see that the Mercedes stands up for about a half-second longer, before the Merkava mounts it and crushes it. That's what I call sexy video. "No parking within 48 hours of suicide bombing. Violators will be flattened." You had to wonder if Palestinians go in for car sex—'cause if they do, just imagine one of those Merkavas—sixty-one tons of ethnic hate, turbo-drive—grinding down a row of Pals hard at work producing the next generation of human firecrackers. Itchy & Scratchy with ethnic headgear. Pretty damn cool.

About those Merkava tanks. The Israelis build some real pretty weapons, but the Merkava is their best. It was built by people who were actually in a war. The engine is in front so it'll take most of the shock of a MBT round. The whole tank, front to back, is immune to RPGs. And it has room inside for a whole squad of infantry. That's important, because it means the Israelis are the only army in the world that actually plans to keep its troops alive till they get to the battlefield. See, most armies imitated the Russians, who sent their troops out in "battle taxis" like the BMP fighting vehicles—and those things blow apart if you hit them with anything more lethal than a rock. The "light" (meaning "cheap") aluminum armor turns into instant shrapnel when an RPG round hits it. Once you've seen the results, you'd rather go into battle in a Yugo.

The Americans tried to copy the Russians and came up with the Bradley infantry fighting vehicle, which is like a BMP only about a thousand times more expensive. And still can't take a hit from an RPG. All it's good for is turning a squad of soldiers into beef stroganoff in about one millisecond. But the Israelis thought for themselves, and they came up with the Merkava, a tank that can fight *and* transport infantry under real protection. They were the only army to admit, "Hey, this isn't WW II." You can't take casualties like those anymore, not with everybody glued to the TV moaning every time a few dozen soldiers get wiped. Survivability, that's the biggest thing now. And the Merkava was untouchable. You used to see those Merkavas idling on a hilltop or car-crunching down the streets of Ramallah like Panzers in 1940. They'd just sit up on a dry hilltop, real cocky, just looking around for camera crews to target. It was beautiful.

But the Israelis lost two Merkava 3s in a month. That's just not supposed to happen. The Pals set up mines big enough to kill a Merkava, then waited patiently for the right moment. The point is that the Pals are getting tough—and, scarier yet, they're getting smart. They've killed two unkillable tanks, and then there was one Pal sniper who picked off seven Israeli Defense Force (IDF) soldiers and three settlers and then got away. That wouldn't have happened ten years ago.

The Pals used to be a total joke. The PLO–people said it meant "Perfect Losers Organization." Worst guerrillas in the world. They were big on chanting and wearing headbands with those Gadhafi-style woof slogans, stuff about tearing out entrails and eating your enemy's eyeballs with Tabasco sauce and that crap. But that just proved how weak they were. Think about it: Who uses that kind of high-school woofing? Weak places like Libya–see my earlier chapter, where Gadhafi drew that "line of death" in the Med. It was a line of death all right–for his little kid, when the F-14s went in. When the Americans or the Soviets wanted to wipe someplace out, they gave it a nice, family-oriented name like Welcome Villages or Shared Harvest. That's what you do if you want to kill big numbers of people, up in the seven-figure range.

The Pals got tough, thanks to Ariel Sharon. It's weird–funny in a way–how he trained 'em up to take him on. He sent the IDF into Lebanon in 1982. The Israelis were at the top of their game. They were amazing! Their air force sliced and diced the Syrians without losing a single plane. They made it look so damn easy, the Americans tried to join in–and wham, the U.S. Navy lost two A-6s in a few hours. Of course, only the navy would be dumb enough to send A-6s into a SAM-rich environment. That's sorta like taking a VW camper van on a windows-down tour of Compton on a Saturday night.

The Israelis cut right through Lebanon and only lost about four hundred soldiers, which was less than Israel lost in car crashes that year. They shelled the Hell out of Beirut and booted the PLO all the way to Tunisia. Reagan just drooled and smiled at 'em. They could do anything they wanted.

And then this weird thing happened: A sixteen-year-old Shiite girl in South Lebanon got in a car packed with TNT and drove it into an Israeli patrol. And everything changed. One of the Israeli generals said on TV, "We're going to regret coming here. No Palestinian drove a car full of explosives at us, not in thirty years of war."

Back then, the only suicide bombers were those crazy Tamil Tigers in Ceylon. They invented the whole suicide-bomber look, with the vest of C4 and string fuse. But everybody figured it was just

Hindu weirdness, like, if you believe in reincarnation, what's one life? You just have to stand in line for a while till you get a new one.

Then this Shiite girl in Lebanon showed that it wasn't just Hindus who could die well. The game was on for real. Amal and Hezbollah had all the martyrs they needed. Boom! goes the U.S. Marine barracks in Beirut, the French barracks, Bachir Gemayel's headquarters. Suddenly, everybody wants to be a martyr.

It was those Shiites who taught the slack Pals what fighting was about. And it didn't happen quick. The Pals were slow learners. For ten years, they watched the Shiites drive trucks and bikes and cars into Israeli checkpoints without getting the idea. They started their intifada in 1987, but all they did was throw rocks and get killed. There's nothing wrong with getting killed; I know that. It's a big part of getting a rebellion going. Starts things off big, gets people excited and all that. But sooner or later, you can't just settle for dying. You got to kill also. Throwing rocks at tanks looks good on TV, but it doesn't make a big impression on people as tough as Sharon.

The Pals . . . they're a little slow, as I said. So it took them till 2000 to copy the Lebanese Shiites' suicide bombers.

Which reminds me of this great segment I saw on the news: a camp for "training suicide bombers." I mean, how hard can it be? "You see, Ahmad, here is the string. Now, when you get to the bagel stand, you pull the string like so. And the next thing you know, you will be in Paradise attended by sixty-two virgins." You don't have to be a Prussian general staff aide to master the subtle military skill of pulling a string.

But eventually, the technique got through to the Pals. Like Bela Lugosi in that Ed Wood movie: "Pull ze string! Pull ze string!" The explosive vest came into fashion among stylin' Pals from Gaza to Nablus, with roofing nails for decor. And 800-odd Israelis later, Sharon's visit to the ol' Dome of the Rock didn't look so clever anymore. Of course, the Israelis have been killing Palestinians at a rate of four or five Pals for every Israeli. But that's a really bad ratio for guerrilla war. You want a ratio of nine or ten natives for every settler in that kind of war. Even then, it's a bad risk. The British killed twenty Kikuyu for every settler and still lost. Peasants have a big birthrate, and when martyrdom is the only career choice in the neighbor-hood, you can afford to lose a lot of kids for the chance to pick off a few settlers. People with something to lose don't like dying.

And that's where it comes back to the Merkava. A great design, yes. But the whole greatness of the design advertises the weakness of the Israelis: They don't like taking casualties. So when I say that, all the rational American readers are probably going to go, "*Nobody* likes it, you jerk!" Except that's totally untrue. Lots of places like taking casualties. The Shiites—they never felt prouder or happier. The Russians under Stalin—they died crying for joy. All you happy people, you think everybody's like you! Lots of people want to die. I want to. Lots of people—there's more like me than like you, you smug bastards.

So for now, there's the Pals taking casualties and laying the bodies out and howling and pretty much strutting, and there's the IDF hunkered down in their Merkavas crunching up cars but not really with the guts to crunch whole populations, whole towns. And if they don't do that, they lose. You can't win a war without a license to kill lots and lots of people. Killing two or three a day won't do it. That's less than a thousand a year—pathetic! The Merkava is a way to protect Israeli soldiers more than it's a way to kill Palestinians. See, in that way, it's a defensive weapon. Whereas an AK-47, with a Pal standing in the street firing at the Merkava, is an offensive weapon. Not that it can hurt the Merkava, because it can't. But it says, on camera, "I want to die and to kill." And the Merkava says, "Yikes, you people are crazy, go away." A tank vs. a rifle is an unequal battle—but not always in favor of the tank.

SYRIA:
PLENTY OF NUTHIN'

FIRST, A LITTLE end-zone gloating: I scooped the big papers' military correspondents again! And all I do is sit at home and watch the networks' war coverage. But I watch smart. I watch careful. Not like a lot of you guys, who believe every crap story out of the Pentagon press/psy-ops factory.

In a 2003 column, "Lynch Mobs and Apaches," I said the AH-64 Apache attack chopper that was supposed to replace armor in the original Rumsfeld Gulf War II plan didn't cut it in battle. And sure enough, a week later, *Slate* ran an article by Fred Kaplan, "Chop the Chopper: the Army's Attack Helicopter Had a Bad War."

The good part about the Kaplan article was he was "embedded," so he got the skinny on what happened. Here's his version:

> The U.S. Army's only disastrous operation in Gulf War II (at least the only one we know about) took place on March 24 [2003], when 33 Apache helicopters were ordered to move out ahead of the 3rd Infantry Division and to attack an Iraqi Republican Guard regiment in the suburbs of Karbala. Meeting heavy fire from small arms and shoulder-mounted rocket-propelled grenades, the Apaches flew back to base, 30 of them shot up, several disablingly so. One helicopter was shot down in the encounter, and its two crewmen were taken prisoner... After that incident, Apaches were used more cautiously—on reconnaissance missions or for firing at small groups of armored vehicles. Rarely if ever did they penetrate far beyond the front line of battle.

Kaplan went on to say how it was the poor old A-10 that did CAS for the rest of the war: "Though the statistics aren't yet in, the A-10s seemed to do well in Gulf War II, especially now that the Army, Air Force, and Marines are more inclined to coordinate their battle plans."

I should find a bookie to take my bets. I'd be making money on this war.

Meanwhile, I'd been checking out the Syrian Army, because, back in 2003, Syria was being set up as the next target, with Bush's people claiming that Saddam and his WMDs were in Syria. (How quickly you all forget.)

Have you seen any proof of WMDs in Iraq? I haven't. Nobody even seems to ask anymore. That's what I mean about how trusting you suckers are.

But anyway, it doesn't matter whether those WMDs are in Syria or not. If Bush's people want to invade, they'll invade. Trying to stop them back in April 2003 would have been like a girl telling Mike Tyson that second base was as far as he was getting on a first date.

If they do hit Syria, it'll be because of this idea they have in D.C.: Make a "crescent of democracy" stretching from Iraq to Syria and on to Lebanon, all the way from the Persian Gulf to the Mediterranean. Now that democracy is bursting out in Iraq, all we have to do is franchise it out to Lebanon, the bloodiest, most messed-up country this side of Afghanistan. Should be a piece of cake.

That was sarcasm, by the way. But the first part of it, blasting the Syrian Army—that part really will be pretty easy, as far as I can tell. Like a lot of Arab countries, Syria has a decent-sized army: 215,000 full-time soldiers and another 200,000 reserves. But then, as you may remember, we were all supposed to be scared because Iraq had "the fourth-biggest army in the world." That was before we found out that it was more like the fourth-biggest looting and fleeing team. If I were commanding an American unit, I'd rather fight 100,000 Iraqis or Syrians than 100 North Koreans or Vietnamese. Because the Asians would fight, and the Arabs wouldn't, no matter how many there were.

The only time the Syrian Army even looked good was in the first days of the 1973 Yom Kippur War, when the army took the Israeli lines in the Golan Heights. Judging by what I've read, it wasn't so much that the Syrians attacked well as that the Israelis' intelligence had failed totally. So the Israeli lines were nearly empty—everybody on leave for the holiday—and the Syrian tanks just had to drive in. But the Syrians were so weirded out at the easy way they'd rolled in, that they sat there, jabbering about how it must be some clever Israeli trick. The Egyptians, who really were fighting well down in Sinai, supposedly begged the Syrian commanders to do their part of the co-ordinated attack by sweeping down from the Heights and attacking

Galilee. But the Syrians just sat there on their plateau, scared shit-less. The Israelis finally woke up, warmed up the tanks, and rolled back the Syrians in a few days. If the United States hadn't ordered the Israelis to stop, they would've headed all the way to Damascus.

Once the Syrians were sure the Israelis weren't going all the way to Damascus, they started talking big again, trying to get the Egyptians to attack Israel. I read a great line in one Egyptian's story about this: "The Syrians were willing to fight Israel right down to the last Egyptian." And the Egyptians weren't buying it anymore. They made peace and left the Syrians to deal with Israel on their own.

The Syrians' next showing was their worst. In 1982, the Israelis invaded Lebanon to force out the PLO. The Syrian Air Force sent ninety of its Russian fighters to take on the Israeli Air Force. The result was the biggest turkey shoot since the last battles in the Pacific in 1945. The Israelis shot down every one of those Syrian planes without losing a single plane themselves. 82–0. That's what you call a decisive score. The Israelis went after the big, expensive, Soviet-built Syrian air-defense network next. They knocked out seventeen of nineteen Syrian SAM sites in a day—and again, they didn't lose a single plane doing it.

From there on, it just got worse for the Syrian armed forces. For one thing, they depended on the Soviets more than they depended on any other country. All their hardware was Russian, and they haven't been able to maintain or repair it since the USSR went out of business. Like a lot of Russian client states, the Syrians went for the big, impressive numbers instead of coming up with a sensible force mix. They bought five thousand Soviet tanks, half of which were T-55s, old enough to draw a pension. The newer ones, T-62s and T-72s, could be tough with real soldiers manning them. But the Syrians turned most of these newer tanks into wheeled artil-lery, basically putting them up on breeze blocks like old cars in a Mexican neighborhood and letting them rust.

The air force is in even worse shape. Losing ninety planes out of ninety in your last war can't be good for morale. Besides, the Syrian Air Force is all-Soviet, nothing but Sukhois and MiGs. And you can't get Soviet repairmen to come to Damascus anymore. That's fatal to a fighter fleet. Tanks (especially Russian tanks) can run for a while without an overhaul, but fighters take more fuss than race-horses. You can pretty much take it for granted that the Syrian Air Force won't be flying if there's a war. And once you give an American invasion force total air supremacy, it's all over.

There's one wild card, and that's WMDs. Saddam didn't have any, but the Syrians might. After their air force and SAM network got smashed in 1982, they invested in bio- and chemical-weapon components. It was like a poor man's nuke program—a last-ditch Hell weapon to use if anyone invaded. There's a lot of back-and-forth in the literature about whether they do or don't have this stuff.

The thing is, even if the Syrians do have some chemical weapons, there's no way they'll ever use them. They're not crazy. They're cowards, but they're sane cowards.

AFGHANISTAN:
WHAT WENT RIGHT?

I WANT TO compare our two latest wars, Afghanistan and Iraq. Everybody's writing about what went wrong in Iraq, but the really interesting question is what went right in Afghanistan. It's hard to remember now, but most people thought Afghanistan would be the tough one and Iraq would be a cakewalk.

Think back to October 2001. Smoke was still coming up out of the WTC ruins. Every day, there was a new anthrax case in the papers. Osama bin Laden said he had lots of new tricks ready for us, and there wasn't much reason to doubt him after what he'd pulled off. We were going to invade Afghanistan, "the graveyard of empires," and take on the guys who'd wiped out a whole British army a hundred years back and gutted the Soviets in the 1980s.

We started bombing the Taliban lines on October 7, 2001. The bombing didn't seem to be doing much good at first. The Talibs seemed too crazy-mean to scare. Our first two ground operations were disasters. First, we inserted one hundred Rangers and Delta guys into Mullah Omar's house. He wasn't home. Then we wasted our biggest local asset, Abdul Haq, a one-legged mujahedeen hero who was going to deliver the Pushtuns to us without a fight. We choppered him into the border zone, where his kin hung out hoping he'd stir up the locals against the Talib. Instead they grabbed him and cut off his head.

It looked bad. All our enemies were cheering up. But we were cool and slow, the way an empire has to be. We kept trying new methods, and suddenly one of them clicked: On November 9, 2001, Mazar-I-Sharif, the key city in northern Afghanistan, fell to the Northern Alliance.

We'll find out what did the trick up there when they declassify the documents in ten years or so. My guess is, after we figured out that bombing wasn't going to do it, and the Northern Alliance couldn't do it on the ground, we went to Plan B: shipping a few tons of gold bars to local Talib commanders to desert. It was a good investment, because a week after taking Mazar, our proxies rolled into Kabul.

The Talibs found themselves bottled up back where they started, in a big pocket around Kandahar to Kunduz. We did our next smart thing there: We told the Northern Alliance to stay put while we cleaned out the Talib from the air. You have to know when to let your local proxies do some killing and when to tell them to back off. This was a time to keep them on the leash, because if they'd gone into the Pushtun zone, they'd have started another hundred-year vendetta. Instead, we did the killing from the air. Nice and impersonal, those B-52s. You can't hold a grudge against an Arc Light strike.

But when five hundred captured Talibs jammed into an old fort near Mazar killed a CIA interrogator and swarmed out, we had the sense to turn loose our Northern Alliance friends, who were drooling at the thought of gutting all those Talibs. All we asked was that they handed us our fellow American, that little hippie John Walker Lindh. (Gee, I hope the jarheads aren't being too mean to him down in Gitmo.)

Check this out: Mike Spann, the CIA interrogator who was killed in that prison riot, was the first American killed in combat in Afghanistan. That's how well we were doing. We'd been kicking the shit out of this graveyard of empires for more than a month and hadn't lost a single man.

Since the Talibs fell, we've been playing around with the hard-core Talibs left in the border provinces, refining our methods, playing it cold-bloodedly like we should. When the Talibs want to be martyrs, we send a GBU to help them. When they hole up in a cave, we take our time, use the local proxies like hunting dogs to keep them denned up, and then play around with ordnance mixes until we've dropped the cave roof, burned out their oxygen, or paid some locals to go spelunking with grenades. It's war the way empires are supposed to do it—more like exterminating roaches than wasting your troops in one-on-one encounters. We've got a good kill ratio, something like fifty Talib for every American we lose. That's how it should be when it's F-15s vs. cavemen. And all this cave fighting will come in handy if we ever have to do the ultimate Tomb Raid, North Korea.

It's not a matter of eliminating the Taliban from southeastern Afghanistan. We're not trying to do that. It's impossible; it's not even a sensible goal. Talibs are just Pushtuns with attitude, and you're never going to turn Pushtuns into Quakers. You're never going to close the border with Pakistan, either. You're probably never even going to find Osama or Mullah Omar. It's enough that you keep them working full time to stay alive, with no spare time for making offensive plans.

Most of all, it's important that you see what you're doing clearly and coldly. And we've done that in Afghanistan. Nobody who matters in D.C. was seriously trying to bring democracy to Afghanistan. We're just keeping the savages contained, picking off the troublemakers, buying off the real threats, keeping our intelligence up to date by going on Talib-hunting parties with the locals. We lose a soldier or two in the hunts—we've lost five troops in southeast Afghanistan since August. But that's a good loss for a big empire.

Not just acceptable but good, because it keeps our special forces lean and alert. Paktika is better than any combat simulator, and the Talib are kind enough to play Red Team for free.

Compare what we did in Afghanistan with what we're doing in Iraq, and you can start to see what went right against the Talibs and what's wrong with our Iraq adventure.

First thing, we took Afghanistan seriously. We were scared of going in there, and that saved us. Too bad we weren't scared of Iraq. Nobody said taking Kabul was going to be a cakewalk, like that idiot Kenneth Adelman said Baghdad was going to be. Everybody knew the Afghans were crazy medieval-ass bastards, and we treated them that way. We were flexible, trying lots of different methods till we saw what worked and leaning to our strengths, cash and air power. We went in quick and got out quick, and left it to the Europeans to stick around policing Kabul before anybody could decide to start picking our guys off at street corners.

Iraq was a fantasy story for Bush's people right from the start. The neocon commissars like Richard Perle and Paul Wolfowitz went around saying we'd be "welcomed with open arms" in Baghdad because we were bringing "freedom and democracy," two things that sell worse than women's soccer in the Middle East. I don't know where they got this insane idea. It's got something to do with Israel's wanting Iraq out of the way; Perle and Wolfowitz are Israeli-Likud policy wonks from way back.

They're also the kind of neocons who really and truly believe that everybody in the world is actually an Ohio Republican, or would be if they got the chance. And this fantasy that Iraqis are Ohioans under the skin (or the mustaches) kept us from seeing Iraq for what it is: one big, dusty gang fight just like Afghanistan.

The worst thing is, *democracy* means we can't do the obvious imperial move: playing tribe against tribe like the Brits used to. We should be playing the Kurds against the Sunnis and letting the Shiites run their own patch of ground for once. The Shia, our natural allies, happen to be the majority in Iran and the oil-producing areas of Saudi Arabia. "Shia Arabia"—now there's a catchy name. Instead, we're doing this lame Peace Corps daydream, singing "Kumbaya" in the middle of a gang fight.

There's another reason we can't see Iraq as clearly as Afghanistan. More like three reasons tied up in one: Cheney, oil, and money. Cheney wants our troops to stick around like unpaid security guards for all his Halliburton kickback cronies while his buds suck out the crude, drive the price per barrel down, and teach the Saudis some humility. The idea is, we give these crazy oilmen a few hundred billion in tax money now, and maybe they pay us back someday with the money they get from the Iraqi oil fields. It's fantasy stuff—they'll never pay it back. But that's what oilmen are like. Trust me, I grew up around oil people. They just want new wells, new fields, new financing. They don't care if the well pans out. If it does, they're rich. If it doesn't, they take it out of your taxes. All they want is to keep it moving, starting up, moving to the next country. Cheney's boys will be busy playing with the Iraqi fields for a few more years, so they're going to want the U.S. Army to stick around Iraq for a long time, being sitting ducks to take the heat off Exxon geologists staying at the Baghdad Hilton.

Stand back and squint at the two wars, and you see something weird: We did well against the tougher opponent, Afghanistan, because we didn't want anything from the place. We wanted Iraq to be a lot of stupid, dreamy stuff, voting booths and cheap gas. You pay for dreaming on duty.

AFGHANISTAN:
LET 'EM EAT HAMS

IF YOUR EXTERMINATOR says he just killed two hundred rats down in the basement, is that good news or bad news?

On the one hand, it's good those rats are dead. On the other hand, I thought we got rid of them years ago, and now there's hundreds? What's going on?

That's the big question everyone should be asking in Afghanistan. In September 2006, NATO claimed we killed five hundred Taliban near Kandahar. That's a mighty impressive body count, sure, but if 'Nam taught us one thing, it's that body counts are a bad sign—for all sorts of reasons, starting with basic common sense: If we're killing that many, how many more are running around out there?

They say with rats that if you see one, that means there's about forty more in the vicinity. I suspect you can use the same ratio for Taliban. That's what Mohamed Arbil, a former Northern Alliance commander, said shortly after NATO's September 2006 claim: "If [NATO] killed that many, the Taliban must have thousands of fighters on that front."

Afghanistan is now enemy territory again. The Taliban has re-formed (as opposed to *reformed*), and according to one Brit officer who's fought in both Iraq and Afghanistan, the fight against the Talibs is already *way* hotter than the war in Iraq.

The truth is, Afghanistan's been slipping away for some time now. I'll own up; I should've been spending more time on it myself. In the time since I wrote the previous chapter, I have been vaguely feeling that it was going bad. But other places were hotter or funnier, so I let it go. Besides, as hard as I've been on my country's war leadership, I didn't really believe that we could possibly be so stupid as to blow the one thing we did right. But as far as I can tell, that's what happened to the U.S. command: Since the Iraq invasion in 2003, it's lost interest in Afghanistan. Iraq's got U.S. military paralyzed, and any energy left over is going into finding a way to invade Iran. Which won't be easy, seeing as how we have exactly zero troops left over from Iraq.

So it's like our command got one of those brain puzzlers Captain Kirk would use to fry alien computers: How do we pacify Iraq (impossible) while invading Iran at the same time (double impossible, does not compute, frying noises, smoke coming out of computer). Right now, there's so much smelly smoke coming out of the Pentagon it looks as if another Boeing hit the place, but it's just the defense intelligence sections' brains frying. There just isn't much high-command brain power left to pay attention to Afghanistan.

That's the key here: paying attention. I'm starting to think that we just don't have the patience and focus to do counterintelligence (CI) warfare. It's much easier to deal with enemies who know when they're beaten. Who know the rules, as laid down in history books. You pound them into the ground, shake hands, and dump a few planeloads of foreign aid on them, and everybody's friends again. It's like a nice, clean boxing match.

CI warfare is more like that style of fighting the Brazilians introduced into the UFC (Ultimate Fighting Championship): The game only starts when you've got the guy down. You know how those guys like Royce Gracie fight? If you've never seen it, it's like this: You throw a punch at him, and the next thing you know, he's on his back kicking you in the legs. If you're expecting a stand-up fight, you're doomed. Your only choice is to jump onto him and grapple it out, which will take a half hour at the very least. That's why they don't run UFC on TV much anymore: too damn boring and slow. It's more like watching bad gay porn, two guys lying on top of each other, sweating. Except they don't even move enough to make good porn. It's all in the wrists, slow as molasses, getting a little advantage until the other side taps out.

We were spoiled by initial success in Afghanistan; we got the Taliban down and then just stopped paying attention. Dunno if you remember this far back, but after 9/11, when it was obvious we had to go in there and root out Osama, everybody was saying Afghanistan was unwinnable, the graveyard of empires, and so on. And the campaign seemed to stall at first, till we took Mazar-I-Sharif and sent the Northern Alliance rolling into Kabul. Boom, game over, victory party, let's go home.

Except the new wars just don't work that way. The tough part was really just beginning. The biggest problem once we took Kabul was tribal. Reporters are always calling the Taliban Islamic extremists, but it's way simpler than that: The Talibs are Pushtun, and our allies in the Northern Alliance are their old tribal enemies the Tajiks, the Uzbeks, and a few free-agent Hazaras.

The Pushtuns are the biggest tribe in the country, if you can call them that, by far. Afghanistan is 42 percent Pushtun, and the second-biggest group, the Tajiks, are only 27 percent. Pushtuns are—now how can I say this nicely?—insane. The craziest Taliban rules, like demanding that every man have a beard at least ZZ Top length, aren't Muhammad's rules; they're just Pushtun tribal ways.

It's like if the Baptists took over in Fresno, they'd make it God's rule that every guy had to have an extended cab on his pickup, and if you asked where in Scripture it says that, they'd just shoot you. That's the Pushtun way: total tribal insanity, all the time. They're so "sexist" that feminists might like them, because they don't even think of women as sex objects. To a Pushtun guy, nine-year-old boys are the sexiest thing on earth.

Professor Victor Davis Hanson might approve, because from what I've read, his classical Greek heroes felt the same way. The Pushtuns are so classical that to them, women are just labor-saving and baby-making machines.

And never mind peace; these Pushtuns may be gay, but they sure ain't sissies. They love making war, and they're real good at it.

Also, they don't get the whole literacy thing. They're not interested in becoming entrepreneurs or learning self-esteem or personal hygiene or compassion or any of that crap. And let's be honest, the joy they felt running around Central Asia blowing up Buddhas and blasting infidels is the same joy a frat boy feels running around a ten-kegger party with a bra on his head. It's pure fun 'n' joy, Pushtun-style.

So once we'd taken Afghanistan, we had this leftover problem, which was that nearly half the population consisted of these lunatics who had no stake in peace, didn't want peace, and thought peace was a lot of newfangled nonsense only fit for heterosexuals, foreigners, and assorted sissies. Especially because "peace" came to their town on tanks and armored personnel carriers driven by their old enemies the Tajiks and Uzbeks.

Worse yet, right behind those tanks came American do-gooders whose idea of pacifying the Pushtuns was doing incredibly naive stuff like starting a TV news show with female anchorpersons, or whatever you call them. I'm not making this up. First thing the U.S. occupation officials did in Kabul was start a news station with some nineteen-year-old Pushtun girl as anchor. That was our idea of winning hearts and minds. That's what was going to calm down those bearded angry dudes: seeing a perfectly salable daughter telling them the news, as if she was the one laying down the law.

I get tired of having to say it, but I'll say it again: Not everybody thinks like we think. Not everybody wants what we want. The Pushtuns want (a) somebody to kill; (b) women kept in their place, somewhere between the clay oven and the livestock; (c) nobody reminding them that there are other ways to live.

And our idea of pacifying them was to rub everything they hate right in their face, with their old enemies as enforcers. You have to wonder why the Pushtuns didn't explode even bigger, even sooner. Well, basically because we handed off the job to some of our allies who did a pretty decent job of keeping the lid on as long as they could. There was a good British contingent up there, who not only did its usual great job of soldiering but also handled tribal relations pretty well. Along with them, the Aussies and even the Canadians were on the job.

Too bad we didn't give the Brits total control of the so-called global war on terrorism and let them play it their way. I can tell you what the old nineteenth-century Brits would've done. Problem: huge, restless tribe (Pushtun) smarting from recent defeat and totally uninterested in peace. Solution: ship every Pushtun of military age to the Sunni Triangle as honored guests of the British Empire, and give them enough ammo to make the place as quiet and boring as Mary Poppins's bedroom.

The Pushtuns would be happy as the Seven Dwarfs, whistling while they worked on quieting down the Sunni; the Sunni would be . . . well, maybe not happy but definitely quiet—"quiet as the grave," as the saying goes. And the Brits would step back into the shadows and let them fight it out till the end of time. A great system, worked for centuries.

Of course, nobody we sent up there was cold-blooded enough to do anything like that. We figured, once the Pushtun warriors saw that anchorwoman up there—Mary Tyler Moore in a burqa with five-o'clock shadow—they'd see the American light and start eating hot dogs and apple pie. Great plan.

That left the whole mess to those poor bastards, our Brit friends. You know, we should get down on our knees and apologize to the Brits for making them trust us, making them believe we Americans actually had a clue and were leading them somewhere. You can see they've finally figured it out, that Bush and Cheney never did know what they were doing, but now the poor, trusting Limeys are as deep in the shit as we are. I guess it's some kind of poetic justice, because we've done to them what they did to hundreds of other tribes: luring someone else into doing the dirty work. But it's no way to treat an ally.

Afghanistan was slipping away month by month, while those commonwealth officers tried to hold it together with rubber bands. All the money and troops were fed into Iraq, which was hopeless from the start, instead of Afghanistan, where it might have worked. The Americans just couldn't pay attention once the big, showy campaign to take Kabul was over.

In fact, I just saw a movie that showed we weren't even paying attention in Iraq. It's called *Gunner Palace*, and it's one of these handheld documentaries by an embedded ham. The idea is, the reporter hangs with a unit of GIs whose headquarters is one of Uday Hussein's former playboy mansions in Baghdad. There's a huge swimming pool and a lot of glitzy decor, and you can tell the reporter thought he was going to get famous for the irony or whatever: gritty, gory soldier stuff with a background of Saddam-era luxury, etc.

I don't think this reporter even understood what he was filming. Seriously. There's a voiceover about how this unit of typical American young men copes with the dark and violent chaos of

Iraq, blah-blah-blah, but that's not what the movie shows. What it shows is hams. Showoffs. A bunch of dudes who don't know where they are, don't care, don't speak a word of the language, and don't want to learn it.

All that these dudes are interested in is hamming it up American-style for the camera. The only time they get excited is when the reporter lets them do their little routines: heavy-metal solos or comedy skits from the whites, rap rhymes from the blacks. No, let's be fair here. In a wonderful sign of advancing integration, there's one scene where a black GI does a rap with backing electric guitar from this white guy, the class-clown type who's onscreen for what seems like an hour. I personally would have had his humorous ass shoved up against the nearest wall and shot, but this embedded cameraman loved him, couldn't get enough.

Halfway through the movie, there's a scene where the unit learns its lead interpreter, their go-to guy when they're asking for info in the neighborhood, the guy who translates every word they hear, is a traitor. An insurgent working for the other side.

That blew me away! But in the movie it's treated just like a little setback, another ho-hum problem of life in Baghdad.

Jesus, doesn't anybody have a clue about CI warfare? Your interpreter is *everything*. He's worth more than all the Bradleys and Strykers you have. He's more important than bullets. He's the whole war. If he's a traitor, everything you've done has been worse than useless! Your local sources are blown. Your plans are known. Every local who was naive enough to trust you is dead or soon will be. The rest have learned a big lesson: Never, ever talk to the Americans.

But in the movie, the scene where they arrest the interpreter is just another excuse to ham it up. The officer in charge ties the plastic cuffs on his wrist and keeps asking, "OK, do you want to be my *guest* or my *prisoner*, Ahmed?" And Ahmed doesn't even answer, it's such a stupid question, such an insane question.

Ahmed is worrying about how long he'll have his fingernails, what they'll use to remove his eyeballs, how hot the poker they jam up his ass is going to be, and this ham is actually trying to be his pal. Finally Ahmed mumbles, "Your friend, your friend…" and the ham gives him a big smile, all pleased. Nobody in the unit from the commander on down seems to realize what a disaster this is. They don't even seem to want to extend their intel network in the area.

Even in the middle of a firefight, guys turn away from their machine guns to ham it up for the camera, like this is their big moment, their screen test, instead of combat. I don't think it's pork that the Muslims hate so much; it's all the hams we've imported into their land.

I'll tell you something I don't usually like admitting: The first time I saw *Apocalypse Now*, I hated it. I thought it was pure libel against all the GIs who fought so hard in Vietnam, making them out to be attention-deficit types who couldn't focus on the war for more than ten minutes. Because that's what that movie is about as a military document: showing how if you don't focus in CI warfare you can't win. The only guy in the whole movie who focuses on the war is Martin Sheen. That's why he's totally alone, while the rest go surfing or have their barbecue or jerk off over the Playboy bunnies the USO flies in.

Well, I still think the movie was unfair to 'Nam vets, because at least till Tet, a lot of our guys worked hard at learning the language and blending into the landscape. But I have to admit that maybe that hippie bastard Francis Ford Coppola was right in the long run. Maybe we just can't pay attention long enough to win in the long, slow grind of CI.

And maybe Coppola's point about Colonel Kurtz was right: It's not that we need more troops in Iraq. Fuck no. After watching these hams screw everything up, I'm dead sure that's the last thing we need. We need a few thousand soldiers who speak the language and don't have any qualms about doing all the dark, bad things that have to be done to hold on to occupied territory. And backing them up we need maybe ten thousand guys trained for the Phoenix Program: pure assassins who will kill anybody they're told to kill, on the quiet, without anyone's ever finding out. Basically, we need warriors who don't want to make it in show business.

THE WAR NOBODY WATCHED

✳ IMAGINE A WAR that went on for eight years, caused more than a million casualties, and went through five distinct phases, with every kind of combat you could ask for, from huge tank battles, human-wave offensives, artillery duels, and amphibious assaults to exotic stuff like naval battles and dogfights with squadrons of MiGs and Sukhois up against American F-14s and F-4s.

Sounds pretty great, right? Well, if you're old enough to remember 1980, it happened right in front of your eyes. And if you were like most Americans, you probably weren't interested. It's the Iran-Iraq War I'm talking about here, and most people barely noticed it.

The reason we ignored this war was simple: Nobody in America could stand even thinking about Iran. We'd just got through listening to our wimp excuse for a president, Jimmy Carter, try to get the hostages back from the Islamic crazies in Tehran by asking real nice. Then he finally authorized a teeny-tiny rescue mission with a lousy eight RH-53Ds, and the mission ended up with some filthy mullah holding up a dead GI's burned-up arm and laughing. I remember that the picture on the news made me so sick I had to go to my room and just lie there thinking about nuking every city in Iran, one a day. I spent a lot of time in the periodical room of the library looking up standoff nukes in *Jane's*, going, "Yeah . . . start with Khomeini's favorite town, Qom: whoosh! Suddenly there's no Qom. Next day pick someplace bigger, use a bigger nuke. . . ."

We were supposedly the biggest and baddest country in the world, and we couldn't get our people back from a few dozen hairy amateurs. It was sickening. I swear to God, when I heard how this asshole Carter won the Nobel Peace Prize, I felt like puking. He's one of these thin jerks who lives to be a hundred, so you keep hearing about him going around building shacks for Third Worlders, getting filmed looking all holy, showing off when he could just write a check with his latest speech fee and fund a thousand shacks for these poor bastards.

We voted him out in 1980, but we still couldn't stand to hear about Iran. So when they announced that Iraq was invading Iran, most people just said, "Great, I hope they kill a lot of Iranians," and left it at that. Nobody wanted details.

I remember thinking—I was only a kid—"Hey, it's like a bowl game to decide which country with a four-letter name beginning with I-R-A gets to be top dog. The 'Ira Bowl' or something."

Now that we've got a little experience of our own in Iraq, it's easier to understand how the Iran-Iraq War started. Start with a map, and you can see that Iraq looks like a funnel narrowing down to the Persian Gulf. That's the most valuable real estate in the country because it's Iraq's only sea access and it's also where many of the best oilfields are located. And it's Shia territory. Iran is Shiite, and Khomeini was like a living god to all the Shiites. He already hated Saddam for booting him out of Iraq after the shah exiled him.

Saddam saw his chance. As we found out in 1991, Saddam's a gambler. And the odds looked good for him to take the western part of Iran away from Khomeini back in 1980. The Islamists running Iran were amateurs, a bunch of noisy students and ignorant mullahs. They'd executed most of the shah's officer corps and put the rest in prison. So Saddam figured the Iranian army would be headless and easy to destroy. Same calculation Hitler made about Stalin's army.

The Iranian air force used to be feared all over the Middle East. It was the only air force outside the United States to have the F-14, the most advanced interceptor in the world. Iran had some of the best pilots east of Israel and a big fleet of F-4s. But after Khomeini's mullahs started butting in, the elite pilots fled or got executed, the United States put an embargo on spare parts (the one effective thing we did against Iran), and soon most of the Iranian air force was expensive scrap rusting in the hangars.

Saddam had another hole card: the Iranian Arab minority. He figured two could play the destabilization game. If Iran started stirring up the Shia majority in Iraq, he'd just return the favor by getting the Arabs in Khuzestan (western Iran) excited about seceding.

So on September 22, 1980, Saddam launched the biggest surprise attack since the Egyptian thrust into Sinai in 1973.

Saddam had the Arab-Israeli wars in mind, too. He was especially thinking about the Israelis' brilliant preemptive attack on the Arab air forces in the first hours of the 1967 war. He sent his MiG 21s and 23s to destroy Iran's F-4s and F-14s on the ground. But he didn't have Israeli pilots, air-to-surface munitions, or intelligence. The F-4s were in reinforced bunkers, the MiGs couldn't carry enough of a bomb load to finish off Iran's big airfields, and a few hours after the attack, Iran had F-4s in the air, attacking the Iraqi armor columns. Just like Stalin after the Nazis attacked, Khomeini had to release dozens of pilots from death-row cells, shove instant rehabilitation and pardon certificates into their hands, and beg them to get into the cockpits and win one for Ali.

The Iraqi ground attacks went pretty well in some sectors, and not so great in others. It was a long front, from Kurdistan to the Persian Gulf. As Saddam's army was built on the Soviet model, it was good at the stuff the Soviets did well, like massed artillery fire and coordinated armor attack. But there was one bit of really bad news for the Iraqis: The Arabs in western Iran didn't revolt on cue. In fact, most of them were loyal, fighting with the Persians against the invaders. (Like I've said before, never trust any plan that says "and then the natives will welcome our troops with open arms," no matter whether it's Saddam or that asshole Richard Perle saying it.)

Iraq took the Shatt-al-Arab, the key waterway in the delta, and grabbed half of Abadan, the most important oil town along the border. Then the attack bogged down.

The Iranians had some basic advantages. For one thing, Iran has a much bigger population than Iraq. And Iran's morale was good from the start. There's nothing a Shiite likes better than sacrifice, and here was a case where you could give your life and save the homeland. The boys came running. Lots of them even brought their own burial shrouds with them—couldn't wait to get into that once-and-for-all nightie.

The Iraqis started to flinch. They liked it when they were roaring over Iranian villages in their T-55s, but house-to-house fighting against crazy Shias isn't most people's idea of a good time. The Iranians noticed something that really got their blood up: Although the Iraqis were decent soldiers, they didn't like dying.

By November 1980, the Iraqis were stalled all along the border and the Iranians were getting excited. All those "students" who ditched their homework to hassle American diplomats had a new enemy to fight. The saps all joined up and headed for the front.

The Iranians had three separate armies: the regular army, the Revolutionary Guards, and the militia. They competed with each other, and there was the usual interservice crap, but all three wanted to fight. The regulars wanted to clear their names, the Revolutionary Guards wanted to get their sixty-four virgin concubines by dying ASAP, and the militia folks wanted to defend their homes.

The key word is *defend*. Defending and attacking are whole different ballgames. If you're going to attack, you need highly trained troops, but if you're only asking your troops to defend, you can sometimes get a good performance out of amateurs. The Iranians couldn't match the Iraqi armor, but they had more guts and initiative in small-unit engagements. By the end of 1981, Iran had pushed the Iraqis away from Abadan.

From then on, the Iraqis were on the defensive. They dug in their tanks, a dumb, coward's move that took away their mobility and showed how plain scared they were.

And the Iranians kept coming. Like the Russians in WW II, they just didn't mind dying, and it started to spook the Iraqis. Saddam flinched first: In the spring of 1982, he pulled all Iraqi forces back to the 1980 border. All this did was get the Iranians excited. They kept coming, with a huge human-wave attack on Basra. The poor militia bastards, with no training or coordination, just ran at the enemy yelling about Allah. They died like flies, up against Iraqi tanks and minefields. It was one of the most bloody, stupid assaults since 1945.

Saddam knew he had to do something. Well, you know the saying "When the going gets tough, the tough go shopping." Saddam went shopping through every Warsaw Pact weapons factory that would let him and his oil money in. He bought everything from MLRSs (Multiple Launch Rocket Systems) to T-62s, but the big-ticket item was a whole fleet of the new Soviet Mi-24 attack helicopter.

If you've read about what the Mi-24 did to the Afghans (before we gave them an edge with the Stinger), you can imagine what a fleet of Mi-24s did to the Iranians' human-wave attacks in 1983. It was a slaughter, and the Iraqis proved that even if they weren't much good at dying, they were good at killing. In one Iranian human-wave attack, the Iraqis flew two hundred Mi-24 sorties, hosing down the poor Shiite bastards like crop dusters going over a wheat field.

With Saddam giving them all the dozers they wanted, the military engineers turned the marshes on the border into artificial lakes, like giant moats in front of the Iraqi lines. And Saddam told his commanders they had one more weapon: gas. The Iraqis started using mustard gas, the sickest weapon of WW I. Even the Nazis never dared to use it, but Saddam's troops used it to break up mass infantry attacks. And nobody much cared. That's the story of this whole war: Nobody outside the two countries gave a damn about what happened.

From 1984 on, the war was like a stuck LP. The Iranians wasted lives like Foch and Kitchener on the Western Front, and the Iraqis tried to kill as many as they could without showing themselves or taking any risk.

With the land war frozen, both sides started using their imaginations, looking for other planes of engagement. They found one: the oil depots and tankers that carried Iraqi and Iranian oil to their main clients in Japan.

An oil depot is basically a big explosion waiting to happen. There's nothing in the world easier to blow up than an oil depot, pipeline, or tanker. Saddam started slamming Kharg Island, where the Iranians had a huge depot, early in the war. By the time the war ended, Kharg had been hit by nine thousand Iraqi sorties, which has to be some kind of record.

One of the shiny new toys Saddam had picked up on his shopping trips was the Exocet, an antiship missile that the French were peddling to anybody who had a coastline and a grudge. Saddam started using these missiles to blow up any tanker carrying Iranian oil. Iraq attacked nearly a hundred tankers in 1984, scaring the Hell out of the Japanese but not the Iranians.

Iraq was desperate to find some way to hurt these crazy Iranians enough to make them back off. So it tried the old standby, bombing cities, trying to kill as many civilians as possible. That was the debut of the Iraqi Scud attack. The Iraqis fired two hundred Scuds in 1988, trying to force the Iranians to negotiate. Just like the Scud attacks on Israel in Gulf War I, these attacks were all hype, noise, and publicity, good for scaring civilians but with zero military significance.

The year 1988 was a good one for Saddam's forces. They'd had time to get over their fear of the crazy Persian suicide squads and to rehearse the sort of massed-armor attack their army was designed to do. And the Iranians had used up most of their own armor and artillery. In the last year of the war, the Iraqis won big battles and pushed back into Iranian territory.

The Iranians were finally tired of the war. Everybody who'd wanted martyrdom had found it a long time ago, and they finally accepted the UN ceasefire offer.

And there was Saddam, with this huge army, all dressed up and nowhere to go. He'd learned his lesson about messing with Iran, but Iran wasn't the only oil-rich country in range of his tanks. There was little Kuwait, a big pile of oil and gold with no army to speak of. Saddam had some huge bills to pay for all that matériel he'd put on the AmEx Gold Card, and a wrecked oil infrastructure that didn't have a hope in Hell of generating enough income to make the debt.

It must have looked like a total no-brainer: Send the tanks to Kuwait, grab the oil and the gold, and your troubles are over. It was one of those plans that look foolproof on paper. Just ask Paul Wolfowitz about that. I hear from one of my army moles that it took an hour to pry Wolfowitz's fingers off the air conditioner he was hiding behind in his Baghdad hotel room after the rockets hit.

LEBANON:
BACK TO THE FUTURE

ON VALENTINE'S DAY 2005, somebody blew up the former president of Lebanon with a suicide Buick. The bombee was a billionaire named Rafik Hariri, a local boy who'd made good. He went to Saudi Arabia with nothing, made friends with the royal family, and came back worth $4 billion. There's a whole lot of money in the construction business in Saudi Arabia. Just ask the bin Ladens—that's how they made enough money to send little Osama on those expensive jihad tours.

What gets me is why anybody with Hariri's money would go into politics when they could be tanning in Maui. Especially Lebanese politics. There's no place in the world with a gorier history. Their motto is "One detonator, one vote." I guess these billionaires just get so cocky they think they can't be killed.

Or maybe the previous few years sort of lulled Hariri into a false sense of security. Lebanon had been quiet for a while. The Israelis had pulled out of South Lebanon in 2000, and the Syrians took their troops out of Beirut a year later. Things were cooling off, and rich Arabs were even starting to book weekends at the Lebanese beach resorts.

But you can always count on something to go wrong here. The whole country is a mirage, anyway, shoved onto the locals by the Brits and French after WW I. Until 1918, it was just another province in the Ottoman Turkish Empire. The Turks owned most of the Middle East, and the Arabs stuck to local clan loyalties. Nobody had any idea that there were "countries" like Iraq, or Syria, or Lebanon.

Then came WW I. The Ottomans made the mistake of siding with Germany, so the Brits started infiltrating the Turkish Empire, stirring up the Arabs. And the British were real good at it. (Still are, for that matter. You'll notice that their part of Iraq is a lot quieter than anybody else's.) The Brits know how to handle Arabs.

If you've seen that great old movie *Lawrence of Arabia*, you may remember the ending, when Peter O'Toole stomps off in his white dress because he knows the Brits are going to betray their Arab allies. Well, that's pretty much accurate. All through the war, the Brits promised everybody everything. They promised the Arab nationalists there'd be one big, united Arab republic stretching from Iran to the Mediterranean; promised the desert warrior chieftains (Lawrence's boys) a big kingdom covering the same ground; and promised the Jews a homeland in Palestine, right in the middle of that republic, or kingdom, or whatever they were calling it.

When peace broke out in 1918, everybody showed up wanting what they'd been promised. The Brits started making deals fast, divvying up the whole neighborhood into "countries" called Syria, Iraq, Transjordan (Jordan), Palestine, and Lebanon.

So on the map, there was this new "country," Lebanon. But on the ground, there was nothing but a bunch of ethnic gangs ready to turn on each other in a second. Lebanon has some of the weirdest militias in the world. What makes it unique is that a lot of the Arabs here are Christian, not Muslim. They call themselves Maronites, and they hung on all through the Muslim conquests, sticking close to the Lebanese hills and mountains—good defensible positions.

Many of these Maronites emigrated in the 1800s, and a lot of Muslim Arabs moved in and out-bred them. If I've said it once, I've said it a thousand times: In the twentieth century, birthrate was the most powerful weapon of all, and the Muslims, especially the Shia, had a phenomenal birthrate. Pretty soon, the Maronites were on the defensive, and it was chronic war between their gangs and the Muslims. Real nasty war, too, like the Balkans in a smaller court: massacres, assassinations, rapes, tortures—and naturally, no real battles.

It's not just Christian vs. Muslim, either. We're talking Arabs here, so naturally the lineups are shifting all the time. Some of the nastiest massacres were by one Christian militia against another. I read this one account—man, I'll never forget it—about how one of the Christian warlords found out his fellow Christians in another militia were having a big picnic on the beach, so he jumped them right in the middle of the volleyball game. What happened after that was pretty sick, even for Lebanon: First the attackers mowed down the men of the rival clan. Then they took the leader of the beaten militia, dragged him over to where they were keeping his female relatives, and made him watch while they gang-raped all the girls and women and then slit their throats one by one.

Now try imagining what happens when you introduce a whole new player to a game like that. That's what happened in 1948, when Israel was created and hundreds of thousands of Palestinian refugees fled north to Lebanon. Suddenly, it was a multisided war: Maronite Christians vs. Sunni vs. Shia vs. Palestinian vs. Syrian. We sent American troops to calm things down in 1958, and Lebanon chugged along, more or less, until the big blowup in 1975. That's when the Lebanese Civil War started. Eighteen months later, about forty-five thousand people were dead, another two hundred thousand had been wounded, whole villages and neighborhoods just vanished, and the country was a Syrian province, patrolled by an "Arab Deterrent Force" that was 90 percent Syrian troops.

Militarily, it was a tough fight to follow, like a giant gang fight in New York City. The Christian militias called themselves the Lebanese Forces, and their mostly Muslim enemies were the Lebanese National Movement. After a year and a half, the only sure thing was that the Christian militias, who started out with the advantage in training and weapons, hadn't done as well as expected. The Muslims, and especially the Shia, fought better than expected. The PLO had actually tried to stay out of the fight in the beginning, but got drawn in after the Christian militias took a Palestinian refugee camp in East Beirut and did what came naturally—killed everybody they could catch, that is. The PLA, the armed wing of the PLO, jumped in against them at that point and turned the tide. The Muslims took a lot of Christian hilltop villages and looked to be winning.

At that point, in the spring of 1976, came one of the weirdest turns in the war: The Syrian Army intervened *against* the Muslim forces. It took a lot of heat from other Muslim countries, but Syria was thinking about its own interests, not Islam, and it didn't want a radical Palestinian Islamic state to its west. Some of the hardest fighting of the war came when the Syrian Army went up against the Palestinian/Muslim forces.

It's worth remembering that Syria's not as simple as the Arab-baiters on U.S. TV make it out to be. A lot of guys in the CIA, like this Robert Baer guy who wrote that Saudi exposé, consider Syria a serious force against Muslim craziness in the Middle East. The Syrians proved they were serious about that by wiping out the Muslim Brotherhood in Aleppo, along with a whole lot of unlucky civilians, when the Brothers tried to stage a religious uprising. It's a real mistake to lump the Baathist secularists in the Syrian government with Iran and Libya—they're different animals.

At the level of weapons and tactics, Lebanon had some important lessons for future warfare. For one thing, it was mostly an urban war, and what we're relearning in Iraq right now is that we'd better find out how to do irregular urban warfare if we're going to have a future running this planet. There are more than six billion humans around, and we take up a lot of space. Nobody can afford to assume future war will happen on open ground.

People assume that Lebanon was just small-arms combat between little squads of infantry, but that's wrong. Thanks to the flood of weapons in the Middle East, there was some serious armor involved in the urban battles. And it turned out that tanks weren't the best weapon for street fighting. Instead, the militias favored their Soviet antiaircraft cannon vehicles, the ZSU-23. With its two- or four-barrel 23-mm cannon firing hundreds of rounds in the time it would take a tank to get off a shot from its main cannon, the ZSU-23 could be used to wipe out snipers in an apartment building without risking troops. They'd just pull up in front of the building and start hosing it down, like window washers. Once they'd stitched up every floor, you could moonwalk to the front entrance without any trouble. Of course, it was bad luck for any civilians still trying to live there, but that's one of the grim features of urban warfare: The civilian is always a human shield, like it or not.

The other weapon that proved itself in the street fighting . . . Well, I probably don't have to tell you by now: It was the ol' reliable RPG. Simple to learn, unbreakable, light, and devastating. A magnificent weapon, as we're finding out the hard way in Iraq. It ended a lot of stalemates in the Beirut fighting. RPGs trumped small arms every time.

Small arms are called small for a reason: They have to be perfectly aimed, or lucky, to hurt you. One thing you'll find in reading accounts of combat in built-up areas, or urban canyons, as they call them in contemporary military studies, is that with all that cover, nonsniper fire is usually ineffective. Guys fire hundreds of rifle rounds at a shadow down the street, and it just keeps firing back. That's where the RPG came into play. The militias found that instead of wasting ammo, it was better to get an RPG up, point it in the general direction of the enemy, and then advance when it went off. Even if it didn't kill the enemy, the blast put their opponents out of action for a good long time, long enough to overrun them. Unfortunately, that's something else we're relearning in Iraq: even when an RPG round misses, it breaks your concentration, opens you up to small-arms fire.

The U.S. Army is doing some interesting stuff with urban tactics these days. I recommend this site on Military Operations in Urbanized Terrain (MOUT):

http://urbanoperations.8media.org/.

The Web site's section on new weapons is especially useful in the next chapter. There, we look at the recent past of this cool little beachside Hell of a country, including the Israeli invasions of 1978 and 1982, the U.S. intervention in 1982, and the three-sided Shia-Christian-Israeli war in South Lebanon.

LEBANON, PART 2:
HEZBOLLAH-BOOM!

ON OCTOBER 23, 1983, a truck drove into a Beirut high-rise full of U.S. Marines and blew up. The building collapsed; 241

marines died in a few seconds. Most of them didn't even know why they were there.

So it pays to know a little history if you're going to mess with Lebanon. In the previous chapter, I started wading through the bloody Lebanese story from independence through the civil war of the 1970s. This time, I'm going to talk about the 1982 Israeli invasion and the monster that came out of it: Hezbollah.

Lebanon is like West Africa: There's not a series of separate wars, but one long, slow tribal war that flares up and cools off from time to time, but never goes away—like athlete's foot.

War is just demographics in a hurry. And Lebanon's demographics are as wobbly as the San Andreas Fault. A hundred years ago, the majority in Lebanon was a bunch of diehard Christian Arabs who called themselves Maronites.

But their majority was shrinking fast. A lot of Maronite families had emigrated (to run cheap menswear stores in the United States, mostly), and a lot of Muslims had moved in. The Muslims didn't emigrate as much; they just didn't have the money.

So they did what poor folks do: stayed home and had babies. Pretty soon the Muslims were the majority. Nobody knows exactly how big a majority, because nobody's taken a census in Lebanon for fifty years. For one thing it's too dangerous—you wouldn't want to go knocking on doors in Beirut, asking total strangers touchy ethnic and religious questions for minimum wage, would you? For another, the Christians don't want anybody counting noses, because they know most of those noses would be Muslim.

The best guesstimate, made by the CIA in 1986, says the Muslims (Shiite, Sunni, and Druze) are about 75 percent of the Lebanese population. The Maronite Christians are only about 16 percent, with another 8 percent Christian "other." I don't know what religion these "other" 8 percent are; I just hope they're not Jehovah's Witnesses, because they have some stupid rule against blood transfusions, and in Lebanon, you never know when you may need a pint or two of O-positive.

The biggest, fastest-growing group in Lebanon is the Shiites. They'll have an absolute majority soon. And they're pro-Syrian.

That little demographic might help you understand why the so-called Arab Spring of 2005 is now only just a faint memory. The people then demonstrating in Beirut on TV, waving those tree flags, were Maronites. Although they're richer, more media-savvy, and more photogenic than the Shiites in the slums, the Maronites constitute only 16 percent of the population. And their tribe is shrinking every year, while the Shiites are growing.

When there's a weak group like the Maronites on top and a strong, growing one like the Shiites underneath, everything can seem calm and stable—till something breaks up the status quo. The first big disruption in Lebanon was the flood of Palestinian refugees and PLO guerrillas fleeing Israel in 1948. The second came when the Israelis got tired of being shelled and raided by the PLO and decided to invade Lebanon.

Israel's first big raid into Lebanon to root out the PLO was in 1978. Militarily, it was a cakewalk. The PLO was never a really dangerous guerrilla army. It had a few great soldiers, like the guy who single-handedly flew a hang glider into an Israeli camp and shot a half dozen IDF guys before being killed. But good soldiers don't make a good army. You need good units, and the PLO was always better at collecting money than fighting. Israel cut through the Palestinians' camps in South Lebanon and set up a ten-mile buffer zone, putting northern Israel out of mortar range.

The UN came on as comedy relief—its usual role. It huffed and puffed and inserted a five-thousand-man force called UNIFIL (United Nations Interim Force in Lebanon), with troops from great military powers like Ireland and Fiji proudly wearing the blue helmet and shouting the UN battle cry, "Don't shoot, I'm neutered!" For the next thirty years, these guys hunkered down in the hills, getting shelled and shot by everyone in the game, doing no good at all, making complete asses of themselves. I swear they'd make a great sitcom—it would make MASH look like warmongering.

The 1978 incursion went so well that the Israelis started thinking about bigger plans. An easy victory can be dangerous—it can teach you the wrong lesson. Like the one the Israelis learned: "If a medium-sized incursion was good, a big giant invasion will be even better!" They went for it in June 1982: A hundred thousand IDF troops blasted right into Lebanon. In command was my fellow fat man, Ariel Sharon. Sharon's a tricky guy; he promised the Israeli cabinet he was only going to sweep the PLO out of South Lebanon, but he planned to go all the way to Beirut. He figured nobody argues with a winner.

And he did win—at first. The Israelis' performance was flat-out spectacular, especially in the air. The Syrian Air Force sent everything it had against the Israeli attackers. And lost everything. The Israelis had learned to use RPVs, unmanned recon drones, from the USAF. The USAF had invested billions of dollars in these cool little gadgets, but wouldn't use them. They weren't sexy enough—nobody climbs to three-star rank by managing little kiddie planes like the ones you see nerds flying in the park on weekends. And they didn't cost enough—the USAF likes stuff that costs billions. These things you could get at a hobby store, damn it!

With a limited budget and a real war to fight, the Israelis didn't worry about any of that crap. They used the little remote-control planes for recon and as decoys to distract the Syrian air defense radars. In a few days, the Israelis shot down eighty-two Syrian aircraft without losing a single one of their own.

On the ground, things were going nearly as good. The IDF surrounded Palestinian camps and bases, bombarded them, captured and processed the civilians, and sent anybody suspicious to internment camps—little mobile Gitmos.

The ground war wasn't as clean and pretty as the air war. The Israelis wanted the Palestinians out of the area for good, so they pretty much bombed first and asked questions later. They'd leave garrisons to watch the displaced Palestinians, but the main force was pushing north to Beirut as fast as Sharon could whip 'em.

When the IDF reached Beirut in the summer of 1982, it had a tactical problem: Go in and grab Yasir Arafat and the rest of the PLO leadership at the risk of taking casualties in urban fighting, or try to force them to give up by shelling the PLO districts? The IDF has always been careful to avoid casualties—Israeli casualties, I mean—so it opted for Plan B: Shell the city till Arafat was smoked out. It got ugly; big, crowded city full of civilian refugees, massed bombardment with phosphorus and cluster bombs. Nobody's sure how many casualties there were, but estimates run from twenty to fifty thousand.

It worked, though: Arafat and his officers settled for a deal that had them transferred to Tunisia, out of the Middle East. And the PLO was broken in Lebanon.

Just as the Israelis were celebrating (the war had great ratings at home: 80 percent approval), everything went bad.

Like us in Iraq, Israel had a man they planned to put in place: Bachir Gemayel, a very scary, double-tough Maronite warlord. He was just getting used to being called "Mister President" when he was blown to bits in his headquarters. That was it; no more plan.

The Maronite militias mourned in their own way: by killing people. Two days after Bachir was killed, the IDF sent his militiamen into a couple of Palestinian refugee camps. They killed everyone they found—about a thousand refugees, most of them women and children. Worse yet, all the TV cameras in the world were in Beirut, so everybody saw it. Not good for PR.

The real trouble was just getting started: The Shiite reaction came next. Sharon and the IDF had barely even noticed the Shiites in their drive to Beirut. It was the PLO they were after. That was a big mistake—like chasing a cockroach around the kitchen without noticing the rabid pit bull in the corner. After a few years of fighting crazy Shiites, Sharon must've been outright nostalgic for the days when he had a nice, harmless enemy like the PLO.

The Shiites didn't like these infidel invaders any more than the PLO did—and they were way, waaaaaaaaay better fighters than the Palestinians. Hezbollah, "the Party of God," was started by Lebanese Shiites under Iranian command—and it started hitting its enemies hard, using the classic Shia suicide bombing technique. (Back then, suicide bombs were still a shock.) From there on, it's just boom, boom, boom.

Boom number 1, April 1983: Hezbollah suicide bomber destroys U.S. Embassy in Beirut; 63 people killed.

Boom number 2, October 1983: Hezbollah suicide bombers bring down high-rise housing U.S. Marines in Beirut; 241 marines killed. Exactly twenty seconds later, Hezbollah suicide bombers hit French barracks, killing 58 French paratroopers.

Boom number 3, November 1983: Hezbollah truck bombers destroy Israeli headquarters in South Lebanon, killing 60 people.

It took the Israelis a while to realize what a disaster the invasion really was. Like us in Iraq, the first stage was such an easy victory that they thought they could do anything. Turned out that by booting the PLO out of Lebanon, they'd tilted the gang-bang balance in favor of the Shia, the newest, most ready-to-die gang-bangers on the block. And the Shia didn't stop hitting the IDF until it abandoned its last "buffer zone" in South Lebanon in 2000.

When the Israelis started getting hit by Shia bombers in South Lebanon, they tried the oldest trick in the book: Hire some local mercenaries to take the heat off your troops. That's how this very weird little mercenary force, the South Lebanon Army, got created. It was an IDF proxy force doing the dirty work in South Lebanon: manning the outposts that were most likely to get bombed, running the prison/interrogation centers—fun, people-oriented work like that. Good pay, must have own life insurance. The SLA's officer corps was Maronite, but most of its soldiers were Muslim—guys who were sick of living at home and wanted a steady income. They were not too popular with the locals, as you can imagine. When Israel decided to evacuate the region in 2000, it had to make special arrangements to find someplace for all twenty-five hundred SLA soldiers, either in Israel or overseas—as far overseas as possible. Because, as I've said before, Shiites never, never forget a grudge.

If this story makes you kind of nervous about Iraq—well, you're right. Hezbollah is stronger than ever now, still tight with the Iranians and Syria. We may be able to kindle a couple demonstrations in downtown Beirut, but don't be fooled. Out there in the slums of the cities and the little villages down in South Lebanon, there's an endless supply of martyrs waiting for their chance. They may not be telegenic, but they make a kind of lasting impression.

ASIA

FAG VS. FAG:
THE INDIA-PAKISTAN PHONY WAR

WILL INDIA AND Pakistan ever finish the catfight and get on with a real war? "We live in hope," like my grandma used to say—but don't hold your breath. Listening to the Indian and Paki generals shaking their little fists at each other, with their little moustaches going up and down, hearing the Indians talk about how their patience is "almost" exhausted—it just gets me down. This fag-slapping shit gives war a bad name.

I used to live next to a house full of Pakistanis in Santa Ana. They were all brothers or cousins or something and ran this pirate cab company, and they fought nonstop—but I never saw a single punch thrown. It was this weird Pakistani style of fighting: They'd yell for hours before they escalated to slapping—weird downward slaps, like elephants hitting each other with their trunks. After a couple minutes of that, they'd each retreat about five yards and look around for automotive parts to throw. They'd keep throwing till they were tired or till they accidentally hit one of the half-fixed taxis parked in the yard. That was the only thing that sobered them up: hurting a car. When they drew blood on each other, they'd cheer, but if they broke a windshield, they'd instantly stop fighting and run up to the car moaning and sobbing.

The way those cabdrivers fought is the way India and Pakistan fight—maybe it's in the genes. It's always low-intensity, low-risk skirmishing, like these "mortar duels" the networks keep reporting from Kashmir. Mortar duels are the perfect combat for cowards, because the mortar is a very high-trajectory weapon, so you can fire it over hills and never even see the enemy face-to-face.

I'm not knocking mortars; they can be powerful weapons in the hands of a real army. The East Asians are particularly good with them. A mortar barrage from Chinese or Vietnamese troops is a serious deal. But that's because East Asian troops take the risk of lugging their tubes right up to the front line, where they can do quick range finding and walk their fire right up to the enemy positions.

The mortar barrages you hear about on the India-Pakistan line are nothing like that. These are from mortars dug in way behind the front line. The aim isn't really to hit any enemy troops but to make a lot of noise, a lot of chimpanzee-style hooting. At most, they aim at a fixed target already plotted. Like a village. Border villages make great targets, because they're not going anywhere and can't fight back. So both armies blow up huts on the other side of the border and kill a lot of livestock.

Somebody should do a history of livestock killing as an element of military history. In the fifteenth century, the Germans called soldiers "the horse-butchers' league" because it was basic tactics to kill knights' horses—by taking them out of the saddle, you cut their speed and mass by two-thirds. In "primitive warfare" like what you see in Africa, killing the enemy's cattle is the worst blow you can inflict. And in Kashmir right now, the main target for the brave mortar-men of both armies is livestock. You mortar a village, and you'll only kill a few villagers; the rest will duck inside, get down on the floor after the first shells hit. But cattle can't duck, so they inevitably get shrapnelled into hamburger.

And the really sad thing is the villagers—on the Indian side of the border, anyway—can't even eat the sacred-cow meat. That's one good argument for Islam, I guess: At least you can eat the cattle casualties. Or maybe not, because the Muslims have that whole halal deal, where you can only eat animals killed in the proper Muhammadan manner. I doubt if an 82-mm mortar is an Imam-approved slaughtering device.

Religion—ain't it wonderful?

Anyway, the point is, the longer these two chickenshit armies mortar each other, the less likely it is they'll ever get down to business with a real war. The mortar duels are military masturbation, a way of letting off steam. When you mortar each other for months and months, you're signaling the fact that you're scared of a real fight.

The Indian Army has the weapons and the numbers to win. It has plenty of hardware and 1.1 million men, roughly the number of riders on the average Indian train. But It's hard to believe that the Indian Army has the right spirit when you see the troops drilling in those wacky uniforms, doing the Monty Python moves they got from the British. Goose-stepping, swagger sticks, little moustaches—it's pathetic. You keep looking around for John Cleese as officer-in-charge.

True, the Indians have beaten the Pakistanis three times out of three (in 1947, 1965, and 1971). But look at what happened the one time they tried fighting a real army: the India-China War of 1962. India decided that its new status as world power required it to grab a few square miles of Himalayan wasteland from China. The Indians worked themselves up into a war frenzy and attacked the Chinese. The Chinese, who don't do woofing, just quietly flattened the Indian Army. It was a rout: moustaches and swaggersticks sprinting downhill so fast the snow was still on their helmets when they hit Delhi. After that, the Indians decided they'd stick to picking on someone half their own size: the Pakistanis.

The Pakistani Army only has 550,000 men—just about the number of spectators crushed to death in the average soccer match in Karachi. Pakistanis talk big—what do you expect, when the name *Pakistan* means "land of the pure"? But they've lost three out of three to the Indians. The Pakistani Army is one of those Third World armies that specialize in protection money, not war. The army runs the country, and the intelligence service, the ISI, runs the army. And the ISI doesn't want a real fight. It would rather shake down the local drug dealers and let the Kashmiri jihadi groups they control raid India. It's safer and cheaper. Besides, they know they'd lose a real war. As long as the Pakistanis act through the jihadi, they can keep denying any involvement at all. In other words, it's the usual cowardly standoff.

But we're supposed to believe it might get serious this time, because the ruling party in India are so-called Hindu militants. Uh . . . yeah. Hindu militants! I can't help it, that phrase just cracks me up every time I hear it. What does a Hindu militant do, anyway? Scream "You bastard, you ate my grandfather!" at the drive-through window of the New Delhi Burger King? The only thing these "Hindu militants" ever did was burn down shops selling Valentine's Day cards. Don't ask me why. Maybe Vishnu told them to. All I know is, militants whose big atrocity is burning Hallmark cards don't sound too scary.

The other reason we're supposed to be scared is: The Nukes. Oh no, nukes! Like everybody's supposed to faint the moment nukes get mentioned. People act like the moment somebody's got one nuke, that country has "got nukes." It doesn't work that way. Nukes are not guppies—they don't breed on their own. You have to build a stockpile, one at a time. The Pakistanis only have about twenty. Suppose they use 'em all, and every nuke kills five hundred thousand Indians. The Indians lose ten million people—1 percent of their population. I said 1 percent!

India has about two hundred nukes, so it could wipe out Pakistan. But the Indians won't, because they're too chickenshit. And Pakistan won't nuke them, because that's the one thing that might piss the Indians off enough to act.

So nothing's going to happen. It's just another big media fake, like skinheads and Y2K.

If the Indians were going to do something, they would've done it when the Pakistani/Kashmiri terrorists attacked the Indian parliament back in 2002. Bodies everywhere, RPGs blasting the government headquarters—and all the Indians did was screech that their patience was "almost" running out. And that's all they'll ever say: They're "almost" ready to fight.

As a former elementary-school bully, I'll tell you a little secret: There is no "almost" in a fight. When you're fighting somebody who "almost" hits people, you can relax. He won't do shit.

I wish I had better news. I wish I could tell you there was a chance of a war worth watching down in that hellhole subcontinent. But there isn't. They'll probably wipe each other out someday, but till then, it's just going to be dead cows and villagers, and dumb generals in secondhand British uniforms talking big for the camera with their little moustaches going up and down, up and down.

NEPAL:
PEACE, LOVE, AND MASSACRES

EVER WANNA GO to Kathmandu? Not me. I was never a hippie. The hippie types always talked about heading off to Nepal for spiritual enlightenment, but it sounded like my idea of Hell: a bunch of grimy beggars grabbing at you, yelling gibberish, trying to sell you yak dung as prime-grade hash. Some of the old acid casualties in my community-college classes had been there and always said it was a real deep experience, but it didn't seem to have done those zombie trolls much good. Most of them were on SSI, paid by the State of California to watch reruns of *Gilligan's Island* and not bother anybody with their acid flashbacks.

The first sign most people had that things weren't so peace 'n' lovey in Nepal was June 2001, when the whole Nepalese royal family got wiped out over dinner. Turned out to be the old story: Bratty son wants to marry a local slut, Dad says no, bratty son has a tantrum. Except this little prince had his tantrum with an automatic rifle. One of those classic dinner-table arguments: "Dad, can I marry Devi?" "No, no, no. Now eat your curry." "'Scuse me . . . gotta, um, wash my hands." And before Daddy and Mummy and sisters and brothers can dig into their chicken korma, the li'l prince is back, peppering the whole dining room with lead. The whole family wiped out before the entrée.

You gotta hand it to the prince, though. I mean, that's love. "Honey, I shot the folks." I bet his girlfriend was real touched. Nothing says "I love you" like wiping out your entire family.

Still want to go to Kathmandu? Well, it gets worse. Way worse. That hot-tempered prince wasn't the only person in Nepal sayin' it with automatic rifles these days. They've been having a big, bloody, serious Maoist revolution. Man, Bob Seger is gonna be bummed. I still can't really believe it myself. Maoists in Kathmandu? Nepal is where rich, liberal assholes like Dianne Feinstein go "trekking." You don't expect guerrillas to thrive at twenty thousand feet with the Gurkhas and the Sherpas.

But it's a fact: Nepal has a Maoist insurrection, and a big one, too. Been going on since 1996. It started out in the classic way: The local Communist Party split between the peaceniks who just want to go on handing out leaflets and the hotheads who want to start fighting now. The hotheads won out, the Nepalese commies split up, and the two or three dozen university types who always dreamed of being the local Che Guevara headed for the hills to radicalize the Nepalese peasants.

The intellectuals found the peasants already pissed off, in the mood to go out and kill some landlords. You don't think of Nepal as having masses of oppressed peasants, but some of the stuff I've been reading is pretty gross: people selling themselves and their whole families to the local landlord just to get malaria medication. Seriously. A peasant gets sick, figures anything's better than dying, and uses his family as collateral for the money he needs to get malaria medication. It's a lose-lose bet: If the peasant survives, he and his wife and kids are the property of the local loan shark.

Slavery was actually legal in Nepal till a couple of years ago. You could buy whole families if you needed household help. Sometimes the debts were a hundred years old: Granddad had bad luck with the dice, so all his kids, forever and ever, were slaves. Little kids working eighteen-hour days, every day, for no money, for life. Hell, with a life like that, Ann Coulter would turn into a Maoist.

So if you're living a miserable life as a Nepalese slave, and a nice clean-cut Maoist recruiter sneaks into the village one night and tells you it's all gonna change and all you have to do is learn a few of Mao's little inspirational haiku and hack your landlord to death ... well, I have to say, I'd join up myself. And these recruiters were university types, all clean-cut and inspiring. The peasants must've been dazzled just to see 'em, Nepal's finest, paying attention to them and their grubby villages. They joined up, and the revolution started cranking.

Mao's battle plan is simple. It can be adapted to almost any country as long as you've got the basic ingredients: mean landlords, hungry peasants, educated city people who couldn't care less what's happening in the countryside. In other words: if you've got a really fucked-up agricultural country. Nepal had that.

Mao's plan doesn't take military geniuses to make it work. What it does take is lots and lots of discipline and patience, because you must avoid battle until the odds are overwhelmingly in your favor. So the first rule is: No Hotheads Need Apply.

Step one is to work the villages. The university-trained commie recruiters fan out into the villages and radicalize the locals—which isn't too hard when the landlords have been buying and selling peasants like mules.

The next part is harder: You set up a shadow government. You don't attack the local police or army at this stage—you try to make them irrelevant. Instead of taking complaints to the cops, peasants take their quarrels to a People's Court that meets in a shed at night. Instead of paying regular taxes, you pay people's taxes to a guy who comes around at night with a notebook and a bag. The idea is to isolate the cops, tax collectors, and other informers—to "put out the eyes" of the government in the area, so that by the time you're ready to attack, the government won't have any intelligence system worth the name and you'll take the ruling elite completely by surprise.

Of course, it's never as neat as the way Mao laid it out in the little red book. People talk, the cops know something's going on. And in Nepal, "cops" doesn't mean a squad car with two guys in it. The Nepalese police are organized in paramilitary units dispersed in barracks across the countryside, with dozens or even hundreds of men armed with automatic rifles, heavy machine guns, light armored vehicles, and air cover on request. These cops know that if they lose their grip on the villages, the police will wake up some night to find their barracks overrun. The cops start bringing in likely suspects and working out on them, using whatever form of torture is traditional in these parts.

The ruling elite had ninety thousand cops/soldiers against at least ten thousand guerrillas. That's not good odds for the government. Conventional wisdom says you need at least ten soldiers for every guerrilla, but that's assuming your troops are as good, man for man, as the guerrillas. The Nepalese cops/soldiers aren't very good. The leader of the rebels (who's from the upper class himself, naturally) predicted that "The king's army will not fight for very long."

The landlords knew it, too. They could feel their grip on the locals getting weaker. Scary graffiti on the walls, people not bowing and scraping the way they used to ... They started calling their cousins in Kathmandu, begging them to send more troops. It all started heating up.

But when the local version of the IRS stops getting taxes from the peasants—that's when the authorities really get grim. You can mess with the army and the cops, but don't mess with the tax collectors. When the government stops getting taxes, it uses the only leverage it's got: It sends the army to get the money at gunpoint. The Maoists do the same thing to the villagers at night. Not a happy time to be a Nepalese villager, especially when the rebels are known to use some pretty extreme penalties for late payment of tax—such as crushing people's arms and legs with big rocks.

Squeezing the peasants between two forces like this is part of Mao's big plan. The idea is to drive the peasants so damn crazy they'll finally be ready to fight. The soldiers actually help the Maoists at this stage by lame attempts at reprisal: They'll almost always grab the wrong people, torture them, and end up radicalizing whole families, whole villages. The Maoist cadre won't be touched; it's hiding deeper in the hills. But every time the cops beat somebody to death, all his cousins become recruits. So the meaner the cops get, the stupider they get and the better for the revolution.

This is where that old commie line about making omelets and breaking eggs comes into play big-time. The more the cops and soldiers terrorize the locals, the more isolated the army ends up in its sandbagged barracks. Nobody feeds the army intelligence anymore; it's holed up, always on the defensive, no longer capable of choosing the time and place for combat.

That's when the slow, boa-constrictor Maoist plan switches over to the offensive. The Maoists focus on numbers and surprise. In May 2002, the Maoists attacked a police barracks in Gam, in western Nepal. There were at least a thousand guerrillas, yelling, waving torches, shouting slogans. They overran the base and hacked to death every cop or soldier they found, at least seventy dead. The Maoists lost maybe two hundred—if you can believe the cops—but that's not important. A victory like that spreads through the villages instantly. The peasants—and remember, these people are used to being bought and sold like cattle—suddenly realize they can take on the army and win.

But where did they go from local victories like Gam? That's the problem. Suppose the Maoists beat the Nepalese Army. Would India let that happen? India thinks of Nepal as sort of a kid brother—annoying but part of the family. The Indian Army may not be good enough to fight a real war, but it sure as Hell could squash the Maoists in Nepal. India has had a lot of practice with this sort of war, in other hellholes like Bihar. The country could easily bring in enough troops for the twenty-five-to-one ratio you need to flush out and destroy rural guerrillas. And India's on a venture-capitalist high right now, not in the mood to tolerate retro-Maoists right next door.

And it's not likely the original Maoists, the Chinese, are going to help the guerrillas. They've got other things on their minds: profit margins, export ratios—money, money, money. I kinda like imagining a meeting between one of these Nepalese gung-ho Maoist rebels and today's Chinese leaders: "You, the party of Mao, must help us overthrow the landlord elite!" "Um, sorry, but all our cash is tied up in short-term Citicorp bonds. How would your revolutionary peasants like to invest in our new Shanghai enterprise zone?"

It must be kind of discouraging to be a Maoist; who can you count on these days? The only real friends the Nepalese Maoists have are the leftovers of those crazy Peruvian guerrillas, the Shining Path. Remember them? They were like the one-hit wonder of 1980s guerrilla warfare: dynamite-throwin', machete-choppin' Incas who made Peru a lively place.

And with friends like Shining Path, well . . . you ain't got no friends. So the Nepalese Maoists are up against it in the long run. They may win inside Nepal, but their talk about "planting the red flag on Mount Everest" ain't gonna happen. Where would Dianne Feinstein go trekking? The folks who run this world wouldn't let anything get in the way of their expeditions up K2 or Everest. They'd bribe the Indian Army to waddle in like a big fat sumo and squash the Maoists.

And there wouldn't be a damn thing Shining Path, on the run down in Peru, could do to help. But that brings me to the last big mystery here, the same one I started out with: the hippies. I mean, what is it with hippies and high-altitude peasant rebellions, anyway? First it was Shining Path—remember back in the late 1980s, all the hippies were wearing those wool Inca hats that looked like wool versions of fourteenth-century man-at-arms helmets? And now, in all the little grimy coffee places where the local alternos hang in Fresno, they're all wearing those ratty cloth over-the-shoulder bags you get from Nepal.

What is it with these people? Is there like some kind of romance to low-oxygen poverty and dirt?

Well, they'll get their chance to do the Nepal treks. In 2007, the Nepalese elite got smart, or scared, enough to do the one thing that snuffs out commie insurgents: buy them off. Nepal abolished the monarchy, taking away the focus of the peasants' hatred, and invited the Maoists to share power. Which means sharing money. Which means the Maoist cadre will slowly get accustomed to limos, butter chicken microwaved for breakfast, and Blackberry. Money is what poisoned Maoist insurgencies all over Asia, and it will work in Nepal—especially because the two world powers flanking Nepal are both cash-crazy.

You can get away with communism on an island, maybe. That's what saved Cuba from our wrath (that, and the Soviets' ICBMs). But a landlocked South Asian country can't buck the trend like Cuba did. Not when all the rich hippies want to go there and love the place to death.

BERSERKERS WITH RED STARS:
NORTH KOREAN SCENARIOS

BACK IN EARLY 2003, when war nerds like me were ready to lose hope, with the Iraq invasion getting put off more times than Michael Jordan's retirement, I'd drive home from my Hell-job cursing every old lady in the fast lane, hoping to pop on the TV and see the new GBUs (guided bomb units) with the Baghdad-cams . . . and instead there'd be nothing but more weak Pentagon promises.

Then, boom! The North Koreans announced that they're restarting their nuclear weapons program and they don't care who knows it, the U.S. Army canceled leave for all the troops in the DMZ, and we've got something to look forward to again: an all-on war, finally.

I mean bush wars are fun, but you get sick of reading about African militias hacking up villagers and carrying around sacks of hands and feet. You want a real war, starring a couple of countries with more than a half-dozen high-school graduates between them. Some real soldiers, with weapons a little more advanced than Kalashnikovs and machetes.

And if anybody can give us that kind of war, it's Korea. The rest of the world may have turned into lapdogs scared of their own shadows, but not the Koreans. They're crazy people. They'll tell you so themselves.

I used to know some Koreans in Bakersfield, because they went to the same Pentecostal church. There were some far-gone folks in that congregation, but the Koreans were the most God-crazy people in the place. Especially the Korean girls. Most of the white girls or Latinas were pretty relaxed outside of Sunday services, but everybody knew you shouldn't even bother talking to a Korean girl unless you were "one with God," meaning your idea of a hot date was holding hands at an ice-cream place and quoting Scripture at each other.

At my high school, one Korean guy, whose claim to fame was that he supposedly memorized the whole New Testament, jumped a Mexican gang guy for making fun of God. He got stomped, but he was in there fighting to the end, biting and screaming and clawing and yelling about Jesus. People left him alone after that. Not because they were scared of him as a fighter, just because everybody respects real hard-core craziness.

So I understand North Korea. They're just like the Koreans in Bakersfield, except they went for Communism instead of Christ. If pure craziness could win wars, Kim Jong-Il's army would kick ass. The problem is, I'm not sure morale alone will do it. Not anymore. Back when you fought with axes and spears, the crazier side usually won, like the berserkers. But craziness won't keep you alive when you're up against fuel-air weapons, cluster bombs, bunker-busters, and all the other high-tech killing toys the North would have to face if it ever does the ol' banzai charge across the DMZ.

And morale won't make up for real infrastructure problems, of which the North has lots. Like no air force worth mentioning. The only way North Korea could get tactical surprise would be to send its men over with what they could carry; they couldn't resupply even if they did make it past the DMZ.

A war on the DMZ would be bloody—I mean for us as well as them—but the North would lose. No question.

The real question is what would happen if the North Koreans decided to play dirty. Which they would. The only thing North Korea does well is train secret agents and infiltrators. Its agents do what they're told, up to and including suicide. They all carry little poison pills they're supposed to take if captured. Lots of countries give these pills to their agents—but the North Koreans and the Tamil rebels in Sri Lanka really take them.

Koreans are real smart, too. Over the past fifty years, North Koreans have come up with lots of different schemes, some scary, some just ridiculous. These people swing for the fences every time. They will go anywhere, try anything, and do all sorts of craziness just for a chance to kill a few South Korean politicians or American imperialists.

The most famous North Korean attack happened in Burma (or Myanmar, as you're supposed to call it now) in 1983. The North Koreans knew that the South Korean president and most of his cabinet would be visiting Rangoon (if you're still allowed to call it that), so they sent three top agents down there to wipe the whole Southern leadership out at once—the Michael Corleone approach, for you *Godfather* fans. After planting a huge bomb at a shrine the South Koreans were scheduled to visit, the North Koreans set it off by remote control. The president survived, but eighteen other South Korean officials were blown to bits, along with a lot of Burmese.

The Burmese were sorta cheesed. They broke diplomatic relations with North Korea. But the North didn't seem to mind. Kim Il Sung didn't play safe. He went all out, and damn the consequences.

The North Koreans don't mind killing off a few civilians along the way, either. They're willing to break as many eggs as necessary to make the proverbial omelet. In 1987, North Korean agents planted a bomb on a Korean Air flight, and 135 people were killed. Kim Jong-Il, who's just as hardcore as his dad was, supposedly ordered this operation himself. He decided that blowing up a randomly selected Korean Air flight would be a good way of scaring tourists off going to Seoul for the 1988 Olympics.

A lot of North Korean operations have that feel of family jealousy about them: The North, all forlorn up there starving and freezing to death, can't stand it when the South gets another prize, like being picked to host the Olympics. That's when North Koreans get really crazy.

The story of the agents who planted the bomb in the plane tells you something about how well-trained and crazy North Korean agents are. The job was given to two agents, a man and a woman. Both of them took their poison pills when they were caught. He died like he was supposed to, but her pill must've been stepped-on cheap stuff, because she survived. She's practically the only one ever captured alive. North Korean agents are harder to keep alive in captivity than great white sharks.

The North never managed to kill a serving Southern president, but it wasn't for lack of trying. In 1970, one Northern agent was blown up trying to plant a bomb at a cemetery the South's president was due to visit. Four years later, an overseas Korean came to Seoul and tried to kill the president, but only managed to kill his wife.

These were small operations. Some of the North's other operations have been really big, more like irregular warfare than terrorism. The biggest were in the 1960s, around the time of the Tet Offensive, when the North Koreans were trying to copy the tactics that were working for the North Vietnam Army and Viet Cong (VC). In 1968, a team of thirty-one Northern elite troops in South Korean Army (ROK) uniforms almost bluffed their way into the presidential palace in Seoul before they were spotted. Twenty-eight out of thirty-one died in the firefight that followed, either killed by ROK troops or by suicide.

That same year, the North landed a really big force, 120 men, on the east coast of South Korea. The story is classic Korean stuff: dead serious, bloody as a slaughterhouse, and, all the same, kind of comical. The North Korean infiltrators were trying to start a Vietnam-style uprising, but without any of the patience or finesse the VC had. They just herded all the local villagers together at gunpoint and announced that all the men would join the Korean Workers' Party and all the women would sign up for the Women's Union.

But the villagers were Korean, too, which means they were natural-born extremists themselves—and since they were from the South, they were natural-born anticommunists. So a ten-year-old boy announced that he hated commies. Naturally, the North Korean troops were offended, so they killed the kid. This did not help in their struggle to win the hearts and minds of the locals, a few of whom snuck off to tell the South Korean Army about the new visitors. The ROK surrounded the village, and the Northerners, naturally, fought to the death.

Out of 120 infiltrators, exactly 7 were captured alive, probably because they were unconscious from wounds and unable to finish themselves off. There hasn't been an army so stubborn about not being taken alive since the Imperial Japanese Army went out of business.

No matter how many times it fails, the North still seems to like the coastal-infiltration technique. After all, Korea's a peninsula with a complicated rocky coastline—lots of places to put men ashore without too many spectators. Who knows how often they're surfacing to drop off new agents? We only hear about a few of their failures.

The biggest recent one we know about was in 1996, when a Northern sub dropped off twenty-six men, some in ROK uniforms, some in civvies, and all lugging guns. They even brought rocket launchers, which might've been kind of a giveaway when these guys were trying to blend in with the locals. Just imagine some wild-eyed child of Kim Il Sung's regime, all got up in slacker clothes, trying to act casual walking in from the beach still sopping wet with a big RPG-7 over his shoulder. He runs into a South Korean fisherman and tries to do his best imitation of a harmless surfer: "Hey, dude, everything cool? *Gouge out the eyes of the imperialist*—Whoops, I mean hang loose, dude!"

That's what I mean about the North having focus but no finesse. The Vietnamese would've sent their men one at a time, unarmed, and given them a few months to get jobs and settle in. But those Kims—they're just impulsive guys. They want it all now.

Naturally, these twenty-six clueless infiltrators were spotted and hunted down. Only two of the twenty-six were captured alive. But the interesting thing is that eleven of the twenty-four dead were supposedly shot by their officers because they refused to kill themselves. Maybe team spirit is weakening up North. Still, you should never assume your enemy is going to fall apart. In general, overestimating the enemy is safer than underestimating him (with some notable exceptions, like General George McClellan, who infused the Army of the Potomac with all the fighting spirit of Jimmy Carter and always assumed, thanks to his inept military intelligence, that Lee had three times more troops than he could ever really put on the field).

My favorite Northern technique is the tunnels. The South Koreans found the first big tunnel in 1974 and detected a couple more in 1975 and 1978. These weren't little crawl spaces; they were big enough to shunt whole divisions of light infantry past the forward ROK-U.S. defense line. One of the tunnels came up only forty-four kilometers from Seoul. You have to assume there are some still undiscovered. Imagine a couple of divisions of North Korean maniacs popping right up out of the ground miles behind what we thought was going to be the front lines. There goes your resupply right there. According to defectors, the North considers each tunnel as powerful as a nuclear weapon.

Which brings us to the biggest question: Does the North have nukes, and will it use them? The North Koreans want us to think they do, that's for sure. After all, it's the fear of nukes that makes all the liberals shove sacks of rice at North Korea: "Here! Eat it, just don't detonate those nukes!" And U.S. intelligence has its own reasons for pumping up the North as nuclear threat. The bigger the threat, the bigger the DoD budget. So it's not so easy to know who to trust here. But there seems to be agreement that the North does have at least a few nukes. Big, clumsy ones, but functional.

A lot of so-called experts are trying to reassure people by saying that these nukes are too big to load onto a missile. What these guys keep forgetting is that poor countries like North Korea have to be more flexible in their strategies. So OK, maybe they can't do missiles—but who ever said a missile is the only way to deliver a nuke? How about just smuggling one into an enemy's harbors in a fishing boat?

If there's one thing that Marxist-Leninist regimes are good at, it's espionage. How do we know that the North hasn't already brought a nuke into Seoul? There could be one (or two, or three) sitting in a rented storage shed or buried in somebody's garden, waiting for Kim Jong-Il to send the page.

An even wilder scenario is that Kim and his little coven might decide to go after bigger game—like Los Angeles or San Francisco. That's the WMDs we should be worrying about. All this talk about Saddam's WMDs is crap. Nobody's willing to die for Saddam. His army proved that in Gulf War I. His secret agents around the world turned out to be a myth. But North Korea has real secret agents, crazy enough to kill themselves on command, blow up civilian airliners, and plant bombs all over the world. These are smart, disciplined, educated people, miles better than the Allahu-Akbars in Al Qaeda.

If anybody could bring WMDs into the United States, it's the North Koreans. How many fishing boats from Asia come into Oakland or San Pedro every year? You weld a nuke inside the engine of an old trawler—what are the odds anybody'd be able to find it? The only way customs agents ever find anything is when they're tipped off, and the odds of anybody in the North Korean secret police dropping a dime on their bosses are exactly zero-point-nada.

So when you look back over the North's record, you get two strong impressions: First, it's overhyped as a conventional army. If the North tried a conventional attack across the DMZ, it would get zapped like ants sprayed with Raid. No question. Second, North Koreans are underrated as terrorists. They don't play by the same rules that we play by, and they're not cowards like Gadhafi and Saddam. Or loudmouthed hicks like Osama.

In fact, what I admire most about North Korea is the way it flips off the whole world, right to its face. Here's a BBC headline from January 2008: "N Korea Defiant on Nuclear Issue." Just look at the first and last paragraphs of this article to see how consistently "fuck y'all" North Korea has been: "North Korea has pledged to strengthen its 'war deterrent,' days after it missed a [2007] deadline for declaring its nuclear activities." In other words, the North told the world, "We're going to make *more* nukes, and screw that treaty we signed!"

Now, the final paragraph of the story, with a totally typical hodong American response to this insult: "US envoy Christopher Hill is due back in the region on Monday in a bid to move negotiations forward." Yeah, that should scare the North Koreans into dropping their nukes, all right.*

Ya gotta love 'em. The world may be turning to chickenshit woofing and white-collar crime, but in Pyongyang, there are people who'd just as soon bite your windpipe open as look at you, real berserkers with red stars on their caps. Our last decent chance for a classic, full-on war.

BURMA:
THEY AIN'T LIKE US

ONCE YOU START learning about war, you get a different idea about what's normal. If my life … driving to work and watching TV … If that's normal, then a place like Burma is as far from normal as you can get. But the more I find out about the world, the more normal Burma seems and the weirder my life in Fresno looks.

Burma is a place where war is a permanent fact of life. There are wars between the Burmese and all the little tribes they stomp on to stay in power. There are wars between the Christians and the Buddhists. There are wars between the opium dealers who run the army and the freelancers in the hills. There may even be a few Communist rebels left in the mountains, gathering around the ol' red flag. Burma has wars the way Fresno has Armenians.

Burma is one of these multiethnic places, and that usually means trouble. My social studies teachers used to talk about the wonderfulness of multiethnic stuff, but let's be honest here: What "multiethnic" really means is if your car breaks down in the wrong neighborhood, you get beaten to death with your own tire iron.

---

* BBC, "N Korea Defiant on Nuclear Issue," BBC News, January 4, 2008, available at http://news.bbc.co.uk/2/hi/asia-pacific/7171096.stm.

And that's exactly how it works in Burma. If you look at a map of the country, you can get a quick idea of how the tribal splits work. It's basically a long river valley surrounded by hills. The Burmese, the big dominant tribe (70 percent of the population), grabbed the good land down in the river flats, and the other tribes had to head for the hills. Literally.

Now they get called "hill tribes," like they have some kind of romantic attachment to high altitudes, but that's not how it happened at all. If you live by farming the way people used to, you want the flat land by the river, because the silt makes good soil and the water means you can flood the rice paddies. When your tribe takes the river flats, anybody from the old tribes who's not dead scrambles off into the hills to live like goats for the next few hundred years.

What makes it so hard for us to get is that in California, the rich people live up in the hills on little, windy streets, and the ordinary people who drive pickups live down on the flats. But that's because we don't have to make a living from our own land. If we did, the rich people'd hire mercs to wipe out the nobodies down on the flats.

You can't say when the wars started in Burma—because they never stopped. The Burmese fought the Mongols (and lost), fought the Chinese (won a few, lost a few), and even got invaded by the Sri Lankans. If you don't think that's weird, have another look at your map and see where Burma and Sri Lanka are. The Sri Lankans managed to burn the Burmese capital to the ground in spite of the fact that most of their fleet got lost trying to cross the Indian Ocean. In the late nineteenth century, the British invaded Burma, so as not to be left out of the fun. They burned the capital down again, messed the place up like they usually do, and then wanted the Burmese to turn into loyal Limeys when the Japanese tried invading India through Burma in 1941.

The Burmese weren't buying that, and started an anti-Brit, pro-Jap guerrilla group led by a guy who renamed himself Ne Win, which supposedly means "bright as the sun." (Sounds more like "no-win" to me, but nobody asked me.) The Japs occupied the country from 1941 to 1944 and the Japanese Imperial Army did its usual job of turning friends into enemies. Ne Win and his comrades, hunkering down in the jungle, decided that even the Brits were better than these crazy Japs. When the Brits turned the Japanese back at the battle of Kohima in 1944, and pushed them out of Burma, Ne Win's BIA (Burma Independence Army) helped out. In fact, Ne Win did everything right in the last two years of WW II. He ended up with an army strong enough to convince the Brits to leave peacefully, and fast, in 1948.

After he and the BIA took over, there were parades, everybody cheered, and everything went to Hell like it always did in these Third World guerrilla dictatorships. Like every other tropical big guy, Ne Win went from smart guerrilla leader to total loony. From 1948 on, he shared the top job with some other army brass, but in 1962, he staged a coup and became uno. That's when these dictators get really weird, and Ne Win lived up to the stereotype. He had the Burmese currency issued in denominations of 45 and 90, because 9 was his lucky number. He took baths in dolphin's blood because some witch doctor told him it would help him handle the royal concubines better. He tried to turn the place into a quiet farm country, banning all foreign influence—sort of like a soft-core Pol Pot. Naturally, all that happened was that Burma ended up poor, isolated, and pissed off.

Meanwhile, all this "national liberation" talk sifted down to the other tribes, and they started thinking about liberation from the Burmese. In the South, there was a long, slow, bloody war between the Karen tribe and the Burmese Army. The Karen had a lot of handicaps, starting with the fact that their tribe has a girl's name. They're a small tribe, about 6 percent of the population, with no weapons or allies. But the army managed to piss them off enough to start fighting. Naturally, they used the national-liberation tag to name their little club: the Karen National Liberation Army (KNLA). Because the Karen are mostly Christian, and the Burmese mostly Buddhist, it was sort of a religious war. The KNLA was never strong enough to fight the Burmese Army openly, so it slunk around a strip of jungle on the Thai border, moving from one side of the border to the other to keep the heat off.

The other tribal rebels, the Shan (8 percent of the population), live in northeastern Burma and grow a little opium. More than a little, in fact. The Burmese Army doesn't like that—it wants to corner the opium market for itself.

Up in the northwest, where Burma meets India, there's another slow bush war between the Nagas and the Burmese and Indian Armies. The Nagas are classic hill-tribe material: They slink around the little bits of jungle still left and try to live the old ways. Since they started fighting in 1954, two hundred thousand people died in this war, and nobody even heard of it. The war in India finally ended recently, when a new Indian government actually bothered to notice the Nagas. Turned out that this was about all they wanted, and the conflict was settled fast.

Nothing that sensible is going to happen in Burma. When Ne Win finally resigned in 1988, Burmese students rioted out of sheer relief. They thought things would get better fast. Instead, Ne Win's comrades killed thousands of students. By the time Ne Win died in 2002, this bunch of shadowy generals was in complete control.

They call themselves the State Law and Order Restoration Council, the kind of really boring name Southeast Asian groups pick. It's a real Southeast Asian thing, keeping everything quiet and staying out of the spotlight. Pol Pot wouldn't even let people take pictures of him.

The only political celebrity in Burma is the famous dissident lady, Aung San Suu Kyi. Like a lot of Third World heroines (Megawati, Benazir Bhutto, Indira Gandhi), she comes from a big political family. She's had it easy so far, under house arrest. Before she was freed (May 2002), all she had to do was stay home and look pitiful. Now, everybody's expecting her to sweep in and turn Burma into a happy land full of strip malls and SUVs. But the more you look at the history of the place, the less likely that looks.

And you know what? The world doesn't need another Fresno. Believe me.

ACEH VS. THE BORG

WELL, WE'VE GOT a real hot war going. The only trouble is, it's another bush war in a tropical hellhole. Even the name of the place is annoying. It's spelled *Aceh*, but pronounced "Ah-che," like a commie sighing over Che Guevara.

Worst of all, it's in Indonesia.

Indonesia is one of those places that don't make sense, never did make sense, and never will. It doesn't even have a shape. You could probably draw the outline of the United States with your eyes closed: a big wedge wider at the top, and Florida flopping at the bottom right. Same with Mexico: a long triangle twisting southeast. OK, so try drawing Indonesia.

Indonesia doesn't have a shape. It's a bunch of islands that don't have much in common beyond hot weather and spiders the size of dinner plates.

You always hear it's the biggest Islamic country in the world, which is true, but Indonesia also has a lot of Christians, like the East Timorese, and even Hindus (on Bali). And like I keep saying, no matter what your social studies teacher told you, it's *not* normal for "people of different faiths to get along and respect each other." What's normal, everywhere in the world, is for people of different faiths to spend Friday nights sharpening up their machetes and taking a few practice swings with Dad's crowbar so they can go trash the "people of different faiths" on the other side of town on the weekend. And maybe, if they get lucky, steal a sofa or a Samsung VCR from the richer crosstown infidels.

That's what was happening in East Timor. The locals were Christian—picked it up from the Portuguese who'd occupied the place for hundreds of years. The Indonesian Army (TNI) doesn't like Christians much (which is cool with me—I don't, either), and it doesn't like people whining about not wanting to be part of Indonesia anymore. So it killed a few hundred thousand Timorese to show the locals the benefits of being Indonesian. And the damn ungrateful Timorese still opted out. This is the kind of bad-mannered behavior that pisses off TNI no end.

And now it's happening in Aceh. The Acehnese are turning their backs on the glory of being Indonesian and saying they want out. But in Aceh's case, it's not about religion. The Acehnese are as Islamic as the next guy, maybe more. In fact, one of the things that got them so mad is that it was the Acehnese who did the fighting and dying when the Islamists were trying to "Islamicize" Indonesia back in the 1950s—you know, before it was cool to be a Talib. And now the Islamists in power in Jakarta are trying to stomp on Aceh.

The Acehnese are the ones who brought Islam to the whole country, in fact. If you look at the map, you'll see that Aceh is on the northern tip of Sumatra. It's the natural gateway from the Indian Ocean, and that's how Islam arrived.

Aceh was also one of the last places to fall to the Europeans in the 1800s. When all the rest of Indonesia was already under Dutch control, Aceh was independent. The Dutch finally invaded in 1873, but it wasn't till 1912 or so that they stomped out the last Acehnese resistance. And in the process, the Dutch lost ten thousand soldiers. Not a bad record for natives with flintlocks fighting a modern European army.

(You have to remember this was when the Dutch still had guts. For a tiny country, they used to be pretty tough. Fought the Spanish, the British, the French—and actually won a few along the way. They weren't the sad hippie bastards they are today.)

So the Acehnese have a lot of pride. They don't like being bossed around by other Indonesians any more than they liked being shoved around by the Dutch. And that's what's happening: the Javanese trying to boss the rest of Indonesia. It's Java that actually runs the country. The bigger chunks of land like Irian Jaya, Borneo, and Sumatra have zero power or influence. That one little pimple, Java, runs the whole three-thousand-island mess (if you can say that anybody runs it).

Java is the most densely populated island this side of Singapore. And the Javanese are like the Borg from *Star Trek*: They want to take over everything. Since the Javanese don't believe in birth control, they've got one of the highest birth rates in the world. They send the surplus kids out to the other islands to make sure the rest of Indonesia gets more and more Javanese every generation. By now, some islands in Indonesia are more than half Javanese, even though fifty years ago, the locals would have never even seen a Javanese.

This is one of the things that pisses off the locals in Aceh. They say the Javanese are taking over the fishing villages on the coast and the rice-growing fields on the hills. Which leaves the Aceh folks with exactly nothing. They feel like trespassers in their own country. Since rice and fish are all they eat, they can't have dinner without paying some Javanese invader.

It's not just rice and fish, either. Aceh has some of the richest natural-gas fields in Indonesia, and the locals say it's been an all-Javanese operation from the get-go. The Javanese who run the Indonesian government make a deal with ExxonMobil and send over Javanese hard-hats to build the gas rigs. My dad was a spot welder, so I can testify there's a whooole lotta money in laying and welding gas pipe. And all that money goes to the Javanese—just like all the gas money they get from ExxonMobil (well, a lot of that goes to ExxonMobil's shareholders, too, but you already knew that).

And the biggest sleazes are the officer corps of TNI, the Indonesian Army. TNI likes having a few bush wars going. It helps the officers' careers and makes truckloads of cash for the army.

Like any standing army, TNI has an officer corps eager for promotion. And the best way to get it is to be transferred to someplace like Aceh, or Irian Jaya, where the locals are rebelling. You're not really at much risk of getting shot, because the guerrillas are hopelessly outgunned, but you can get a big body count and a promotion. So troops stationed in Aceh have good reason to kill as many locals as they can.

There's also a lot of money in it.

The Indonesian government only gives the army about one-fourth of the money it needs. It's up to the army to go out and get the rest. So every last man in the TNI, from general down to private, is looking for a better deal. ExxonMobil pays TNI millions in protection money for its gas fields. That goes straight into the generals' pockets. The lower you go in the table of ranks, the smaller the grift. A major might shake down a Chinese merchant (Indonesian Muslims hate Chinese like poison). A private might have to settle for "searching" a few huts and taking anything he can drag back to the armored personnel carrier.

It stands to reason, if you want to keep the protection money coming in, there has to be something you're "protecting" your customers from. That's why TNI likes having low-level insurgencies popping up here and there—like in Aceh. It gives the army a reason to stay in power.

And it needs that, because ever since Indonesia's big crash in 1998, TNI has been on thin ice. First the Javanese themselves rioted against Suharto and his army cronies; then the word finally got out on all the horrible shit TNI was doing in East Timor. People started asking why Indonesia needs this big, corrupt, incompetent bunch of thugs in the first place.

TNI doesn't like questions. It's used to running the country. It's been doing so since 1965. Not many people remember it now, but the first big "Islamist" rebellion happened in Indonesia in 1965. Sukarno, the Pinko dictator who ran the country, was getting a little too Pinko to suit the army or the CIA (which has always been real, real close to TNI). So with CIA help, the army started agitating garrisons all around the country to kill any commies it could find. The army stirred up the civilians, too, about how the commies were going to abolish religion.

In a few months, the PKI (Indonesian Communist Party) was wiped out. I mean wiped out. Nobody is sure of the casualty figures, but the best guesses are around five hundred thousand people. Some were commies, some were pesky neighbors ("I'll teach you to play that jungle music on a work night, you bastard!"), and some just had furniture somebody coveted ("I want that sofa, you commie, you!").

From 1965 to the late 1990s, Suharto fronted for the army, and everybody was happy—everybody in Langley, that is. But when the

USSR went under, it got harder to pretend that every time TNI wiped out a village, it was fighting communism. Then the mass graves in East Timor started getting shown on the U.S. evening news, and life got even harder for the TNI brass.

Now TNI is stuck. The only way these army guys know how to do counterinsurgency is the old, sloppy way: Surround a village, shoot anyone on the known-rebel list, torture the kids to get more names, rape the women and girls, burn the school, and leave with a stern warning that next time, they won't be so nice.

To be honest, that's how counterinsurgency warfare works everywhere. But it's not pretty and sure doesn't make good TV. Now that everybody and his dog's got a video camera, it's tougher to do things the good ol' way.

That's what's been happening in Aceh: real old-school counterinsurgency blood 'n' guts. Literally old school: TNI seems to be specializing in burning schools. It has burned down almost every school in Aceh. It has taken a lot of men and boys out of the villages and shot them. No doubt the army used standard TNI interrogation methods to get more names: beatings with rifle butts, electric shock on a wire stuck into your penis hole, that kind of thing.

Meanwhile, the rebels, GAM (for the group's Indonesian name, Gerakan Aceh Merdeka), have laid low. That's standard guerrilla warfare, too: When the army comes in hard, you vanish. This means you let your own people get terrorized by the troops. Like I said, it ain't pretty, but it's the way things are done. From GAM's way of looking at it, TNI is doing a great job of recruiting more GAM soldiers. Every time TNI shoots somebody, his brother volunteers to join GAM.

Nobody's sure how many men GAM has, but most estimates say five thousand at least. That's pretty big for a guerrilla force, but I hear they're not very good soldiers yet. They do small ambushes mostly, and kill maybe ten TNI soldiers per month. But they do have what every guerrilla group needs more than guns: a good network of informers all over the province. A guerrilla war is about intelligence, not so much combat. That's why TNI raids villages: to get information. And that's why GAM doesn't defend the villages: It doesn't want battles; it wants the locals even more pissed off at TNI, so they'll become informers for GAM.

The trouble is, wars like this turn into long stalemates real easy. This could go on for twenty, thirty years. TNI officers will stage a few offensives, brag about the body count, and go back home to Java with a medal and some loot. Then GAM will play up the locals' anger, recruit some more guerrillas, and ambush a few dumb privates who don't even know where they are. That's the way it goes, and it can go on like that forever.

East Timor would still be bleeding if the UN hadn't finally stepped in. What happens next on Aceh doesn't depend on the locals or the TNI. It'll be decided by what happens in the rest of Indonesia—especially if the other rebellions get hot—and what's decided in Washington and in the UN. Until something big and dramatic happens far away, this will drag on, a nice little war that makes a few TNI officers rich and a whole lot of villagers dead.

And not one damn battle worth filming.

SRI LANKA:
TERRORISTS WITH AN AIR FORCE

POP QUIZ: Who were the first suicide bombers?

It's sort of a trick question. Depends on the style of suicide you're talking about. If you count kamikazes, then the Japanese air force gets the honor, if it is one. If you mean vehicular mass-manslaughter—guys in trucks or cars bumping over the curb to double park 'n' explode outside U.S. embassies, then the real trendsetters were the Shiites who drove their truck into American, French, and Israeli bases in Lebanon in the early 1980s.

But if you're talking about simple pedestrian suicide bombers, the kind who stroll around wearing those fashionable TNT vests, the ones who drift into fast-food strip malls in Jerusalem and pull their instant-hamburger string . . . well, it's pretty clear who gets the credit. That distinction goes to those underrated killers, the Liberation Tigers of Tamil Eelam, or LTTE for short. The LTTE did its first walking suicide bomb in 1987, killing forty-odd government soldiers in some hellhole called Nelliyadi.

Nobody's heard of the LTTE. I'm not sure why. It's big enough, and lethal enough, to deserve more coverage. Maybe it's because most of the people I see around Fresno are too damn stupid to even know where Sri Lanka is, never mind figuring out who's fighting who over there. I have to interrupt myself here to curse out Fresno a little.

You know, when it's cool and rainy, I can almost stand the place. But the heat—I just can't take it. It's bad enough being fat in cool weather, but when the heat comes on, it's fat people who suffer the worst. Sweating all the time, folds and wads of greasy skin. You make yourself sick. I make myself sick. Every store window you go past turns into a mirror, and you see yourself waddling by like a jerk in that stupid white acrylic XXL dress shirt, with the tie choking your fat red throat, big armpit stains—and skinny joggers go by and they're not even sweating.

But it's not just me. I swear to God, everybody in Fresno gets about twenty IQ points stupider as soon as the hot weather starts. Yesterday, I spent forty minutes trying to get home, just sweating onto the plastic car seat. I'm ready to kill somebody and I look around—everybody's sitting there all patiently, listening to Christian pop on the radio and humming along. Bunch of smiley-face morons.

Then I look past the cars, and right where the tract homes stop, it's nothing but desert. Like a line: one side housing, other side wasteland. I start realizing, Nobody should be living here. It's worse than a desert. At least a desert has some integrity. A desert you could respect. Fresno doesn't even make it as a desert. It gets about five lousy inches of rain a year, just enough to keep us out of desert rating. It's "semiarid." No class at all.

That's why I get all enthused about being a war nerd in the summer. The hotter it gets, the more I want to hear about war and death, and the bigger the better. That's why Sri Lanka sounds good to me right now. It's a good, big war and went on for a good, long time. Good graphics, too—like the shot of a guy's head all by itself on the ground, looking happy.

Sri Lanka's one of those tropical hellholes that changed its name when the Brits left. People used to call it Ceylon—like the tea—but I guess Sri Lanka sounds like fireworks and apple pie to the local crowd. Ceylon or Sri Whatever is a little droplet-shaped island off the southeast tip of India. And it's one of those wonderful multi-ethnic countries where people spend most of their time killing each other. The players here are the Sinhalese, who are maybe two-thirds of the population, and the Tamils, who are the other third. The Sinhalese hang out in the south and west of the island, and the Tamils stick to the northeast. The Sinhalese are Buddhists, the Tamils are Hindus.

The Brits did their best to fuck the place up, naturally. They picked the Tamils to be their little helpers, which made the Sinhalese majority hate the Tamils more than they already did. Naturally, when the Brits pulled out in 1948, the Sinhalese jumped at the chance for some payback. They made Sinhala the official language and stomped on the Tamils every way they could. The Tamils started getting pissed off. The LTTE was founded in 1976 with the goal of setting up a separate Tamil state in the northeast of the island, and by the late 1980s, the Tigers had a booming business in suicide bombers.

One of the theories on why the Tamil were so good at suicide bombing was that Hindus just don't mind dying that much, since they expect to be back, reincarnated as a Malibu baby, real soon. That sounds like bullshit to me. Fact is, nobody minds dying till it happens to them. Nothing easier than getting high-schoolage idiots to put on a uniform and walk into bullets—doesn't matter whether they're Muslims or Hindus or Baptists.

But Buddhists . . . that's different. Funny thing about Buddhists. They've been losing out all over the world. It's too bad, too. If I had to respect any religion, it'd be theirs. For starters, their God is a fat guy. I like that. And they're quiet, at least. The Sinhalese are the only Buddhist-majority tribe in India. The Tamils, though, they've got lots of relatives in South India, where there are hundreds of millions of other Tamils. And lots of these mainlanders send money to the LTTE to buy bombs and guns to help "liberate" their "homeland" in the north and east of the island. Too many Tamils and not enough tigers. There's not a single actual four-legged tiger left in Sri Lanka.

It's like the California grizzly: They put it on the state flag right around the time they wiped out the whole species. I'd trade the whole population of Fresno to have a few grizzlies wandering around the Sierras.

But the population of Sri Lanka doubled in just thirty-five years, and they wiped out the tigers. Now the only tigers are the Tigers in camo fatigues who prowled around the island ambushing government troops from the early 1980s to the truce of February 2002.

That's twenty years of war. Something like sixty thousand dead and a lot more hurt, blinded, or maimed. Big doin's—till you remember the population doubled in one generation. The higher the birthrate, the easier it is to write off five-digit casualty figures.

The LTTE has a huge pool to draw from. It gets a dozen volunteers for every soldier it takes. Even so, the Tigers are huge by guerrilla standards. They've got at least seven thousand soldiers and fifteen thousand full-time civilian auxiliaries.

But that's not the most amazing part. What blows me away is that they've got an air force. No kidding, they're the only guerrilla army in the world with an air force. It's not much, a few helicopters and some prop planes, but it still counts. Kinda reminds me of an old joke you get on Web sites about terrorism:

Q: How do you define terrorism?

A: Violence by people who don't have an air force.

They've got a navy, too, and this one's for real, medium-sized by world standards and world-class in terms of morale. Called the Sea Tigers, they've got at least two thousand people. They've got a dozen fully armed freighters, hundreds of small fiberglass boats with tiny radar signatures, and a special frogman squad.

You get the feeling these guys are serious? Well, this is how serious they are: They've got a tank brigade of their own. About a dozen T-55s. OK, that's a pretty old tank, but it's a damn good one. Imagine going up against a couple of them if you were a Sri Lankan army patrol with nothing but rifles. If you're a 'Nam war fan, you might remember that one thing that small U.S. units strung out in the jungle feared most of all was the NVA coming in with tanks. Which happened a few times, wiping out several small U.S. outposts. You just don't expect the guerrillas to come in with heavy armor, so it can be devastating when they do.

One more little indication that these guys don't play around: Every Tamil Tiger carries a cyanide capsule into battle. You're supposed to take it if you're captured—and these guys actually do. There's only two armies I know if in the world where they actually use cyanide capsules: the Tamil Tigers and the North Korean People's Army. That's some serious company to be keeping.

Up against the Tigers is the Sri Lankan Army. It's nothing special. On paper, it's bigger: 150,000 troops, seventy main battle tanks, five hundred armored personnel carriers (a weird mix of M113s and BMPs), a decent-size navy, and a small air force. The tanks are mostly T-55s, which means the army doesn't even have a technological edge in tank battles against the Tigers.

The air force uses a sad Argentine CI ground-attack plane called the Pucara. The Pucara had a pretty sorry record in the Falklands War: Every Pucara the Argentines had was either shot down, destroyed on the ground, or captured. In exchange, the entire fleet of Pucaras shot down ... one British helicopter. I bet those Tamils are just quakin' in their boots every time they hear those heavy-duty Argentine engines getting closer.

The mainline fighter is the Kfir, a weird hybrid Israeli design. Basically, the Israelis stole everything they could from the Mirage, then stole the rest from U.S. designers, and called the result a new Israeli-produced fighter, the Kfir ("Lion" in Hebrew). It's the sort of big steal the Israelis seem to get away with time after time, and it's made them a lot of money in sales to Third World air forces.

But the air force can't win a CI war. Vietnam proved that pretty damn clearly. It's the morale of the army that makes or breaks a CI campaign, and the Sri Lankan Army ... well, it's not the worst, but it's not the best, either. The war was mostly fought on the Tamils' terms, with the army just trying to keep up.

The Tamils started ambushing army patrols around Jaffna, their key city, in 1983. By 1987, the Indian Army landed and pretty much forced the Tigers to sign a peace deal. The Tigers decided that they were better off not trying to fight the Indian Army, so they signed. The Indians, who knew they'd gotten into a real bad mess, paddled home before the ink was dry on the peace treaty. The Tamils only waited till the Indian Army sailed home before restarting the war.

This was their high point: the early 1990s. They did a classic bit of power projection across the straits by assassinating Rajiv Gandhi in 1991, just when he was about to become prime minister of India, because they didn't like his anti-Tiger policies. Just to keep things fair and not show any favoritism, they also assassinated the prime minister of Sri Lanka in 1993.

The Sri Lankan Army had its best moment when it captured Jaffna in 1995. This wasn't guerrilla warfare; it was classic, massed armor attack against fortified positions. The United States had a hundred-odd military advisers helping the Sri Lankan Army by this time, and it showed. But the Tigers are cold-blooded, flexible fighters. Once they realized they'd lost the conventional war, they went back to unconventional warfare, setting off suicide bombs in the Sinhalese cities down south and ambushing army patrols. Soon the Tigers had the army bottled up in the Jaffna peninsula and were pressuring the army's supply lines all the way down the island. In 1996, they set off one of the bloodiest single terrorist attacks in history, a huge truck bomb they drove right into the Central Bank in Colombo. At least a hundred people died, and fifteen hundred were injured. Worse yet, these casualties were rich people! Solvent! People who mattered! This was the kind of thing that made your ordinary Sri Lankan real tired of the whole damn war.

By 2002, even the Tigers were tired. They couldn't destroy the army, and the army sure as Hell hadn't destroyed them. The Indians were getting tired of taking care of a half-million Sri Lankan refugees, the CIA wanted the whole mess done with so it could focus on not finding Osama, and there was a new peacenik administration in power in Sri Lanka. All around the world, guerrilla ethnic armies were winding down and switching to politics. The Tamils saw the way things were going and got the best deal they could.

From that time until 2005, it had been a lot of yelling and walk-outs, but not war. Not yet. But groups like the Tigers think in terms of decades, not months. They're committed to the long-war theory, just like the VC were. In this strategy, peace is just a break between rounds.

SRI LANKA:
THE BIG HATE MO'

JUST LIKE I had predicted, the war in Sri Lanka flared in late 2005. At least the participants got it on again with an enter-taining premiere series of battles. Instead of the usual boring ambush intro, the main Tamil guerrilla force, the LTTE, staged a big comeback extravaganza in a harbor near Jaffna, at the northern tip of the island. The Tigers sent up to twenty small vessels full speed ahead toward a Sri Lankan naval patrol.

You'll recall the LTTE ranks as maybe the only guerrilla force in the world with its own air force and navy. Its air power is nothing much, but the navy, the Sea Tigers, is another matter. This group is serious. In line with the Tamils' proud heritage of kamikaze attacks, the Sea Tigers launched several of their suicide boats—little one-man speedboats with a nose full of high explosives.

This time, though, it looks like the Sri Lankan gunners were ready for them. If you believe the official version, it was one of those live video games, with machine gunners on the naval patrol boats lighting up the Tamil attackers, killing "up to one hundred" Tigers and sinking "up to twelve" of their boats.

Come to think of it, the wording of these stories is more important than the fuzzy, fake numbers they list. So here's a typical story, written on September 2, 2006, and describing that engagement. As part of your war-nerd training, I'm gonna ask you to read it and see what you make of it.

Accounts Differ in Sri Lankan Sea Battle

COLOMBO, SRI LANKA (UPI)–Sri Lanka's military says it sank a dozen Tamil Tiger rebel boats in an all-night sea battle Saturday off the northern Jaffna peninsula.

The Navy said about 80 Tigers were killed in the fighting that began with a rebel attack near Kankesantuari harbor while government forces suffered only two wounded, the British Broadcasting Corp. reported. However, the pro-Tamil Tiger Web site TamilNet said two Navy fast attack craft were sunk and another damaged. Its sources said about 30 government sailors were missing. The two sides have been in conflict on the peninsula for the past month, but neither side has officially withdrawn from a 2002 truce.

The key phrase here is in the headline: "Accounts differ." Ain't that the truth. In fact, that's why war-nerding isn't as easy as it looks. A true war nerd has to sift through mounds of PR from all sides, as well as their lackey outlets in the mainstream media, to get any sense of what's really going on. Whose version of this battle do you believe? If this is the first and only story you've read about this war, then you've got no hope. The best you can do is look at the news agency that filed it. In this case, it's a UPI story. UPI is an American service (now owned by the Moonie empire), and America doesn't care one way or the other about Sri Lanka (although we have loaned training officers to the Sri Lankan Army).

That's good, because it means the hack who wrote the story doesn't have an axe to grind here. It's different when you're reading American reporters' stories from wars we've got a stake in, like Iraq or Afghanistan. Whenever you read AP, Reuters, or UPI stories from there, take any claims of victory over the locals with about two tons of salt. Same thing when you read British news-agency stories out of Ulster or Basra, or Colombian army claims about FARC casualties: Just assume the body counts are inflated and at least half the "victories" never happened.

But here, thanks to the fact that U and I and UPI couldn't care less how many Ceylonese rub each other out, you don't have to factor in the writer's—or the editor's—favoritism. All you have to do is choose between the versions from the two sides: the Sri Lankan navy and the Sea Tigers.

First clue: The navy is crowing louder and claiming a bigger victory than the Tamils are. (The navy claims it killed eighty Tamils and sank twelve Tamil boats, whereas the Tamils are only claiming two Sri Lankan navy boats sunk and thirty sailors killed). So it's likely—not sure, just a good hunch here—that the navy came out ahead in this one. Especially because if you read that story carefully, you get the impression the navy broadcast its version whereas the Tamils just responded on their Web site, like they'd prefer not to talk about this rumble on the sea at all. Still, you should just lop off about half of the navy's claimed numbers, so figure it actually sank six Tamil boats and killed maybe forty insurgents.

Decent numbers for these days. We don't get Stalingrads anymore, folks, and we hardly ever get naval battles at all, so be grateful.

We also don't get nice, crisp starts and endings to wars anymore. That seems to bother a lot of people, because several readers wrote me asking why the peace treaty in Sri Lanka between the government and the Tamil Tigers broke down. That's like asking why a Yugo breaks down. It breaks down because that's what Yugos *do*. Like I said earlier, these treaties between governments and guerrilla armies are just a time-out, not the end of the game. Usually, neither side expects the treaties to last, or even wants them to. In fact, the only suckers gullible enough to think they're really solving the problem are the do-gooder Jimmy Carters and Scandinavian diplomats who broker the treaties.

In Sri Lanka, it was the Norwegians who dragged the Tamil guerrillas and Sinhalese government to the table and got them to sign on the olive-branch line. I guess that's what Norwegians do now that going a-Viking ain't an option: Sail the seven seas ruthlessly imposing peace treaties with a half-life shorter than some subatomic particles. I bet the Sri Lankans went screaming, fleeing for the hills, when they sighted the dreaded Norwegian banner flying from the mast of some biodiesel-powered Greenpeace frigate carrying Norwegian mediators into the harbor. "Help! Foreign invaders trying to impose peace!"

Eventually, though, feuding tribes like the Tamil and Sinhalese figure out they've got nothing to fear from signing the pieces of paper these blond busybodies shove in front of them, because the EU's guilt-ridden bureaucrats will shovel money at you if you go through the peacemaking motions for the press.

Before the ink is dry on the treaty, you've got Airbuses full of rice and penicillin darkening the skies. All for free, or rather for profit, because the locals never see any of it. It goes straight into the carefully guarded warehouses of the guerrillas' wholesale operations. Every guerrilla movement that lasts past its first manifesto has some very cool heads running things behind the scenes. And the most carefully run, orderly places in the country, sometimes the *only* spick-and-span interiors in town, are the secret storage depots where the movement keeps all its donated food, meds, and weapons.

There's another reason these treaties don't last: hate momentum. That's what I call it, anyway. See, people have the wrong idea; they think violence starts when the insurgents set off their first bomb. It doesn't work that way. That's just when the violence first makes the press. There was *always* violence in these places, lots of violence. But as long as the government is strong enough to dish it out, nobody notices. When the people getting zapped nonstop suddenly start zapping back, suddenly it's a man-bites-dog story, a big turn-around, and every TV channel in the world is on the story.

Take a look at the way The Hate between Sinhalese and Tamils built up in Sri Lanka. The Sinhalese owned the island till the Brits decided they wanted cheaper, more docile laborers running their tea plantations. Boom, the British ship over hordes of Tamil slaves from Southern India. The Brits also make the Tamil their teacher's pets, putting them in charge of running the lower levels of the colonial admin.

Naturally, this pisses off the Sinhalese no end, so when the Brits leave, the Sinhalese start taking every kind of small-time revenge they can, like making their language the only legal one, booting Tamils out of their Brit-designed jobs, and yelling "Tamil, Tamil, smells like a camel" when their opponents go by. (OK, I made that one up, but I'll bet there's some playground rhyme a lot like it in Sri Lanka.)

The Tamils' hate boiled over in the 1980s, when the LTTE started up its suicide bombings and ambushes. Naturally, the Sinhalese responded with artillery and air attacks, and naturally, most of the casualties were civvies. They always are. The kill radius of a 155-mm shell is huge, and it's kids and old folks who are the worst at dodging, so they die sooner. And picking up the shredded remains of your sister or cousin makes you an easy mark for the next guerrilla recruiter who comes a-knockin' at your door. So you walk into a bank in Colombo, blow yourself up, and kill somebody's uncle, and he orders an air strike on your home village, and so on and so on. That's momentum. In fact, you could say tribal hate is the only real perpetual motion machine that works.

Funny how many islands around the world have this kind of hate because of the Brits' habit of importing Indian laborers, pissing off the locals, and then picking up and leaving. Take Fiji. The Fijians were happy enough chewing kava and eating anybody who got ship-wrecked on their lovely beaches till Queen Victoria decided they needed to put on more clothes, switch from long pork to mutton, and get out of the way while the Brits imported tens of thousands of Indian cane-choppers who'd work for next to nothing. Well, the Indians didn't have much to do after hours except breed, which they did so well that now Fiji is almost fifty-fifty divided between Fijians and Indians. That's why you hear about coups there every couple weeks. It's all thanks to the Brits' appetite for cheap labor. This was before outsourcing, y'see, so they physically had to drag the Indians to wherever they could underbid the local labor force.

It takes a long time for the hate momentum to build between the imports and the domestics. And the dominant tribe is always totally shocked when the underdogs finally get it together enough to strike back. The Tamils got walked on for years before they organized. Blacks in the United States didn't start hitting back till the 1960s; till then, "race riots" were whites hunting blacks in the cities. Even though they'd been stomped on for centuries, the Catholics in Ulster didn't hit back till they saw the footage from Watts and Detroit. The Israelis walked on the Palestinians and laughed at their feeble little PLO, till the second-generation insurgents like Hamas and Islamic Jihad started playing for keeps.

It's always the same story: It's not "violence" until somebody hits you back. Till then, you don't notice your guys hitting the other tribe. That's just normal background noise. It takes blood, buckets of it, to get a person's attention. And not just anybody's blood—it's gotta be your own, or that of a close relative. Otherwise it's just spots on the sidewalk.

KARGIL:
WAR AS ICE CAPADES

SOME GUY IN India once asked me to write about the 1999 Indo-Pakistani fighting in Kargil, a patch of high-altitude ice in Kashmir at the northern tip of the subcontinent. This is some of the most worthless yet fought-over ground in the world, up where the borders between Pakistan, India, and China smear together like the middle of a pie sliced by a spastic. Pakistan lost the conventional fight for Kashmir in the three Indo-Pakistani wars, and now mostly sticks to funding the thirty-odd militias fighting to eject India, but there have been a few small, conventional battles. The Kargil border battle was the biggest, but as I recalled, it ended in a stalemate—a few hundred dead on either side and no real change in the border.

It didn't seem like much to work with, but he promised me there was some pretty intense fighting, "even hand-to-hand combat!" I don't know why people think hand-to-hand combat is so wonderful. It's usually a sign that something has gone way wrong in the plan. The whole idea is to destroy the enemy before he gets close enough to grapple with you. And hand-to-hand fighting eighteen thousand feet up in the Himalayas makes me tired just thinking about it. It must've been some pretty slow-motion combat, like Tom and Jerry on valium. Lunge, take a five-minute breathing break, lunge again.

At that altitude, nothing works the way it's supposed to. Kargil was the only time two modern armies fought at such an insane altitude. Both armies had to use specially modified helicopters to ferry supplies, because normal models won't fly in that thin air. Artillery ranges were all messed up too, because standard trajectory calculations didn't hold. Shells flew much further than they were supposed to—no wind resistance. Humans don't work too well at eighteen thousand feet, either; guys on both sides were falling over with altitude sickness and frostbite before they even made it to the front.

In most other ways, Kargil was a classic example of why war these days is so frustrating to watch. Instead of India and Pakistan slugging it out with all their strength down on the flat, they settled for this little sideshow in terrain that made large-scale warfare impossible.

Actually, that's why they fought in Kargil: because they knew it was small-time and would stay small-time. By 1999, India and Pakistan both had nuclear weapons. Remember how overcautious those weapons made us and the Russians in the Cold War? Well, it had the same effect on the subcontinentals. Neither country is really all that eager to find out how itchy the other side's button-pressing finger is.

The Pakistanis still want Kashmir back from the Indians—it's a Muslim region, so they figure it's rightfully theirs—but they want to take it in an indirect, deniable way. So the Pakistani intelligence service, the ISI, came up with the idea of infiltrating some "volunteers"—a mix of Kashmiri, Afghan, and Pakistani Islamists—into the heights of Kargil during the long winter. At that time of year, the Indian troops in Northern Kashmir hunker down in their bases and try to eat enough vindaloo to stay warm.

The Indian Army didn't even notice the enemy trenches overlooking them till May 1999, when they started digging their bunkers out from under the snow. Indian scouts—Get it? "Indian scouts"?—noticed that there were enemy infiltrators dug in along a ridgeline on their side of the Line of Control, the border between them and the Pakistanis.

The Indians decided to deal with the problem the sensible way: with air power. Unlike helicopters, jets love high altitudes and the Indian pilots were dying to fly their MiGs against live targets.

That didn't work out too well. The infiltrators used shoulder-fired SAMs to shoot down both a MiG-27 and then the MiG-21 that the Indian Air Force had sent to find out what had happened to the MiG-27. Why you'd send a clunker like the MiG 21-out after a better plane like the MiG-27, I don't know, but they did. Score so far: Infiltrators 2, Indians 0.

One of the most important lessons of this weird little campaign is that even a small infantry force can defend itself against air attack if it's equipped with good SAMs. And somebody (meaning the ISI) had provided the infiltrators with some very good SAMs. I can't help wondering if they were Stingers, because we handed over a whole lot of these top-of-the-line American shoulder-fired SAMs to the Pakistanis back in the 1980s. The idea was they'd pass them on to the Afghans to use against Soviet Mi-24 choppers. And the Pakistanis did give some of them to the Afghans, and those Stingers were a big factor in defeating the Soviets in Afghanistan. There was just one little problem: When we tried to collect all the unfired Stingers after the war . . . well, we sorta couldn't account for a couple hundred of them. The CIA put up posters all over Afghanistan offering cash for any returned Stingers, but didn't get too many takers. I guess some Afghans decided they'd prefer to keep their surface-to-air capability. After all, if you want money, all you need to do is plant more opium poppies; but money can't buy a weapon as magical as a Stinger. And, of course, a lot of Stingers never made it to Afghanistan at all; the ISI kept them to pass on to its Islamic-militant friends for future use.

The infiltrators sent one shot-down pilot's body back to the Indians, but that only made the Indians angrier, because an autopsy showed the pilot hadn't died of injuries in the crash. He'd been shot twice, in the chest and head. The Indian press had a great time playing up that story, and the home folks started getting excited.

The Indian Army was still trying to figure out who was up on that ridgeline, and what they were going to do about it. Over the next few days, there were probes and counterprobes all along the Line of Control. Naturally, there were casualties on both sides—and when the Pakistanis handed back the Indian dead, the corpses were mutilated, eyes and penises missing.

At least that's the way the Indian newspapers told the story. Who knows if it's true. What we're dealing with here is good old war propaganda, and nothing gets the home folks excited like mutilated corpses. It goes all the way back to *The Iliad*, with Achilles dragging Hector's body around tied to the back bumper of his chariot.

Personally, I don't much care what they do with me once I'm cold meat. I'd much rather be mutilated dead than alive. If they had a donor card for corpse mutilation on your driver's license, I'd check the box every time. But for some reason, it drives people crazy seeing a body mistreated. When we ran from Somalia in 1992, it wasn't losing those eighteen men that upset people—it was those pictures of dead GIs being dragged in the dust. After days of probing and air strikes, the Indians finally sent their infantry up to push the intruders out. That's when most of that "hand-to-hand" stuff that filmmakers love happened.

Little wars like Kargil are actually better than a big war for stirring up nationalism back home. When a country is fighting for its life, people are more scared than proud. But as long as the war is a skirmish eighteen thousand feet up in the Himalayas, nobody has to be afraid. People can afford to puff out their chests and get all furious about atrocity stories.

And the Indian press pushed the Kargil story as hard as it could. India is a huge, messed-up country with more than a billion people speaking more languages than there are in all of Europe. You have to work damn hard to keep a place like that united, and the simplest way is to get them mad at somebody across the border. Kargil was like the Alamo for Indian propaganda—kind of a sacred last stand. If you want to see what I mean, have a look at a couple of Web sites I found dedicated to the "heroes" and "martyrs" who died in Kargil: www.angelfire.com/in2/kargil/ and www.kashmir-information.com/Heroes/.

If you read some of the tributes on these sites, stuff about "grim-jawed officers meeting the heroes' coffins," you'd think you were back in one of the great old European wars, before the Europeans got too cool and chickenshit to do patriotism:

> With unrelenting courage and fierce determination, [India's] brave soldiers are guarding the country from the enemy's clutches. Facing danger at every step and hostile weather conditions, they put their lives at risk. Forsaking the comforts of home and family life for a life of hardship and danger, it's their unwavering love for their motherland that spurs them on. This page is dedicated to the brave men of our soil who embrace danger and even death willingly for the sake of the country. This page is the tribute to their indomitable will, their stoic courage, and their intense love for nation . . . [The Kargil campaign] ended with pakistani army (cowards) and its foreign mercenaries FLUSHED OUT WITH HEAVY LOSSES!

I like the way the Web site guy put "cowards" in parentheses right after "pakistani army." Me being a writer myself, I can see that's his way of making sure the reader gets the point. He's also a fan of all-caps, to make sure you get the important bits, like "FLUSHED OUT."

Finding these Web sites really cheered me up, made me realize that just because one part of the world gets all cool and tired doesn't mean it's all over for everybody. Excitement just moves to a new part of the world. We're just starting the era of great national wars in the subcontinent. People there are not tired at all; they've got this big birthrate, a really patriotic press, an economy just heating up, lots of energy—all the ingredients.

There was even a hit film about Kargil in India, a Bollywood blockbuster called *LOC Kargil*. I got a real kick out of reading what the female lead, a woman named Esha Deol, said about being in the movie. If you want to know what all-out patriotism is, forget the poor Jawans (grunts) who died up on the ice, and just listen to her comment: "I would have worked on the film even if they'd only given me a two-minute role." Settling for a two-minute role—baby, that's real sacrifice.

Like most wars these days, Kargil just petered out. The infiltrators had the best of it at first. Indian intelligence had failed to give any warning. Well, that's what military intelligence does: fail. They should just drop the façade and call military intelligence the Department of "Whoops!"

By the time the Indian Army spotted them, the mysterious infiltrators were dug in on the high ground. Not a good position to be in, if you're the Indians—kind of like Bunker Hill, if it was on top of Mount Everest. Attacking uphill in air that thin, while the defenders shoot and shell you—man, that's my idea of Hell.

All things considered, the Indian Army did pretty well. It got aggressive, once it saw the threat, and forced the infiltrators to leave. The infiltrators who stayed died. So did about four hundred Indian troops. I haven't found a breakdown on causes of death, but I'd bet that the cold and lack of oxygen killed at least as many men as enemy fire did.

Once the skirmishing was over, the fight was on the propaganda front. The big question was how much the Pakistani Army had been involved. Naturally, the Pakistanis tried to claim it was all foreign militants who'd dug in on the heights in order to free Kashmir from Indian rule. Naturally, the Indians tried to prove that the whole Kargil war was a Pakistani Army operation from the get-go. And it was. It couldn't have happened without massive help from the Pakistani Army and, more importantly, from the ISI. There were never more than a thousand infiltrators on the heights, but it took tens of thousands of men to handle the logistics for a manned position in hostile terrain like that. The Pakistanis later admitted that one of their local units, the Northern Light Infantry, had crossed the Line of Control and helped the infiltrators, who were mostly locals and Pakistanis—the foreign militants were never more than 10 percent of the infiltrators.

In tactical terms, Kargil meant very little. The battlefield was one of the least-valuable bits of real estate on the planet. If it had fallen, nothing would have changed down on the hot flatlands, where the Indians and Pakistanis actually live.

But war these days isn't about tactical victory. It's about morale and propaganda. In those terms, Kargil was a huge, huge victory for India and a big defeat for Pakistan. It did more for Indian nationalism than cricket, and that's saying a lot. It's damn hard finding anything everybody in India can rally behind. Almost everything in India is the exclusive property of one particular tribe or religion or caste. Remember, India nearly tore itself apart in the early 1990s over whether the Muslims or the Hindus had a right to build a shrine on some extra-special piece of holy turf in Ayodhya.

And that's where losing four hundred men in a high-profile, harmless little war like Kargil comes in handy. Those Web sites I mentioned list the names of every single Indian soldier killed up there. When you consider how many Indians die every day, with nobody giving a damn at all, it's pretty amazing that these four hundred dead guys get so much adoring press.

When you look at the list of names, you see why. Some of the names are obviously Sikhs (Sikhs love armies), but there are plenty of Hindu names and Muslim names—for all I know, there are Zoroastrian names in there, too.

It's a chance to sob together over those dead integrated units—like those good old corny WW II movies where every platoon has this melting-pot roll call: "OK, lissen up, Bernstein, deNapoli, O'Brien, Kowalski, and Running Bear!" And naturally, the most harmless ethnic sidekick in the platoon gets killed and everybody cries, and feels patriotic. I haven't even seen the Bollywood movie they made out of Kargil, but I'm willing to bet it has a scene like that in it.

By losing four hundred men up there, where there are no mosques, Hindu temples, untouchables, or sacred cows, India got a huge nation-building boost at zero cost—a strategic victory out of a minor skirmish.

SOUTHERN THAILAND:
THE LONG GRIND

SOUTHEAST ASIA IS the new hot vacation spot for the ball-bearing backpack crowd. Not only did JI (Jamaah Islami, the Indonesia franchise of Al Qaeda) manage to hit Bali a second time, but the war in Southern Thailand is heating up enough to deserve a chapter. In 2005, the Southern Thailand death toll went into four figures—1,037 killed in action.

UPDATE: Whoops, better make that 1,042. Just now the rebels just killed five Thai Rangers in a classic drive-by shooting at a checkpoint on the Thai-Malaysian border.

UPPER-UPDATE. Whoops! Better double that number for 2007. Drive-by shootings and bombs placed in nightclubs and restaurants seem to be the insurgents' preferred techniques for many of the killings—you want to avoid intense exercise in that climate, so drive-bys are a natural.

A four-figure death toll is big-time these days. It's a sad commentary on the way the world is sliding into wimpery when a puny death toll like that rates a mention. Sixty years ago, they were killing that many men every few seconds on the Eastern Front. These days, we kill the way you piss when you've got kidney stones—a dribble, a lot of moaning and groaning, then another dribble. But hey, what can I do about it? I don't make the wars, I just try to enjoy them.

To enjoy a war like this, you have to lower your expectations. There ain't gonna be any Gettysburgs in this one. Like most of our pissant contemporary wars, it's not about military strategy or hardware, just tribal grudges rubbing against each other like those continental plates, grinding away and flaring up into a massacre now and then.

Southern Thailand is one of those places where ethnic plates are squeezing like the San Andreas Fault. Look at Thailand on a map, and you'll see it's like an apple with a worm dangling down from it. The big apple is the Thai heartland, the river valley where the ethnic Thais grow their rice. The worm dangling down from it is the Malay Peninsula. This insurgency is happening at the very bottom, at the Malay border. The insurgents are Malays, not Thais. Different culture, different religion—Muslims, not Buddhists like the Thais.

To understand Southeast Asian military history, you have to understand that in this part of the world, the key is controlling the fertile river valleys. That's where you can do intensive rice planting, so you can feed more people, meaning you end up with more soldiers.

The losing tribes get pushed away from the river, up into the dry hills, just like Burma (see "Burma: They Ain't Like Us"), which has the same pattern.

The longer the Thai kings were able to hold on to the river plains, the more armies they accumulated—just like holding Australia in Risk. They had to spend some of those armies defending Thailand against their traditional enemies, the Burmese, but the rest were used to push the Thai empire outward, into the northern mountains and south down the Malay Peninsula.

Thailand has been gobbling up little bits of borderland for centuries, like the French kings did in the Middle Ages. The Thais love stories about their kings fighting on the borders against those dirty Burmese.

I just rented a Thai war movie, *The Legend of Su*–... Wait, I forget how to spell her damn name, better look it up ... OK, it's *The Legend of Suriyothai*, and it was about a seventeenth-century princess who fought off the Burmese invaders. The movie made no sense to me at all, but the big battle scene at the end was great, with the princess on an elephant having a halberd duel against the Burmese king.

If I had to fight a duel, I'd pick that style. A fat man has the advantage when it's halberds on elephant-back. Maybe I'll challenge Victor Davis Hanson to a game of elephant hacky sack, and he gets to be the hackee. All proceeds from the ticket sales donated to promoting war and trouble throughout the world.

In the big battle scene, the Burmese elephants had red war paint in the shape of flames coming from their eyes, which was about the coolest thing I've seen this year. I recommend you rent it. Just keep pressing fast-forward for the first two and a half hours or so until you see those red elephants charging through the jungle.

(By the way, if you want a *great* Asian war movie, get this Korean one, *Brotherhood of War*. Stands to reason that the Koreans could do the Korean War better than anybody, and they do. The best battles I've seen since *Gettysburg*, and better yet, it doesn't have that sawed-off stump Martin Sheen trying to fill Robert E. Lee's size 12 shoes, or Jeff Daniels in a walrus mustache trying to do a Cliff Claven accent.)

As they pushed their borders south, down the Malay Peninsula, the Thai kings ran up against the Muslim kingdom of Pattani, and they've been trying to hang on against local rebels ever since. That's what we're seeing now: another flare-up of a war that's been going on for centuries.

It's hard not to take sides on this one. I'm a Thai food fan, a Pad Thai hog from way back. So even though I've never been to Thailand (never been east of the Rockies, in fact), I like Thais. I'll just declare my prejudices here: Those Malays should take off their headscarves and try to be better Thais. It'd be a step up for them.

Of course, that's not how they see it. To the Malays in Pattani, the Thais are Buddhist imperialists trying to make Allah's faithful bow down to fat-man statues. (And what's wrong with that?)

These Southern Muslims were the biggest of all the Thai rebellions in the 1960s. People forget that during the Vietnam era, it seemed likely that Thailand would be one of the first dominoes to fall. If you look at a military map from that period, the only "green zones" (under government control) were the central river valley and the cities.

In Isaan, the dirt-poor northeast province, Communist cadres were working the pissed-off villagers with help from the VC, Chinese, and Pathet Lao. Hill tribesmen funded by the drug barons of the Golden Triangle were sitting in ambush on every scraggy mountain in the north.

But the Muslim rebels of the far South were always the toughest, biggest, and hardest to crush. By the mid-1980s, the Thais had killed all the other insurgencies. There were a lot of factors at work here: The Chinese feud with Vietnam left the rebels with no superpower support, the United States poured at least a billion dollars into CI work, and the Thai king—a smart guy, definitely the best king around—pushed the military to kill the rebellions off with kindness: development projects, counterpropaganda, and a royal amnesty for anybody who came in from the jungle.

But the biggest reason is the obvious one: money. Suddenly, Thailand was the new, cool destination for Northern Europeans eager to get out of social democratic limbo for a few weeks. Skulking in the jungle, swapping malaria parasites with Pol Pot wasn't a good career choice for a Thai when you could work as a diving instructor in Phuket or Pattaya and make enough to impress the girls with a motor scooter and a knockoff Rolex.

Money killed off the commie rebels, but didn't do a thing to the Muslims. That's one of the most important lessons we have to remember: The commies were paper tigers. A few dollars, and they vanished.

But the Muslims won't be bribed. When you've got Saudi boys choosing one-way tickets to the World Trade Center over a lifetime of lying by the pool with your imported Swedish girlfriend in Riyadh, you've got a serious ideology to deal with.

The Pattani rebels have gone through the same sort of change as the Palestinians. Back in the day, the Southern Thais had a PLO-style, semi-commie organization called PULO representing them. But as communism burned out and Islam heated up, the torch got passed to a new generation of Jihadis.

In Palestine, the PLO lost out to Hamas. In Southern Thailand, PULO is as decrepit as the Fresno Rotary Club. The cool new clique is the Pattani Islamic Mujahedeen Movement, or GMIP.

These guys are long on theology but short on tactics. In fact, some of their operations have been just plain comic. In April 2004, Muslims from the village of Su So massed around Thai police stations in the South, waving machetes and knives. The cops told them to hold that pose, got the M-16s out of the gun case, did a few stretching exercises on their trigger fingers, and blasted away. At least a hundred Malays were killed. No cops were even wounded.

Getting slaughtered in a mismatch like that seems stupid to us Americans, but there's a pattern in insurgent warfare here: The first wave is suicidal, the second homicidal. There are dozens of examples, two of the most famous being the first and second intifada in Israel.

In the first intifada, the Pals threw rocks at Merkava tanks and got slaughtered. In the second, they went on the offensive. Same pattern in Ireland in the early twentieth century: In the Easter Rising in 1916, a bunch of rebels in uniform occupied buildings in downtown Dublin, declared themselves a target, and got blown to bits by artillery fire. In 1919, the second wave started, with ambushes and pioneering efforts in urban guerrilla warfare that succeeded in driving the Brits out of Southern Ireland, the first big British defeat.

How does it work? Like all guerrilla warfare, it's about winning by losing. The first wave takes one for the team. By marching out and getting themselves killed, they get the people angry and establish the rebels as heroic martyrs. The rebels' corpses are like fertilizer for the second wave, which consists of cooler heads, guys who are out to kill, not just die.

The grosser the mismatch, the better the propaganda. So in the first intifada, you saw Palestinian kids with rocks fighting tanks. In Ireland 1916, you had rifles vs. heavy artillery. That sort of things stays in people's heads for centuries, especially when the government troops' retaliation gets out of hand and wreaks havoc.

So it was actually pretty smart for the Irish rebels to occupy central Dublin, because heavy artillery isn't exactly surgical, and it ended up destroying most of the city.

So far it looks as if the Thai government is doing the heavy-handed response, laying waste any Muslim village that gets uppity. In October 2004, the army jumped a crowd of Muslim demonstrators, arrested and hog-tied thirteen hundred men, and threw them into trucks like sacks of flour for the long drive to their new prison-camp home. By the time they got there, seventy-eight men had been crushed to death.

That's not smart killing. It might be smart to kill all thirteen hundred—and all their male kin, while you're at it—but it's not smart to kill a few and make the rest into your enemies for life. The Thais are just getting frustrated, the way regular armies always do dealing with guerrillas. And from the Thai perspective, there's never been a better time to get rough with Muslims than now, while the Americans are already pissed off at the Jihadis. So they want to clean up the problem before we go soft again. And if you're a Southeast Asian ally of the United States, you can't help fearing that the Americans will go soft again soon. We've done it before, and they're right to fear we'll do it again.

The really smart move for the Thais would be to set up a puppet Muslim autonomous regime in the South, consolidate its power, and then push it into a civil war with the extremists. That's what the Israelis are doing in Gaza at the moment: leaving suddenly, creating a power vacuum in the hope that Fatah and Hamas will get too busy fighting each other to keep intifada number two going.

It worked for the Brits in Ireland. After losing an urban guerrilla war to the IRA in 1919–1921, they signed a treaty with the moderate faction, handed over heavy weapons, and let the moderate and extremist wings duke it out until both the Irish groups were exhausted. The Brits got fifty years of quiet on the western (island) front out of it.

My guess is that there is no happy solution. The Muslim rebels are doing all the right things to keep the people pissed off and angry. The Thais are doing the only thing they can by killing anybody they think is in on the insurgency, because frankly, you can't kill off these Muslim rebels with kindness (and money) the way the Thais did the other rebellions, the commie-inspired rebellions in the north.

We're going to see a long, slow grind of the ethnic plates in Southern Thailand. Your great-grandkids will be reading the same headlines from there, a hundred years from now.

THE JAPANESE RED ARMY:
WE HARDLY KNEW YE

A LOT OF newspaper columnists are worried that the word *terrorism* is "losing its power to horrify" because we're using it too often. I worry about this, too, only from kind of a different angle. I worry that we're handing out the word *terrorist* to every no-class single-A bushwhacking gang in the world, when it should only apply to groups that have earned it, gangs with a few real scalps on their belts. I'm talking standards here. I'm trying to stop grade inflation, like what happened to the Purple Heart when they started giving it away for paper cuts.

The way I see it, *terrorism* is one of the few really serious, scary, real words left. Curse words don't have any power since the gritty TV shows started using them for effect. All the hate-speech stuff is off-limits. What's left of the old, hard stuff? Just a few words, and *terrorism* is one of the best.

We need to remember what the word really means. We need to look at some old-school terrorists, original gangstas, so we have a standard to measure new gangs against.

And that's why I'm going to tell you the amazing story of the Japanese Red Army, the best pure terrorists, pound for pound, in history.

Serious terror buffs talk about the JRA with maximum respect, maybe even awe. Even the State Department showed their respect for the JRA by making it the first group named to the official list of terrorist groups. So we're talking about Heisman killers here, the can't-miss picks of terror.

I get the feeling a lot of Japanese feel the same way. You know that movie *Battle Royale*? Well, if you don't you better go rent it, because it's got some of the best kill scenes ever, and the victims are popular kids from a high school. What more could a war nerd want in a flick?

Anyway, if you know that movie, you'll remember a scene that shows how much cool Japanese kids respect the JRA. It's the scene where the leader of the nerds shows his friends a little pendant he wears. Unscrewing it, he takes out a detonator. He tells his friends that his radical uncle was planning to use this detonator to blow up the Diet, the Japanese senate.

But the plan fizzled, the uncle fled to make revolution in other countries, and the kid got the detonator as a keepsake. He's obviously talking about the JRA. And what I like about this scene is that there's no whiney antiviolence crap; the kid's majorly proud of his uncle, and his friends are totally impressed. That made me all warm and cheery, like an S&L director opening the vault the day after deregulation kicked in.

Maybe this means the ol' banzai spirit is coming back to Japan. God, that'd be great. The Japanese were among the world's greatest soldiers, fliers, and sailors until they lost heart in 1945. Can't blame them for that, I guess; nukes are a real bummer, no denying it. Millions of dead scattered from the Coral Sea to the Aleutians, Tokyo reduced to burnt bones and ash—it'd get anybody down.

But c'mon, my noble Nipponese warrior pals, it's been fifty years. You've been good too long, like the bumper sticker says. Let's shine those bayonets, dust off those maps of Manchuria, rethink Australia's coastal defenses! Let's be Japanese again, not just confused, spiky-haired tourists and girls who won't wear anything but black!

I've seen enough *manga* and *hentai* movies to know you Japanese men still like the rough stuff, so why not move from animation to, if you know what I mean, live action? Allow me to suggest you start by invading North Korea. Everybody'd love you for it, because they want Kim taken out but don't have the Roe to do it themselves. They'd forgive a whole bunch of Nanjing-style block parties so long as you whacked the Dear Leader in the process.

People have tried, now and then, to convince Japan's wimpy Self-Defense Force to stop acting like a Quaker college's marching band and get mean again. So far, it hasn't worked. My favorite example happened in 1970, a bad time for militarists everywhere.

The man who tried to rouse Japan's military spirit was a writer named Yukio Mishima. A freak, no denying that, but at least he was antipeace, prowar—he had "moral clarity," as they say. Not your typical militarist, though—Mishima was an avant-garde novelist. Haven't read his books, but I'd imagine "avant-garde" means his books make no sense even in translation. He was also a flaming mariposa, gay as a Spartan bath attendant. Worked out nonstop, got very buff (for a Japanese), and was always posing with his shirt off, trying to look Imperial, with that rising-sun flag wrapped around him, or wearing a samurai sword and headband—only he's always got that "Hi there, Sailor" expression, which pretty much ruins the effect.

Still, his heart was in the right place, and I'm not going to do gay jokes, because I realized after high school that in those four lousy years, no gay guy ever called me fatso.

Mishima proved his guts, and I mean that literally, on November 25, 1970, the day he died. He was sick of the new, feeble, peacenik Japan. So he decided to seize a Self-Defense base called Camp Ichigaya, where he hoped to harangue the troops into getting back to old-school Imperialism and militarism stuff, like the good old days of 1939. The rest of his plan was kind of hazy, but he sort of hoped this would ignite something.

Mishima showed up at the base with four guys from his private army, the "Shield Society." An interesting group: not too big, about a hundred members. And I hear Mishima picked them for their looks more than their fighting ability. Great uniforms, though.

What happened at the base that day is just plain hilarious, one of the funniest war stories ever. Mishima's party of five tromped into the commander's office. So far so good. Then Mishima took out his sword. The base commander flinched, so Mishima told him it was "for ceremonial purposes."

Which was a fib, because a second later, Mishima was threatening the CO with the blade while his men tied the poor paper-shuffling Colonel Klink-o-san to his desk.

By this time, about eight hundred soldiers were outside, wondering what the Hell was going on. Mishima went out and started trying to whip the troops into a war frenzy.

Well, as the old showmen used to say, "tough crowd, tough crowd!" James Brown couldn't have got an "Amen!" from that crowd. As for Mishima, they laughed at the poor guy. He couldn't buy a "Banzai!" It turned into a standup comic's nightmare: They started heckling Mishima.

I've seen photos of Mishima making his final speech, and you can see why he bombed with the troops. For one thing, he looks ridiculous, got this 1930's gay tunic thing on, and even though he's trying to scowl all stern like Mussolini, he still has that same gym-mirror pose. He's just not scary.

Besides, it was 1970; the troops were probably stoned. Maybe if Cheech and Chong had staged a coup, they'd've had a chance, but a serious Imperial throwback like Mishima made no sense to them at all.

They started tearing down Mishima's banners. So Mishima stopped, thought it over, and went back into the CO's office. He told the tied-up CO he was going to "shout banzai to the emperor" and did, the old-school way: by kneeling, taking off the tunic and ripping his belly open. His disciples helped ease the pain by cutting his head off—still the best anesthetic around, beheading. Works faster than morphine, lasts longer.

After Mishima's head rolled off, one of his disciples, a copycat, ripped his own belly open and had his head removed. He was probably the kind of kid who'd jump off a bridge if Johnny down the street did.

So here's the scene in the CO's office: We've got two heads on the floor, a really messy carpet they probably had to throw away, and a desk-jockey general. The gen was probably wondering if these wackos were going to add him to the pile of skulls or leave him alive to explain to his superiors how his base got seized by a gay novelist and his four boyfriends. That's a rock and a pretty durn hard place for a career officer.

Mishima's crazy death-day was the last time anybody tried to put any team spirit in Japan's poor old Self-Defense Force. The right wing was worn out, discredited by the war. The army was a joke. So where did young Japanese bloods eager for some action go in 1970? Simple: the far left, the one place where violence was cool and hip.

The people who founded the JRA in the late 1960s were that type, conquistadors disguised as commies. They talked Marx, but they were in it for the blood, right from the start. They had no "people"; the Japanese population thought they were crazy, and the JRA despised the *sarariiman* (salaryman) world. So this was pure splatter, with no ethnic, class, or astrological-sign base to worry about.

The JRA was tiny, never more than a hundred-odd members. But every member was a smart, disciplined, and ruthless killer. That's why I say that pound for pound, man for man, they were the best terrorists ever.

There were other terrorists from middle-class rich countries back then, like the Baader-Meinhof Faction in West Germany in the 1970s and the Red Brigades in Italy in the 1980s. But compared to Fusako Shigenobu's JRA, these Euro-trash terrorists were squeamish dilettantes. Unlike the JRA, they didn't usually target civvies, and settled for the odd kidnap, picking off an official or two per year just to keep in practice. They cared more about the ideological crap than action.

JRA killers weren't squeamish that way. They never hesitated, always tried for maximum casualties. That's one of the weird aspects of their group: If the leaders of 1930s Japan had watched 1970s Japanese TV, the only people they'd be proud to call comrades were these commies of the JRA—because they were the real reincarnation of the kamikaze spirit.

The craziest of all was their leader, a woman named Fusako Shigenobu—a pioneer in blasting the glass ceiling for women as CEOs of terror gangs. So how come she never gets mentioned in those feminist heroes lists? Cowards!

Fusako formed the JRA by quitting a less blood-crazed hard-left party and taking the crazies with her. It was 1970, the same year Mishima did his last one-man show. She was more practical than that dreamy writer. Her boys didn't fool with swords; they stuck to automatic weapons. Because guns work, and swords are for *Lord of the Rings* dorks.

In fact, I just remembered another scene from *Battle Royale* that makes the same point. Remember the scene, early on, when the psycho killer wipes out a bunch of kids on the beach and looks over their weapons to see if they're worth taking. He grabs the AK, naturally, and a grenade—then he picks up a set of nunchucks, sneers at them, and throws them away. You want to kill, get a gun. You want to impress other dweebs, carry a knife. Or nunchucks.

Fusako decided to kick off the JRA with a few spectacular field trips. Like all Japanese, the JRA's new recruits loved world travel. Only they didn't pack a lot of cameras. This was before there was any real airport security, so the JRA could zip around the world doing its version of revolution.

In their first year as a gang, the JRA hijacked a Japan Airlines (JAL) flight to North Korea. It was a battle of the three-letter groups, JAL vs. JRA, and JRA won hands down. The JAL crew flew the gang to lovely Pyongyang with no delay at all.

Yup, you read right: They hijacked a plane *to* North Korea. I don't know if that's comedy or just insane, but you have to admire the sheer gung-ho spirit behind it.

From then on, JAL was the JRA's hijack airline of choice, their flying chauffeurs. In 1973, a mixed JRA and PFLP (Popular Front for the Liberation of Palestine) team grabbed a JAL flight over Europe and diverted it to the Libyan desert, offloaded the passengers, and blew up the plane. There was one casualty, a PFLP woman who got herself blown up with the plane. Must have slept through the pre-explosion announcement that all passengers must disembark using the emergency exits before the aircraft is detonated.

The JRA was also the only terrorist group I know that thought globally, really took that commie "worldwide revolution" stuff seriously. They were always up for a bloodbath in Japan, but if that wasn't happening, they spun their globes and picked someplace else to start blasting. I suspect this was partly because even these wackos realized there wasn't going to be a revolution in Japan. They offered their services to comrades everywhere, free of charge—charity terror.

The first group to take them up on it was the Palestinians, who after all provided Fusako with her inspiration in the first place. They asked the JRA to hit their Israeli enemies, and as usual, the JRA was there with a can-do attitude. The result was a bloody slaughter at Lod Airport in Israel in 1972. Three JRA men flew in to Lod without attracting suspicion, because, hey, it's three Japanese guys in suits, polite and quiet and harmless. Well, the whole notion that Asians are wimps is wrong to start with, and this time the world paid for stereotyping.

Guess where they had their weapons. You won't believe it: violin cases. Yup, like some old gangster movie. Man, people in 1970 . . . well, it's like Beavis and Butthead say: "This movie is from back when people were stupid."

Nobody searched the cases. Nobody did a thing as the polite little guys opened the cases, took out machine guns, and started to, er, play their instruments. They played nonstop, spraying the crowds, until one of the shooters ran out of ammo. His two friends did the comradely, samurai thing by blowing him away. One of the two still alive did a different hi-tech hara-kiri by pulling the pin on a grenade and holding it like a corsage against his chest. The third guy wimped out and tried to hide in the crowd. Not too bright, this guy; "I'm just another brood-spattered Japanese guy mingring with you Israeris, dum-dee-dum . . . fitting right in . . . Hava-nageera-hava-nageera-hava . . ."

This letdown of the JRA bleated. He confessed that the JRA had taken the job on contract from George Habash's PFLP, a small but deadly Palestinian group that was eventually pretty much wiped out by Mossad, one guy at a time. In 1970, the PFLP's yearbook was still full, though—didn't have all those black *X*'s over the seniors' pictures yet—and the JRA showed the Palestinian group the ultimate respect, terror-style, by doing their bloody laundry for them.

The three-man JRA team managed to kill twenty-six people at Lod—not bad for a brief shooting spree. You have to remember, humans are big mammals, good design—hard to kill. Only a shot to the head will do it for sure, and even then, if it's a .22, the victim may live (he'll drool more than a stoned St. Bernard, and he won't be a major contributor to the global economy, but he'll live.)

Unfortunately for the JRA and its PFLP backers, the civvies who died that day were mostly—and I'm sorry, but this is more comedy—well, they were Puerto Rican Christian pilgrims to the Holy Land. Sixteen of them dead. Puerto Rico. Like it's not bad enough already, their tourists get splattered on a holy journey. If only my old parish had been on tour instead—damn, if the JRA had blasted our youth pastor on one of his Israel/Jordan tours, I'd have sent the JRA all the lotus flowers they wanted.

Just to be fair, the JRA scheduled another splatter tour of a Muslim country's airport: In 1976, they opened fire in Istanbul Airport and scored eleven kills. The assault, another favor to the PFLP, was designed to punish the Turks for being soft on Israel. I haven't been able to find out if the eleven dead were Puerto Rican, but I wouldn't be surprised.

In the late 1970s, the JRA started looking at the Asian market, with spectacular results: In 1975, they took hostage a whole diplomatic party in Malaysia and promised to kill them all unless Japan released five of the JRA's imprisoned comrades. Other groups try this kind of thing, but you wonder if they're bluffing. Nobody, but nobody, thought the JRA was bluffing, and five JRA vets were out of their cells and on a flight to Libya faster than a Benihana chef slices up shrimp.

It worked so well the JRA asked their pals at JAL to step aside as they hijacked another flight, this time in Bombay. They demanded a big cash payment and the release of six JRA prisoners—and got it, as promptly as the last time.

And the JRA was tough but fair; they were just as hard on themselves as on the rest of the world. As in, capital punishment for everybody! When Fusako decided the group was getting too slack, she marched them into a remote Japanese mountain retreat, where she conducted her own trials for ideological crimes. As a result of these legal proceedings, fourteen JRA members were given the lightest sentence allowed: death by hanging.

Eventually, the Japanese cops sniffed out their hideout, and the JRA turned that mountain lodge into another Bataan. Two cops died, but the gore was over all too soon and most of the JRA rank and file were in prison (after a good kicking around by the dead cops' friends).

Their glory days were almost over, but they never stopped trying, trying. In 1988 the JRA bombed a GI hangout in Naples, killing five people. What's much more interesting is that about the same time, a JRA vet named Yu Kikumura was arrested on the New Jersey turnpike with a trunk full of bombs. He was planning to blow up a stateside base, sort of a duet with Naples. I wonder what Yu thought of Jersey. Never been there, but from the pictures I've seen, it looks like it could use some radical relandscaping.

By now, the JRA's cadre was getting on in years, mellowing—just didn't feel like killing civvies some days, what with the arthritis and the lower back problems. They were dispersed all over the world, but were so tired they started slipping up, getting caught. The final blow was when Fusako got caught in 2000 and, during her trial, announced that she was renouncing terror and going into politics, trying to take power "by legal means." The State Department even took the JRA off its red list and demoted the organization to "groups that need watching."

Sad, like Jordan's baseball career, a disgrace to former greatness.

The saddest thing of all is that without the guns behind her, Fusako's attempt to talk the voters into electing her dictator of the revolution is as silly as Mishima's standup routine in front of those jeering peacenik "troops" back in 1970. Fusako lasted longer than Mishima did, but she forgot the one thing he did right: When the fun's over, kill yourself before you get turned into a running joke.

Part 6

HARDWARE, STRATEGY, AND NERD DOCTRINE

TOM CLANCY IS NOT ONE OF US

MY FIRST FAN letter was an email from some guy in Michigan who wanted the latest news on Tom Clancy. Yeah sure, that's why I'm here—to help you kiss that rich, fat coward's ass. For a while, I couldn't believe anybody'd be stupid enough to think I'd be a fan of Clancy's. You may think that all war nerds are equal, but they're not. There are three big differences between Clancy and me:

1. Clancy was born in 1947. So he was twenty in 1967. Good age to go to Vietnam. Did you ever hear about Clancy serving in 'Nam? No, you didn't. That's because he spent the war at a safe little Catholic college in Maryland, making sure he had a deferment. "Hail Mary, full of grace, keep me far from Charlie's place!"

   I was born in 1965. Vietnam was over before I got my first pubes. I'd have gone. I'm not saying I'd have been a good soldier. I woulda sucked—but I'd have gone. And died. It probably sounds like bragging, but it's not. I know how I would have died, some dumb way like stepping on a mine. Entrails dragging in a rice paddy. All the cool dudes in the squad laughing at me, listening to Hendrix, passing around a joint while I bled out. But I wouldn't have spent the war hiding out at Loyola Maryland.

   That's the worst part: Maryland! The stupid fuck didn't even have the sense to buy a van and head for San Francisco and the hippie chicks like all the smart draft dodgers did. He spent the 1960s studying accounting. So he's not just chickenshit, he's stupid.

2. Clancy divorced his wife, Wanda, in 1998 so he could trade up for a groupie with a cooler name, "Alexandra." I'd bet he tried on a lot of groupies before he settled on Alexandra and left ol' Wanda and their four kids. Just left and never looked back.

   I don't have that kind of temptation. Not a lot of groupies hang around me. Even the fat Mexican ladies at Safeway flinch when they pass me my plastic bags. The only girls I get to see naked are old whores pretending to get whipped on Web sites like Slave Farm, where they use lipstick streaks on the ass-cheeks to look like stripes from a riding crop.

   So I mean it when I pray for war. Clancy doesn't.

3. Clancy tried to buy the Minnesota Vikings for $200 million, and ended up settling for the Orioles. A baseball team. Football is war for office slaves, but baseball? That's not war at all. That's lawyer stuff.

   By way of reminding you of the differences between Clancy and me: I have $630 left in my account after paying for some kind of electrical fault on the Subaru. I have no idea what the problem was. All I know is, you don't wanna be car-less in Fresno, not with summer coming. I'm more scared of the Fresno summer than von Paulus was of the Russian winter.

   If you think Clancy's a real war nerd like me, how come he was willing to spend $200 million for an NFL franchise—and in Minnesota at that? And if you still think he's for real, how do you explain the Orioles? The NFL is at least about people hitting each other, trying to snap each others' bones. Baseball is about cowardly jocks spitting and snoring. Anybody who'd buy a baseball team is out of the war-nerd club forever.

Think about what you could do if you had that kind of money. Money is what bin Laden used, and he made himself a one-man crusade. Everybody in America is scared of one skinny Saudi. Like my social studies teacher said about Lenin, "You may not agree with his program, but you have to admire his determination." Or look at this Khattab guy who got killed in Chechnya in 2002: Another rich Saudi who became a warlord by buying his way in.

Warlord—God, that's most beautiful word in the language. That's the job you want. With $200 million, you could buy your own army. Take some place like the southern Sudan, where there are a half-dozen ethnic and religious wars going at once. You know how far that kind of money would go in a place like that? You could not only buy your own army, but also buy your own slaves. Yeah: slaves. They have 'em. They make not be the cutest girls in the world, but they're thin at least and they have a good attitude: trained to submit. Ritual scarification. You could have your pick from every village. They'd be honored. "At your service!" No age or consent problems, either. Brand 'em so they don't go astray.

Or you could go to Central Asia—one of the 'Stans. Kirghizstan is nice and cheap, I hear. Or Tajikistan—there's a lot of Slavic blood in the mix out there, and some of those girls look like starved models. Only not snotty like real models. On the contrary, delighted to be chosen for your pleasure.

With $200 million out there on the steppes, you'd be the shah. Ride the steppes all day with an eagle on your wrist and your retinue in attendance, hunting small game and children: "Swoop, my beauteous eagle! Swoop on yon peasant brat!"

Come home at the end of a long day of hunting, dismount onto a kneeling servant, then chill out in your yurt—clap your hands when you're ready to have them parade today's harvest of peasant girls from the local villages past you. Choose whichever you want. Hell, choose two, they're small.

In fact, with $200 million, you could choose real models if you wanted. First, you have to build up a private spy service; once you've got that, you could kidnap any girl you wanted, from anywhere in the world. Take a field trip to Rome, sip your drink at a sidewalk café with a half-dozen Kirghiz slave-catchers standing behind you, and wait till you see someone worth possessing walk by. Then lift one finger, point her out, and say: "That one." A week later, she's delivered to your Transylvania-style castle in Central Asia in a wooden crate. She might have a bit of an attitude in the beginning, but those things can be changed. People in the 'Stans know how to fix a bad attitude. A week in the dungeons, and she'll crawl to you and beg to be of service.

It's not just a dream. There are guys doing it right now. Kim Jong-Il, the Great Leader of North Korea, has talent-spotting teams all over Asia picking out the best girls, kidnapping them, and presenting them to him, gift-wrapped and terrified, in Pyongyang. Supposedly he's a fan of South Korean movies. He uses them to preview the merchandise. Sits there at his private screenings and, when he sees something he likes, tells his agents, "I wish to interrogate her." That's all it takes. They grab her off the streets of Seoul, and when the bag comes off her head, she's in Pyongyang, scariest place in the world, with Kim, this jowly little nearsighted freak, feeling her up, panting and whispering, "Capitalist bitch, you will be now be reeducated by me!" You don't have to like his ideology, but you have to admire his style.

When that sort of indoor life gets dull, you could invest a little of the $200 million in hardware and start a little war of your own. You can get anything you want out there: T-72s are going for scrap-metal prices. People think tanks are useless, but that's way oversimplifying things. Tanks worked beautifully for the Serbs till the NATO air forces got involved. If you're fighting irregulars in a treeless landscape like the 'Stans, tanks work just fine.

So you buy some MBTs, some artillery, go in and just wipe out one of the local clans. That'll get the locals' attention. They love a winner. Make your own flag. Your own uniforms. Convert the whole place to some cool religion, dump that Islam nonsense: Declare the first Zoroastrian jihad, rolling back the inroads of Islam, that imported, flea-ridden Arabian cult. Or . . . I don't know . . . you could revive the old Egyptian gods . . . No, Zoroastrianism would be better. It's more local and pretty cool, too, from what I've read. Worshipping fire, leaving your dead on rooftops to be eaten by vultures. Think of the speeches you could make: "We are the Army of Flames, the Sacred Fire of Tajikistan, and in Zoroaster's name, we vow to burn across the steppes until all is cleansed and ashen!"

Goddamn, think of the possibilities! The CIA would love you: an anti-Muslim jihad! The agency would need C-5As to hold all the cash it'd send you!

A war like that is just a big pyramid scheme: You take a village and distribute the loot and the women to your men. Then you round up all the surviving men and boys from that village, and offer them a simple choice: Join us and be reimbursed with the loot and women from the next village we take, or die right now. It's a very effective sales pitch. Repeat until the whole steppe is yours.

That's how the African armies work. Nobody gets this; they call it atrocities and claim not to understand how human beings can behave the way they do in Sierra Leone and Sudan. But these handwringers are stupid—stupid or just pretending, I'm not sure which. What's so difficult to understand? It's the oldest and most sensible style of war. Compare it with, say, WW I: Which kind of war would you rather be in? Gassed or blown apart in the trenches—for what? What do you get out of it? Now compare that to war Central-Asian or African style: The village over the hill has some cute girls and some nice carpets, so you sack it, kill the men, enslave the girls, recruit the boys, and move on. By the time you're on your third village, you've got such a big rep that the girls are in no mood to object and the boys can't wait to be issued an AK and a license to rape and pillage the next village.

To come out of that wonderful dream to this, to a duplex in Fresno, and the office and the job . . . it's torture.

That's why it makes me so fucking crazy to see Clancy, this supposed war nerd who has all that money to play with, using it to buy a football team. Football! Football is war for wimps. For cowards. For office workers. And that's all he is, Clancy: an office boy, a fat insurance agent who sucked up to Reagan and got lucky.

I may be the loser here, but at least I'm serious. If I had Clancy's money, I would burn and pillage from horizon to horizon. There would be columns of smoke from every direction. I'd become a warlord, not an NFL franchise owner sitting in a corporate box talking about pass defense and smoking cigars.

I wouldn't marry anybody called "Wanda," either. Especially if she was from Maryland. And if I did marry her, if I did do something that stupid and pop out four kids with her, and join the Republicans and talk about family values—then I wouldn't dump her when a better offer came along. It's one thing to be cruel—cruelty is fine—but it's another to be low, to be a hypocrite. I don't hold with that.

So kill her maybe, but don't just dump her for a newer model. That's low. That's office bullshit, lawyer stuff.

Be a warlord, choose a new peasant girl to rape every night—but don't be a sleazy, lying rich fuck, "Honey it's best for both of us, my attorney will talk to your attorney—say bye to the kids for me!" That's low.

Ever since I read that the poor, trusting cow was named Wanda, I've had this image of her in my head. I mean I can imagine what Wanda looks like: like Tom in drag, Tom in a Pat-Nixon wig and K-mart lipstick. Like the fat lady on that Drew Carey show.

I can imagine how scared the poor sow must've been since Tom got rich and famous. They must've been the perfect couple once. Made for each other. She was probably real happy—or as happy as an ugly woman named Wanda can get—back before Tom got famous. She just had to look at the wedding picture on the wall of their cheap condo to feel safe, because she and Tommy looked like twins—the same fat, potato-faced loser smiles. And like good fascist Catholics, they popped out four fat-faced Clancy kids to keep the drive alive.

Then suddenly, Tom is so rich and so famous that his fat face doesn't look so bad anymore to all the PR girls and publishers' reps, and they start coming on to him right in front of Wanda. And Wanda ... I can imagine her trying to get thin and beautiful, compete with the skinny girls who are targeting her Tommy. Wanda working out, trying to live on grapefruit. You know, nobody tries harder or believes the crap more than us fat people. Six months sweating, and she loses three pounds ... and lately, Tommy's spending a lot of evenings with his "fans." His "fans," skinny girls with hip names, not Wanda. All hair and smiles and tight little butts. "Oh, Tom, you're such a genius! You're the bestest writer in the whole woooorld!"

And Tommy has access to these bodies. He can't believe it at first, thinks it's a joke like what the frat boys used to play on him. The kind of girls he used to stalk in college—now they're stalking him. They even pretend to like the war stuff: "Oh, Tommy, it's so fascinating when you talk about the homing capability of the new General Dynamics nuclear-armed ASB sub/surface-to-sub/surface torpedo!"

She expects him to jump her right then, but he keeps talking about the torpedo till the groupie is ready to slit his throat with her martini glass. She knows he's worth something like half a billion, so she's ready to let him shove his blimp body into hers—but she didn't realize there'd be so much talk first. It's worse than the way her stepfather used to talk about Motocross before fucking her. That crap was romantic poetry compared to Clancy and his monologue about navy hardware. She almost thinks it's not worth it—she can go back to waitressing, a little street work on the side, and make enough to keep herself nodding most of the time ... but finally Tom's drunk enough to take the chance, he has his chauffeur bundle them back to the Maryland mansion, where he pops a couple of discreet Viagras to make sure there won't be another embarrassment like that time in college when the ex-nun TA took pity on him and he, uh, let her down.

They drive home, necking in the limo—and there's Wanda, looking out from her "personal" wing of the new mansion, the one Tom told her was "personally and entirely" hers, meaning: stay there and don't bother me. She sees the chauffeur helping her fat man and a skinny girl into Tom's wing of the house, sees the lights go on, and knows the game is over. Tells herself it won't be so bad after the divorce; she won't have to go back to work answering phones in an office. She can join a church and meet a "decent man," maybe.

She doesn't mind if he's partly interested in her money, as long as it's just partly.

Then the lights go out in Tommy's wing of the mansion.

And next morning, Tom's waddling around like a stud porker, tickling his "fan" under the covers and bouncing up to call his money man: "Let's light a fire under that Vikings deal!" He loves to talk that deal-maker patter he learned from Reagan's pals.

She's pretending she's still asleep, still retching a little. It was even worse than she thought it would be. The smells—anybody that rich should be clean, at least. It's too soon to assert herself, so she has to let him prance around in his stupid jockeys, talking big on the mobile. He'll pay later. Once the wedding bells have rung out.

Yeah, that was our Tommy's new love. I hope she tears his balls off with a gardening claw. Just like Birgitte Nielsen did to Sylvester Stallone—remember? She grabbed him, drained his bank account, and ran off with her girlfriend laughing all the way.

And he wasn't even fat and ugly like our Tommy is. Oh, it'll be sweet when the wife #2 makes her move. Tommy'll run back to Wanda and the kids. (I imagine the four kids looking like the kid in *Far Side* cartoons, you know? Fat, freckly faces, big blank glasses, crew cuts.) He'll rediscover family values, blubber about how wrong he was, tell all the talk shows about the importance of being true to yourself . . . till the next groupie comes along.

And the fucker could have been a warlord, a living god of battle, like Khattab or bin Laden. Emperor of the Steppes. And he picks the Orioles—a baseball team, named after a little songbird from the suburbs—instead.

So don't tell me Tom Clancy is one of us. He is the enemy, the fake war nerd, the office version. He lives in Maryland. It's a small state, and he has a big house. He shouldn't be too hard to find, my fellow war nerds. And when you find him—you know what to do.

FUTURE WAR:
HI-TECH TOYS VS. FANGED VERMIN

I KNOW IT'S hopeless trying to guess how war will change over the next century. But it's just as hopeless trying not to think about it. I can't help guessing, though I know I'll probably be wrong. Hell, at least I can be cold-blooded about it, because I know I won't be around personally. My doctor told me it's maybe fifteen more years for me . . . I've got every cardiovascular symptom you get when you're fat and bitter and pretty much hate life. So whatever happens, I won't have to worry. I kinda like that.

It'd be nice to think all you fuckers'll just wipe each other out in an all-out nuclear war.

But you're in luck, all you thin, healthy, smiley bastards: I don't think it'll happen like that. It's going to be weirder, slower, and a lot less *Star-Wars*-y than people think.

It's easy to get all excited about blasters, space battles, lasers, and all that Luke Skywalker stuff. But my job is to give you my best guess on what's really gonna happen. And you know, I'm not even sure war will survive. War seems too good for people like you, you beach volleyball people. Well, one thing's for sure: It won't be the cool sci-fi war you like to think about, you saving Carrie Fisher from Jabba with your Jedi mind bullshit. . . .

Space war—killer satellites, orbital lasers . . . won't happen. Nothing but lame NASA fundraising ideas. Never convinced anybody this side of *Newsweek*. In 150 years, there'll be nobody on the moon, nobody on Mars—just some fragile, expensive tools floating up there, not worth blasting, far too expensive to risk.

Down here, everything will go on getting smaller and smarter, like a math class full of Chinese transfers. It's easy to come up with a future war scenario based on that steady tech advance: no more manned fighters, for example. Lots of RPVs (remotely piloted vehicles), doing everything from surveillance to ground attack. That's not really even futuristic; the Israelis have been doing it that way since they used RPVs to help destroy the Syrian Air Force in three days in 1982 without losing a single plane. The damn things worked so well for the IDF that the USAF finally got dragged along. By now, we can keep a Predator RPV hovering week after week, waiting for a target. When the U.S. Air Force grudgingly gave the Predator RPVs a chance in Afghanistan, the air force had to admit the damn things worked even better than the advocates were promising. These Predators are amazing: too small to spot, damned hard to shoot down, and cheap enough that we don't lose much even if one does get hit. And you know the best thing about RPVs? They don't react to torture. No pilot to go on Iraqi TV looking like Jake LaMotta after twelve rounds with Sugar Ray Robinson and start apologizing for disturbing Baghdadis' beauty sleep.

The trouble with this nice, clean automated-war scenario is that nobody wants to play with us. The United States can play that game, but who else can play it? The Israelis? They're the only real combat-tested RPV-using army. And if it came to a U.S.-vs.-Israel war, let's face it: the U.S. Congress would back Israel all the way, and the United States would have to surrender before a shot was fired.

Try plugging the high-tech, RPV-heavy war plan to a more even-sided war, say, an all-out struggle for world domination between the United States and China ten years from now. The first thing you realize is that it'll come down to production rates. You're gonna lose a lot of hardware in a hurry. Like aircraft in the early days of WW I, RPVs will go from surveillance to attack, and that will lead to interceptor models designed to destroy enemy RPVs. There'll be unmanned dogfights, and since these things are easy to make, the dogfights will be unbelievably massive, maybe hundreds of thousands of individual combats in the sky over the battlefield. It comes down to our factories vs. theirs. If you can replace it faster than they do, maybe you win. It'll all be as harmless as a nerd picnic on the school field Saturday afternoon, with the Asian kids and the pasty white kids each piloting their little remote-controlled MiGs and F-16s and arguing about who killed who, then going off for pizza.

As the two-tier war system develops, the high-tech nations won't even associate war with death anymore. War will be a demolition derby: Our machines beat your machines. Nobody has to die. When the dogfight between a Chinese and an American RPV finishes, nobody will die; the U.S. controller will disconnect from the monitor and have a beer, and so will the Chinese.

Production dominance will tilt one way or the other, at last: You own the skies. They can't send up any more RPVs, and you can. OK, you've won. Now what? Do you start carpet-bombing their cities? What the Hell for? The civilian population won't even matter anymore. Kill a hundred million Chinese—so what?

You want to assert control, though, prove you've won. Whaddaya do, send in troops? Chinese troops landing in Hawaii, or American troops landing on Amoy? It's real easy to see what happens next: The nukes come out, and everybody loses.

Oh wait, I forgot: We're gonna have a nuke-shield over us. Uh . . . yeah. Folks, as long as I'm debunking sci-fi bullshit, lemme tell you the sad news: This nuke shield has a technical name. It's called bullshit. Nobody can be shielded from nukes. Not just because it's impossible to intercept an intercontinental ballistic missile under real conditions (those tests? They were just plain faked, folks!), but because an ICBM isn't the only way to deliver a nuke.

Jesus, just think for a minute. You're Mao. You hate the United States; you have a few big, ripe, homemade nukes; and you want to be sure the Americans know they can't push you too far. Do you build ICBMs? Sure, a few—enough to keep the Japanese and the Russians awake. But you don't really trust those homemade missiles. And—this is kinda the key point, so listen up here—you don't need to. Because a regime like Mao's (or Stalin's or Kim Il Sung's) does one thing really, really well: spy stuff.

And if you've got a good spy service, delivering nukes is a cinch. A pickup truck is a perfectly effective way to deliver a nuke. How many pickup trucks cross from Canada or Mexico every year? You think every one of those gets searched? How many ships call at U.S. ports every year? How many get really carefully searched? How hard is it to carry a nuke to an American harbor in a harmless-looking Liberian-registered cargo ship, then dump it over the side somewhere near the East River, or the Bay Bridge?

I used to know this drug dealer, a really cool guy who'd been a navy frogman. He put those skills to good use: He'd drop a water-tight package of goodies just offshore, then dive back to pick it up once his ship had been searched and let in the harbor. Never failed, he said. If he could do it, you'd better believe Kim and Mao not only could do it, but *have* done it.

And that means there are nukes lying in our harbors and in long-term storage sheds and cemented into the foundations of buildings in our downtowns. So no matter how much the Defense Department bleats about its antimissile systems, you better believe that the United States will never, never be safe from nukes. And neither will any other place that matters, in China or Japan or Russia or Europe.

That means there won't be any total wars of the good ol' WW II kind, except between little backward countries without nukes. So we'll have a two-tier system of wars: very cautious, limited wars between the big players, and bloody messes between the savages. The civilized countries' wars will be great for using up surplus hardware. There'll be dead machines all over the landscape. But the casualty count for humans ... well, it's very hard to predict that. Right now, it's looking low. Why bother killing a few million civilians? Won't settle anything. Just makes you look bad.

The only enjoyable wars will be the mismatches, when the machine armies are unleashed on the savages. We've seen some of them lately: the NATO air forces working out on Serbia, the United States and British planes playing with the Iraqis like a couple of kittens with a half-dead mouse. They're the wars people will enjoy, because the targets are so easy, so undefended, that there are lots of good gun-camera shots.

But these wars have a little weakness: They never solve the problem. NATO killed a few thousand Serbs too stupid to realize their fellow Christians didn't give a fuck about them. And the Serbs pulled back. But the Albanians moved in. You go into a slum like the Balkans, try to fix things up by slapping around one gang—and the gang next door comes in, kills the first gang's families, and takes their houses. It's embarrassing. From what I hear, a lot of NATO soldiers dream nonstop of the day they'll be allowed to fire on the Albanian thugs they're supposed to be protecting.

The answer is obvious: annihilation. The two-tier wars will get really annoying. How many times do you go in (and "you" could be the Chinese, the Indians, or whoever's running the show a hundred years from now) and separate these drunken, small-time thugs? Sooner or later, somebody will suggest the neutron-bomb option. Nothing dramatic, just a Raid commercial on a larger scale.

They'll be provoked. That's a sure thing—before the ruling countries take the annihilation option, they will be *Hell of* provoked. The lower tier will have one weapon: the willingness to die and to kill. You don't need high-tech to kill a lot of people. You think Mohammed Atta could pass a course on jet engineering? Physics? He couldn't have gotten into Solano Community College, where all you need to pass there is two-thirds attendance. The loser countries, the ones that can't do math, are gonna skip shop class, skip the machine crap, and go back to basics: Kill a lot of people. They'll do Columbine on a worldwide scale. All the losers will come to the lobby with guns. Serbs, North Koreans, Tamil Sri Lankans, will walk into the lobbies of the machine peoples' towers like Keanu Reeves in *The Matrix*. They will splatter those security guards, they will smash up the decorative marble, they will disrupt office routine with drums of gasoline and vials of pesticide and rerouted sewage floods; they will turn the cities against their citizens and kill, kill, kill.

And the upper tier will respond. They'll be patient. They'll endure the first twenty or so urban massacres in a civilized way. Then they'll think of the obvious: the Raid solution. Every pesticide commercial they ever saw will occur to them as they decide what to do with the Serbs, the Tamils ... and finally someone in a government office in Beijing or Washington or Delhi will decide to do something permanent about the vermin. Ah yes, the Balkans: nice country. Too bad it's infested with two-legged varmints. Why not clean 'em out? It'll strike somebody as a good idea, sooner or later. And that's how we'll have our first nuclear war: not the old Cold-War scenario where two nuclear-armed nations wipe each other out, but a perfectly logical, one-sided version: China, or India, or the United States, or whoever, will simply sterilize the Balkans. (Or Java, or the South Bronx.)

It won't be pretty, or even glorious. Sorry about that; just trying to do my job. And there's kind of a consolation: There'll be one Hell of a lot of beautiful dogfight footage from all those RPV combats in the skies.

And then . . . well, something else, something no one will predict, will happen. And a big, brand new, bloody mess of a world will be born. But that will be your problem. I'll be safe on a shelf in one of Fresno's many fine crematoria, dreaming of the Thirty Years War.

U SANK MY BATTLESHIP!
GAMES AND WAR GAMES

WHEN KIDS PLAY war, they end up spending less time shooting than arguing: "You're dead!" "Am not! You missed!" It just gets worse the bigger the kids. I remember a D&D-er crying when his character got killed—wouldn't talk to the rest of us for years, still grieving for his dead elf.

The U.S. military has been having exactly this kind of argument, and they're even whinier and more of a pain about it than D&D-ers, if you can believe that, with leaks and counterleaks, planted stories, and plenty of good ol' character assassination. It all comes out of the Millennium Challenge war games staged in the Persian Gulf back in 2002. The big scandal was that the opposing force commander, General Paul van Riper, quit midgame because the games were rigged for the U.S. forces to win. The scenario was a U.S. invasion of an unnamed Persian Gulf country (either Iraq or Iran). The United States was testing a new high-tech joint force doctrine, so naturally, van Riper used every low-tech trick he could think of to mess things up. When the Americans jammed his CCC network, he sent messages by motorbike.

But that was just playing around. The military wouldn't have minded that. Might've even congratulated van Riper, bought him a drink for his smarts, at the postgames party.

The truth is that van Riper did something so important that I still can't believe the mainstream press hasn't made anything of it. With nothing more than a few "small boats and aircraft," he managed to sink most of the U.S. fleet in the Persian Gulf.

What this means is as simple and plain as a skull: Every U.S. Navy battle group, every one of those big, fancy aircraft carriers we love, won't last one single day in combat against a serious enemy.

The navy brass tried to bluff it out, but they were pretty lame about it. They just declared the sunken ships "refloated" so that the game could go on as planned. This is the kind of word game that makes the military look so damn dumb. Too bad Bonaparte never thought of that after Trafalgar: "My vleete, she is now reflotte!" Too bad Phillip didn't demand a refloat after the Armada went down: "Oye, vatos, dees English sink todos mi ships, chinga sus madres, so escuche: El fleet es ahora refloated, OK?"

But the trouble is that everybody in this story has an agenda— starting with the retired U.S. Marine Corps general named Paul van Riper, the hero of the story for most readers. When it broke the story, even the *Army Times* admitted that van Riper has a reputation as an "asshole" who has a grudge against high-tech scenarios like the one the military was testing. He also has a reputation as a guy who lives for the chance to make the brass look bad in war games.

But that's what a good opposing commander is supposed to do. This van Riper may be an asshole, but then most good generals are. Patton wasn't somebody you'd want to be stuck in an elevator with. Rommel was worse; there's a story about how one morning in the desert, Rommel announced to his staff officers, "Today is Christmas. We will now celebrate. Hans, how is your wife? Hermann, how is your wife?" and without waiting for his officers to answer, Rommel said, "That was Christmas. Now—get out the maps."

Even if it's true that van Riper has his own angle on this—some kind of anti-high-tech prejudice—does that mean the brass who "refloated" the ships he sunk are any more objective? Hell no. With their careers are all riding on the success of this operation, the big shots have just as much reason to lie or fudge the results.

The story just got dirtier as it bounced around the Web. The gullible types who believe everything the Pentagon tells them decided to trust the brass—van Riper was just a troublemaker. The paranoid types, the ones who think the CIA controls the weather, took it for granted that the whole war games were fixed from the start.

A lot of the arguments came down to the question of what war games like Millennium Challenge are about. Trusting war nerds were saying on the Web, "Well, the whole *point* of war games is to show up weaknesses! So naturally, when van Riper sank the ships, they made a note and restarted the games!"

It's a nice idea, but kinda naive. Most war games aren't neutral at all. They're supposed to showcase a new weapon or doctrine. Millennium Challenge was supposed to showcase high-tech joint-force doctrine. So when van Riper sank the fleet, you can bet that the guys running it didn't just say, "Well played, old boy! We must make a note of your tactics in order to avert such mishaps in the future!"

What most casual readers won't get is that some of van Riper's moves are chickenshit and don't amount to anything—but others are so damn scary that the U.S. Navy will be trying to live them down for years.

That trick of sending messages by motorbike is a good example of a move that gets lots of publicity and sounds smart but doesn't mean much. OK, you send your messages by bike. For starters, that means they move at miles per hour, unlike radio messages, which are almost instant. That's a huge disadvantage. And what happens if your biker gets strafed? No message—or a captured message. I'd be happy to fight an army that had nothing better than motorbikes to communicate with.

But what van Riper did to the U.S. fleet . . . that's something very different. He was given nothing but small planes and ships—fishing boats, patrol boats, that kind of thing. He kept them circling around the edges of the Persian Gulf aimlessly, driving the navy crazy trying to keep track of them. When the admirals finally lost patience and ordered all planes and ships to leave, van Riper had his grab-bag fleet all attack at once. By all accounts, they sunk two-thirds of the U.S. fleet.

To see why the brass, and particularly the navy brass, is so scared, you have to look at *how* van Riper's simulated Persian Gulf forces smashed the U.S. fleet. That should scare the Hell out of everybody who cares about how well the United States is prepared to fight its next war. And the scariest thing about this is that the lesson it teaches us is a lesson we should've learned a long, long time ago: No large surface ship is going to survive even an hour against a middle-range opponent.

A few years ago, a U.S. submarine commander said, "There are two kinds of ship in the U.S. Navy: subs and targets." He wasn't kidding. Let's look back at some war games involving surface ships and aircraft to see the pattern.

In 1921, Billy Mitchell finally got the chance to prove what he'd been saying for years: Large surface ships without air cover had no chance against aircraft. Mitchell had made himself the most hated man in the armed forces for saying this, but he wouldn't shut up. Finally, thanks to the huge surplus of military vessels left over from WW I, he got his chance. A German battleship, the *Ostfriesland*, and three surplus U.S. battleships were anchored off Virginia to see what Mitchell's rickety little biplanes could do to them. You have to remember how big and tough these dreadnoughts seemed to people back then. They had the thickest armor, the biggest guns, the deadliest reputations of any weapon on land or sea. The idea that aircraft could sink them was a joke for most people. Not to the navy brass, of course; the admirals had done everything they could to keep Mitchell from getting his chance. But pull (Mitchell's father was a former senator) and a little help from the army—a chance to slap the navy in the face—had won out.

The little biplanes buzzed out . . . and sank every damn ship. First a destroyer, then the huge German battleship, and then all three U.S. battleships. And guess what the navy said: "It doesn't prove a thing." Yeah. Sure it didn't. But Mitchell won his point: With Mitchell yapping at its heels and Congress helping him push, the navy finally started moving from battleship-based to aircraft-carrier-based battle groups.

The British didn't pay any attention to Mitchell's demonstration. Their battleships were better made, better armed, and better manned. With an impregnable British stronghold in Singapore and the Royal Navy patrolling offshore, what could those little Jap monkeys do?

Three days after Pearl Harbor, the British found out. A powerful battle group led by the battleship *Prince of Wales* and the cruiser *Repulse* steamed out to oppose Japanese landings in Malaysia. The British hadn't bothered to provide air cover. In a few minutes, both ships were sinking, holed by bombs and torpedoes, strafed, hit by wave after wave of Imperial Japanese Navy planes. The *Prince of Wales* sank so fast, virtually the entire crew went down with her. With its naval screen gone, Singapore the Impregnable fell so fast the British still can't talk about it without blushing.

That's what happens when you have too much invested in large, indefensible surface ships. Aircraft carriers came out of WW II as the kings of naval war, because they could attack and defend themselves with the air wings they carried. But the aircraft carriers are the battleships of the new century: The first time the United States takes its proud carriers into battle with any halfway smart enemy, these huge floating barges are going to go to the bottom so fast they'll take their crews and all their aircraft with them. You know how much we have invested in these things? Each carrier is the size of a small city. Every plane they carry is worth tens of millions of dollars. And not one is going to survive.

That was the real lesson of Millennium Challenge II. And that's what has the navy so furious at van Riper: He blew its cover. He showed all the hicks back home that the carrier battle fleet can be sunk by "small planes and boats."

If this surprises you, you haven't been following the news too carefully. In the Falklands War, the Argentine Air Force, which ain't exactly the A Team, managed to sink a half-dozen British ships, in spite of all the Brits' Harriers and SAMs and radar-aimed close-in defenses. The Argentineans did it very simply: came in low and fast and fired the antiship Exocets they'd bought from the French. And they did all this hundreds of miles off their coast, with no land-based systems to help.

Now think about what the Argentines *didn't* have: a decent submarine force; good ground troops; a civilian population to blend in with; shallow inshore waters to neutralize enemy subs. All those ingredients are present in all the places the U.S. plans to send its carriers: the Persian Gulf, the Straits of Taiwan, the shores of North Korea.

If your local library has copies of *Jane's Weapons*, check out the antiship missile section. There are so many models on the open market, you can get just about anything you want for rock-bottom prices. The top of the line in standard weaponry might still be the old U.S. Harpoon, but you don't need anything that fancy. In fact, compared with a SAM or an antiaircraft missile, an antiship missile is easy to manufacture. That's because surface ships move very slowly, have huge radar signatures, and can't dodge.

Imagine the radar signature of an American aircraft carrier off the Persian Gulf during a war with Iran. The Iranians aren't cowardly slaves like the Iraqis. They're smart, they're dedicated, and they hate us like poison. Imagine how many small aircraft and boats there are along the Iranian coastline. Imagine every one of those craft stuffed full of explosives and turned into kamikazes. Now add all the antiship missiles the Iranians have been able to buy on the open market. If you really want to get scared, add a nuke or two.

U.S. Naval forces are centered on the carriers, which are like the termite queen: Kill them, and the whole thing falls apart. The problem is that there are so many ways to kill a target that big, slow, and expensive. Suppose the Iranians use van Riper's method: Send everything at once, from every ship, plane, and boat they've got, directly at the carrier. Suppose the navy manages to stop 90 percent of the incoming planes and missiles. The result is still a dead carrier, going to the bottom and taking several thousand guys and several billion dollars' worth of aircraft with it.

Now try shifting the scenario to a U.S.-China fight off Taiwan. The Chinese have it all: subs, planes, antiship missiles... Hell, they *sell* that stuff to other countries! I'll say it plainly: No American carrier would last five minutes in a full-scale naval battle off China.

Let's go back to that objection some of you are probably raising: "The navy must've thought of all that!" Yeah, that's probably true—the navy's probably got some very quiet studies showing that its carriers are floating targets. But it's not going to say so in public. The submariners know all about it and laugh about it. They figure that's why the navy put all the real firepower—the nukes—on subs, not surface vessels: because the brass knows damn well that all that floating iron is going to be nothing but a dive site after the next war.

The more you think about it, the crazier it looks. The navy knows—it must know. But it keeps putting billions of dollars—Hell, it's more like trillions—into carriers. For no good reason except their careers, and the whole funding momentum behind these giant floating coffins. If you think that's impossible, just remember the British in 1940. There was plenty of evidence that battleships were nothing but giant coffins. They just decided not to think about it.

And they never recovered from that. That's the thing: You can be stupid and get away with it for a while. But eventually, you're going to pay. Right now, fighting a joke like Iraq, the U.S. navy can probably get away with sending its carriers into the Persian Gulf. But if Iran gets involved, those carriers won't last one day. If they ever approach the Chinese coast in wartime, they'll just vanish. If a carrier-based group steams anywhere near the North Korean coast . . . Well, there won't even be enough left to make a good dive site.

And the sickest part is, the admirals and the captains and the contractors all know it. Goddamn. Maybe we deserve what's gonna happen to us. The only thing is, it won't be the brass who die. It'll be the poor, trusting kids on those carriers who'll die, not even believing what's happening to them when the whole giant hulk starts cracking up and sliding into the water.

MOST VALUABLE WEAPON:
THE RPG

The weapon of choice for the Iraqi resistance is the rocket propelled grenade (RPG)-7.
—GEORGE J. MORDICA II,
USA CENTER FOR ARMY LESSONS LEARNED

THROUGHOUT THIS BOOK, you might have noticed that I don't talk military hardware as much as most war buffs do. A lot of people will talk all day about whether the Russian T-90 or the U.S. Abrams is the best MBT. I don't do that very much, for the simple reason that wars these days don't come down to one model of tank vs. another. It's pretty rare to find a war where both sides even use tanks. Most of the time, it's guerrilla vs. guerrilla, or conventional army vs. guerrilla. The odds of an all-out high-tech war between two conventional armies like the United States and Russia are about . . . oh, zero-point-zero. So it just doesn't matter that much whether their tanks could beat ours in some make-believe replay of the Kursk Salient. If you want to play that kind of war, buy a computer game. God knows there's enough of them. If you want to know how people make war now, in the real world, you need to study people, not hardware.

Sad but true, boys: War these days is more like social studies than metal shop. It's about tribal vendettas, military intelligence, propaganda, money—just about everything except pure hardware.

Don't get me wrong, I love the hardware as much as anybody. I used to spend every free hour, back before there was an Internet, going over those big, heavy reference books in the library: *Jane's Tanks, Jane's Missile Systems, Jane's Combat Vehicles*—Jane got around, whoever she was. I had those big blue books memorized. Seriously, you could open any of the Jane's handbooks at random, read me the name of a weapons system, and I'd recite its stats from memory—Norwegian antiship missiles, South African APCs (armored personnel carriers), you name it.

But eventually I had to face the facts: Most of those weapons are never going to get used. If you look at all the real wars going on right now, you come across the two weapons, over and over: the AK-47 and the RPG-7—both Russian designs and both older than your dad.

They're the weapons that matter, because they're already out there, millions of units, enough to equip every guerrilla army in the world, simple enough that you can teach a peasant kid with hookworm and a room-temperature IQ to fire them, and cheap enough to buy in bulk.

And the RPG is the best of all, even better than the Kalashnikov. This simple little beauty just keeps getting more and more effective. Nothing but a launcher tube and a few rockets shaped like two ice-cream cones glued together, this cheap little dealie has kicked our ass (and Russia's, too) all over the world since back when the Beatles were still together. In fact, more and more guerrilla armies are making the RPG their basic infantry weapon, with the AK used to protect the RPG gunners, who provide the offensive punch. The Chechens fighting the Russian Army are so high on it that they've switched their three-man combat teams from two riflemen and an RPG gunner to two RPG gunners with a rifleman to protect them.

Here's another important stat: Until the IED came into its own, the RPG was inflicting more than half half! of U.S. casualties in

Iraq. This is the weapon that kept the insurgency going until it learned to make shaped-charge IEDs (described in the next chapter). And it's been doing that for one Hell of a long time.

The Soviets created the RPG for use by Soviet infantry squads against U.S. tanks, APCs, and personnel in that big NATO/Warsaw Pact war everybody was dreaming of back in the 1960s. The design was an example of beautiful simplicity. It was a classic of Warsaw Pact reverse engineering. Warsaw Pact weapons designers had this attitude that it was a waste of time to design from scratch when you could count on your spies—and the Russians had the best spies in the world back then—to get you the specs on the weapons other countries had spent billions designing. So they just put together a cross between the two best shoulder-fired antiarmor weapons around, the Wehrmacht Panzerfaust and the U.S. Army bazooka. And that was the birth of the most important weapon in contemporary warfare.

The RPG got its start against our guys in Vietnam. The Viet Cong and NVA used RPGs as squad-level antiarmor weapons, and it worked so well that we never got our money's worth from the tanks and APCs we sent over. Our APC back then was a really lousy dump truck, the M113—basically a light-tank chassis with flat slabs of aluminum on the sides and top.

Sometimes, you can see how good a design is just by the way it looks. One look at an M113, and you can see that this was a lousy vehicle. It was way too tall for an APC, which meant it was a real big target. The aluminum armor didn't have firing ports, so the soldiers inside just had to put their helmets over their balls, close their eyes, and hope the crew would open the hatch and let them out ASAP. The armor was just thick enough to slow the thing down, but not nearly enough to stop an RPG round. Which is no surprise when you know that an RPG armor-piercing round can penetrate 300 millimeters of rolled steel—almost a foot of steel. Not a bad punch for such a little weapon to pack.

GIs who'd seen what an RPG hit could do to an M113 got in the habit of saying, "I'll walk, thanks." The RPG warhead does something called *spalling*, which means the warhead turns the aluminum side armor of an APC into molten shrapnel, which goes zipping through the guts of everybody inside like a Benihana chef's knife, only it's a knife as hot as the surface of the sun.

If GIs in Vietnam did have to ride an M113, they wore a lot of St. Christopher medals and sat on top. They were a lot less scared of getting shot by a sniper than of being hit by an RPG while sitting inside.

We had nothing like it and still don't. We had the LAW (light antitank weapon), another shoulder-fired rocket originally designed to penetrate armor, but it wasn't nearly as easy to carry, because it didn't have the reusable launcher the RPG featured. If you wanted to throw a dozen rockets at an enemy bunker, you had to carry a dozen LAWs along, whereas the RPG gunner needed just one launcher and a sackful of warheads.

'Nam was just the beginning of the RPG's career. Just think back to Mogadishu, 1993. The whole *Black Hawk Down* mess happened because some Afghan Jihadis who'd retired to Mogadishu—guess it was nice and restful compared with Kandahar—showed the Somalis how to use the RPG-7 as an antiaircraft weapon, which its Russian designers never even thought of. The RPG was the key to the whole battle that ended up killing eighteen Ranger and Delta guys (jeez, remember when eighteen GIs dead was supposed to be "unacceptably high" losses?), getting us to bug out from Somalia and getting Ridley Scott's directing career back on track.

First the Somali RPG gunners, firing up from the streets where they'd dug holes to channel the big rocket back blast, hit our Black Hawks, bringing them down in the maze of slums. That drew our troops into the slums, where everybody from toddlers to grandmas started potshotting them with AKs.

The Afghans worked out how to use RPGs as antiaircraft back in the 1980s, fighting the Soviets. I guess it was a little bit of poetic justice that the first helicopters to get brought down were Russian. The Afghans didn't have much to use against choppers except captured Russian heavy 14.5-caliber machine guns, which didn't have enough punch to bring down the Mi-24. And Reagan, the wimpiest hawk that ever flew, waited five long years to give the mujahedeen the Stingers that could take down an Mi-24 every time. So the Afghans started playing around with using the RPG against Russian close air support.

They came up with some great improvisations. There's nothing like war to bring out the inventor in people! One thing the Afghans figured out was how to use the self-destruct device in the warhead to turn the RPG into an airburst SAM. See, the RPG comes with a safety feature designed to self-destruct after the missile has gone 920 meters. So if you fire on up at a chopper from a few hundred meters away, at the right angle, you get an airburst just as effective as SAMs that cost about a thousand times more.

When the Chechens took on the post-Soviet Russian army in 1994, the good old RPG was the key weapon again. By this time, the Russians must've been cursing the name of the man who designed the thing.

In their first war against the Russians, in 1994, the Chechens found out that the RPG is the perfect weapon for urban combat. The Russians sent huge columns of armor into the streets of the city, and the Chechens waited on the upper floors, where they couldn't be spotted by choppers but still held the high ground. They waited till the tanks and APCs were jammed into the little streets, then hit the first and last vehicles with RPGs—classic antiarmor technique. That left the whole column stopped dead, and all the Chechens had to do was keep feeding warheads into the launchers, knocking out vehicle after vehicle by hitting it on the thin top armor. The Russians were slaughtered and had to pull back and settle for saturating the city with massed artillery fires, which killed lots of old ladies but didn't do any harm to the fighters. So, basically, the RPG single-handedly lost the Russians their first Chechen War.

Which brings us to Iraq, now. The first key to the RPG's effectiveness is availability, and it turns out that the one thing Iraq had more than enough of, in spite of all those sanctions, was RPG launchers and rounds. Saddam's army had an official license from the Russians to produce RPGs in Iraqi factories, which made so many that when Saddam went down, there were piles of launchers, with plenty of antiarmor and antipersonnel rounds, in most Iraqi towns. And after the Iran-Iraq War and Gulf War I, so many Iraqi men had trained on the RPG that there were plenty of gunners and instructors to teach the new generation how to use it.

Everything about the RPG design seems like it was designed to be used in Iraqi cities. It's got one of the shortest arming ranges of any shoulder-fired antiarmor weapon, which means you can fire it at a tank coming right down the street. At fifteen pounds, it's light enough for even the wimpiest teenager to run through alleys with. It's simple enough for any amateur to use—the original noncamera example of "point and shoot."

U.S. doctrine for countering the RPG always stressed looking for the flash when it's fired, and the blue-gray smoke trail it leaves. There are two problems with that, though. In the first place, unlike, say, the TOW (a U.S. antitank missile), the RPG is unguided, so once it's launched, it doesn't do much good to kill the gunner. You're still going to get hit. Second, it's not easy to see the blast or the smoke trail in one of these Iraqi "urban canyons." Too many walls to hide behind.

Our doctrine also used to stress laying down heavy fire in the general direction of the RPG launcher, to suppress further firings and hopefully kill the crew. But when you're fighting in the middle of an Iraqi city, that kind of general fire is going to kill a lot of hunkered-down civilians along with the RPG crew. And that doesn't look good on TV. More importantly, it makes you a lot of new enemies among the people whose cousins got shot.

Even if the RPG doesn't disable a vehicle, the blast radius of the antiarmor round is four meters, which means anybody in the area is going to be seeing little birdies for a good few minutes, deaf from the blast, temporarily blind, not to mention very scared and pissed off. Once you've got the occupying troops in a position like that—I mean literally blind and deaf and hating everybody around them—you're in a guerrilla strategist's idea of heaven. Troops in that mood tend to start firing blind, which makes everybody hate them even more, which suits the guerrillas right down to the ground.

IEDS:
THE LAZY MAN'S INSURGENCY

THE YEAR 2005 saw a big jump in the effectiveness of Iraqi insurgent tactics, and it all came down to one thing: switching to the improvised explosive devices (IED) as their weapon of choice.

One of the glorious things about war is the way it makes people think faster. Peacetime armies never learn anything; wartime armies learn new tricks faster than a hungry raccoon. And for the same reason: It's life or death, not just a parade-ground game.

Death was the problem the insurgents were trying to solve. Too many of their guys were getting splattered by superior U.S. firepower in their ambushes. In the early stages of the insurgency, a typical ambush relied on shoulder-fired weapons to kill the two or three GIs per day they needed to wear down the U.S. public's will to fight. Take April 2004. That was a terrible month, as you may recall, the month the kids in Fallujah hung those four roasted Blackwater dudes from the bridge. That month, we lost 140 troops, but only 19 of them, about 14 percent, were killed by IEDs.

Compare that with the second half of 2005, when IEDs caused 63 percent of U.S. combat deaths. October 2005 was typical: Out of 96 U.S. troops killed, IEDs were responsible for 57.

It's a classic case of wartime innovation, responding to losses by changing your approach. The insurgents finally realized that, as long as U.S. forces were patrolling blind, the Iraqis didn't need to put so many of their men at risk in these ambushes. Why not do it the easy way, using IEDs as their low-tech standoff weapon, instead of risking combat with superior U.S. firepower?

The real question is why they got away with it for so long. Well, it's pretty brutally simple: Until we let David Petraeus step in and run an intelligence-based counterinsurgency war, we had *no intel* on the rebels, and a bunch of Westmoreland-type "think positive!" generals like George Casey insisting that we could just keep rolling blind down Baghdad's back streets and eventually the enemy would get tired of blowing up our vehicles. A great plan if you're Stalin, with a secret police scary enough to stifle dissent back home, but not a great plan if you're dealing with a skittish public that winces every time another GI gets killed.

Our lack of intelligence on the enemy was the biggest failure of the war. What still shocks me is that back then, nobody in the U.S. media would even talk about it. The "professional" military correspondents were hypnotized, by years of Department of Defense briefings, into thinking that all military problems could be solved with better hardware. Well, counterinsurgency warfare is about people, not hardware. Until Petraeus came along, we were all hardware and no intelligence, like an all-weekend *Home Improvement* marathon. Made me sick. (The war, I mean, although I hate that show, too.)

Without intelligence on the neighborhood they're rolling through, no convoy is safe, no matter what vehicles it's riding. Even the Israeli Merkava 4, the best-armored tank around, has turned out to be vulnerable to shaped-charge IEDs. The only way to really protect your patrols is to learn who lives in every house along the convoy route, and whose side they're on.

It took the insurgents a while to realize that the IED could be the main course of their attacks, instead of just the appetizer. Maybe they just couldn't believe how dumb the pre-Petraeus American approach really was.

At first, they were using IEDs simply to bring our convoys to a stop. That's the way you use mines or IEDs in classic urban-guerrilla doctrine: to blast the first and last vehicles in the convoy, setting them up for the RPG gunners and riflemen hiding in the roadside buildings. Those are the guys who are supposed to inflict most of the casualties.

You can see the macho appeal of that kind of ambush. It was their version of shock and awe, popping up to blast us. But just like shock and awe, it was mostly show'n'yell. Rifle fire is ineffective even against up-armored Humvees, and though the good ol' RPG did a better job, it still left the crew exposed to return fire when the American choppers and planes swooped in.

See, making your getaway is the real problem in any urban guerrilla attack. Anybody can pull a trigger; the real trick is getting your insurgent squad home safe while the enemy's choppers zoom through the sky and every street is full of troops and armor looking for men of military age. That's one reason suicide attacks are getting so common: You really don't need to worry too much about your getaway.

But not every Sunni in Iraq wants to be a martyr. Most of the insurgents thought more like Patton: They wanted to kill and *not* be killed, which was a problem for the traditional ambush featuring shoulder-fired weapons. Then, sometime in late 2004, a little light bulb went on in some insurgent commander's head: Let the IED do all the work! Given the state of electrical power supplies over there in 2004, this might have been the only light bulb in the whole miserable place that went on, but it was a big one. By just increasing the size of their IEDs, the insurgents get more kills than ever at much lower risk.

In an IED attack, only one man needs to be on the spot—the triggerman. And even he doesn't have to be exposed to enemy counterfire. In a lot of IED attacks, the triggerman detonated the IED from a car parked down a side street and just drove away before the American and Iraqi forces could even start their search. No risk. No casualties. Very demoralizing for our troops, especially since they knew damn well that everybody in the neighborhood was in on the attack, but the soldiers couldn't level the locals' shacks in retaliation. Not just because the "rules of war" say you can't, but because that sort of wild shooting is exactly what the guerrillas hope the occupier will do after an ambush. Nothing recruits new guerrillas faster than an occupying army firing blind into the slums.

The learning curve for the insurgents went up scarily fast all through 2005 and 2006. Their IEDs got bigger and better, and the insurgents learned to use shaped charges. Now here I may as well admit that I've been impressed, in a depressing way, with how well the Sunnis have fought since the insurgency began. I mean, after that shameful performance in the 1991 war, did you expect these bastards to be so sneaky, patient, and smart? I knew this war was a bad idea (and said so, and got slammed for it), but even I never realized it would get as bad as it did.

For a while, American troops could tell themselves that at least they were safe in an M1 with the hatches down. The M1 is a great tank, with excellent crew protection, and the Iraqis had a hard time killing it until somebody—maybe somebody with a Persian last name, I don't know—taught them how to make shaped charges.

To understand why shaped charges are such a powerful weapon, we have to go into the incredibly cool world of explosive physics. I love this stuff. I mean, what red-blooded American boy didn't experiment with explosives? The only reason I ever opened my chem book was to see if it mentioned TNT or dynamite in the index. (It didn't—goddamn hippie teachers.) And naturally, I used the local wildlife, like toads and bees, in my experiments with the killing power of firecrackers.

What I learned was the most important point about the subject: Blast alone doesn't do a good job of killing the target. A bee would wobble off unhurt after one of my Fourth of July daisy-cutters went off right next to it.

Now before you hotheads whose hobby is making pipe bombs in the garage write me angry letters (or send me long, round packages with no return address), I know a blast can kill, if it's a big enough blast. We had a really nasty example of that on August 8, 2005, when a huge IED killed fourteen marines near Haditha. From what I've read, an investigation showed there was nothing special about the IED. It was just three antitank mines stacked like pancakes—the IHOP of IEDs, I guess you could call it.

Take a closer look at that blast in Haditha, and you learn some important lessons about what we were doing wrong at that stage of the war. And the first lesson is, like you might have guessed, that it's intelligence that matters in this kind of war. Or, in this case, counterintelligence: not letting your unit be penetrated by enemy spies. See, the same unit that suffered this terrible IED attack had just had six of its snipers killed in a small-arms ambush. Now you tell me how any enemy can ambush six snipers unless the enemy's completely penetrated the unit. The insurgents knew where the unit's snipers would assemble, and they knew where the vehicle would be passing. That was the United States in Iraq before Petraeus came along: We didn't know a thing about the enemy, but they knew way too much about us.

There was one other reason that a single IED killed so many men: The fourteen guys who died were marines, so they were riding in one of those ridiculous landing crafts the corps uses as APCs. Yep, the corps puts its guys in open-top landing craft even in places like Haditha, hundreds of clicks from the sea. The clunker they were riding in is called the AAV-7A1, and it looks like a giant, armored dinghy. Since it was designed to ferry troops ashore, it sacrifices armor and speed and damn near everything else to an amphibious capability that has no use anymore. But that's the corps for you. Real brave, but not always real smart.

Maybe if those guys had been in a real APC some would have survived. I can't say. But most of the time, guerrillas don't have the surplus matériel or the delivery systems to rely on simple blast effects against enemy armor. You have to make the blast more lethal somehow. So if you're trying to kill soft targets—i.e., people—you pack the bomb with homemade shrapnel: roofing nails, ball bearings, anything that'll shred flesh. A suicide vest tipped with nails is basically a 360-degree 12-gauge.

It works with civvies at a shopping mall or restaurant, but to kill GIs with one of those shrapnel vests, you need to catch them off-guard, somewhere they feel safe. That's what happened in December 2004, when a Jihadi killed more than a dozen of our guys in a mess hall in Mosul while they were having lunch—minus their body armor.

U.S. troops in armored convoys protected by choppers are obviously a lot harder to kill. And that's one of the biggest benefits of IED attacks for the guerrillas: Air power is totally useless against them. There are just no targets for the attack choppers circling after an IED goes off. The pilots know damn well that one of those

Iraqi cars driving away from the scene is carrying the guy who set off the IED, but there's no way to tell which one.

In a strange way, the IED meant Iraq had become a 3-D war. We controlled the air, but the Iraqis literally controlled the underground, thanks to these buried IEDs. These guerrilla movements don't get called "the Underground" for nothing. We flew, they dug, and the surface was up for grabs.

The insurgents' first IEDs were simple, just artillery shells buried in the road, wired up to a detonator. Lots of amateurs were tinkering in their garages, or whatever Iraqis have instead of garages, playing with stuff that goes boom. And naturally, lots of those guys went boom themselves.

Like I said, war teaches people fast, but some of the lessons have to be learned by the next of kin, not the handyman whose bright idea for a new type of bomb turned him into an abstract painting all over his wall.

Sometimes an insurgency has to learn its lessons several times. Take the case of pressure-triggered IEDs. These are basically standard antivehicle mines, with something like a bathroom scale as trigger. People and cars can pass over them unharmed, but if a really heavy (meaning armored) vehicle, or a scooter with a fat boy like me on it, rolls over that scale, the bomb goes off. (Trucks are a problem. Some trucks weigh as much as an APC.) The best part is that you don't even need a triggerman to set it off. You can all be off at the hookah parlor polishing up your alibis when it goes off.

The insurgents in Baqouba used pressure bombs in 2003, but the devices usually failed to go off. Their bomb-makers didn't have the technique yet.

But thanks to all that info-sharing the Internet gives an insurgency, the bomb-makers kept trying, with better wiring diagrams. On October 25, 2005, a pressure bomb shredded a Humvee in Baqouba, tearing four GIs' legs to pieces.

Other units were tinkering with those simple artillery-shell IEDs. The first generation was usually mortar rounds—too light to penetrate our armor. So the insurgents supersized to heavy artillery rounds, big shells that could kill almost anything except the M1 Abrams tank.

The standard view is that the best way to kill a tank is with the main gun of another tank, using special antiarmor rounds. The M1 held up very well against Iraqi tank forces in the first phase of the 2003 invasion: Only eighteen were lost in the advance on Baghdad.

But the insurgents began to figure out ways to disable, if not kill, even the M1. By the end of 2005, at least eighty of them had been damaged badly enough that they had to be shipped back to the Anniston, Alabama, repair depot.

The good news is that the M1 lived up to its rep for crew protection. The Army's Armor Center says less than a dozen crew have died in IED attacks on M1s. At least that many M1 crew have been killed, mostly by sniper fire, riding in open hatches.

M1s are hard beasts to kill. So if you're an insurgent bomb-maker, your ultimate goal is to find a way to kill the M1, destroy it completely, and kill its crew, not just knock a tread off. And that's where the shaped-charge IED comes in. Shaped charges were developed for tank killing and were used in MBT antiarmor rounds and antitank weapons. Their warheads are basically thick cups of soft metal—metals with low melting points, usually copper. The bomb-maker's job is to make sure as much of the force of the blast is channeled to the copper cone as possible. So sometimes, he'll put several 155-mm shells beneath the copper, or pack a whole lot of TNT under it.

When the IED detonates, this copper cup turns into a shaft of superheated metal that can zip right through any armor, even an M1's. That's what they tell me, and I have to believe it.

It's the kind of weird science that used to frustrate me in physics, the sort of info you just have to take on faith. I can't help wondering if they're kidding us civvies about it all. I don't get why a soft metal like copper can penetrate Chobham armor, which can defeat almost any warhead around.

Apparently, the copper isn't even actually molten. It ejects as a solid; it just "behaves like molten metal." I'm sure the insurgent *Home Improvement* tinkerers don't understand the science involved any more than I do. They just hear that it works and try it out.

The U.S. countermeasures, before Petraeus changed our whole approach to the insurgency, were based on coming up with some lame *Popular Mechanics* technological solution, rather than doing the hard work of human intelligence-gathering. In 2005, American convoys began to travel with jammers that made it harder to detonate the IED by cell phone or garage-door opener. Nokia and Genie sales probably dropped suddenly in the Sunni Triangle, but IED attacks didn't. Remember, low-tech is the guerrilla's friend. After the Americans started using jammers, the insurgents went back to setting off their IEDs by wire. Some insurgents went even lower-tech by tying a string to the detonator. Even Tim Allen's bearded sidekick couldn't find a way to jam a string.

Beyond that, Bush's policy was to blame Iran, or Syria, or Satan, or whoever. I'm sure Iran's doing what it can to keep us bogged down in Iraq. Wouldn't you, if your sworn enemy jumped into a hopeless mess right next door? But even if the Iranian secret services are behind the IEDs, what's the point? Only a few truly crazy neocons are still talking about invading Iran, and short of that, all we can do is throw tantrums at them.

Blaming the Persians was just a sign of Bush's frustration. As long as he could, he tried to pretend everything was fine, and besides, it was Iran's fault everything was so screwed up. It wasn't very logical, and it was getting on everybody's nerves. Bush's poll numbers were threatening to explore new ground, dive down into the negative integers, before he faced facts and put Petraeus in command. Petraeus had been the only U.S. commander to realize from the start that guerrilla war has no technical solution. Or even military solution. The only effective counterintelligence techniques are torture, reprisal, and, ultimately, genocide.

Since Petraeus took command in February 2007, we've been fighting a smarter, intelligence-based war, and the IED hasn't been nearly as effective against our convoys. The reason is simple: Petraeus has emphasized going after the guys who are setting the bombs, instead of tinkering around with tech gadgets.

Which brings us to the big question: Can we beat the insurgents? The short answer is still no. Maybe, if everything went just right—steady support from home, consistent backing from the politicians—we could manage it. But at the moment, we're winning hearts and minds the old-fashioned way: We're buying them. With the Sunni minority, Petraeus has managed a tilt that includes huge payoffs to tribal chiefs, basically bribes not to attack us. As soon as this administration goes, or a recession bites us hard back home, that money's going to stop flowing. When it does, or when any one of about two dozen other variables turns malignant, then we're back in big trouble. Guerrillas don't plan to win on the battlefield; in fact, they don't plan on having battles at all, if they can avoid them. They think about the long war. They want it more than we do.

Ask yourself honestly if you care about keeping Iraq. I mean, aside from the home-team pride thing, wanting us to win. Or the oil. I mean the actual place: Can you imagine wanting to live on dry mud flats full of people whose main hobby is yelling?

But to them, it's home; they like it. Eventually, they figure, the First World army will just get tired of the whole mess and go home. That's usually what happens.

To see it their way, don't think in terms of years; think decades. Imagine you travel in time, forty years into the future, to one of those big, expensive bases we're building in Iraq. Whose flag do you see on the wall? My guess would be the Iranian flag. That's only a guess, but one thing almost for sure is that it won't be the Stars and Stripes, or the flag of anybody who likes us very much.

If you take a long squint at modern counterinsurgency warfare, you have to admit it's been a complete failure most of the time. We're at one of those dead stops in military history; nobody really knows where we go from here in dealing with guerrilla forces.

My guess is that genocide will come back. Not a happy thought, maybe, but it's where the grim logic of war is leading. Remember, war forces people to think hard, even mercilessly. And genocide is the logical answer to guerrilla warfare. That was how the Ancients dealt with rebellious towns: wiped 'em out. One of these days, some

First World country is going to get impatient and a problem child like the Sunni Triangle will be a big, radioactive ghost town.

If we don't do it, the Kurds may end up doing it the old-fashioned way they learned from the Turks: one bullet, one village at a time. It's been done before—seen any Armenians up there lately? Probably not, but most of "Kurdistan" used to be "Armenia." A few of the Armenians made it to Fresno, but the rest are buried up there.

After all, we're talking about Mesopotamia here, the place where total war was invented. Hundreds of peoples have been wiped out forever in those parts. All these Holocaust lobbyists get furious if anybody says Jews aren't the only tribe to get genocided, but that's just politics—"Our genocide is better than your genocide!"

The fact is, genocide is, historically, the most common result when one tribe runs into another. And something tells me the next big wipeout will happen right there in Central Iraq.

WOMEN AT WAR AND IN DRAG

WHEN I WAS a kid, girls didn't get to play soldier. War was a boy's game, played with dirtclods, with maybe a nice sharp rock stuck in the clod if you really hated the guys you were fighting. That was the heroic age, the Homeric era of Bakersfield. We had a code, damn it. One time Lisa Royster, this buck-toothed sister of a friend of mine, tried to join the wars and got herself dirt-clodded back to her dollhouse by a rare, united volley from both sides, which just shows you how chivalrous we were.

Now they tell us women have to get equal time, some Title IX deal where the feds have decreed girls not only have to get equal volleyball funding but a full and fair chance of getting blown up by an IED. Which is why we've already had fifty-two American women killed in action in Iraq. Officially, women aren't supposed to be in frontline combat units like infantry or armor, but nobody told the Iraqis about this front line.

The fact is, any U.S. soldier or vehicle, anywhere in Iraq, is a target, so banning women from certain kinds of service doesn't do a thing to keep them safe. It just means your congressional representative can send off a form letter saying Congress did its best to keep our daughters out of the Ramadi Inn where Jessica Lynch stayed before she got fake-rescued. In other words, it's all a crock.

Back in the day, women knew their place in wartime, which was running away screaming when the village got jumped. If they didn't make it to the tree line, well, things were likely to get a little rough, with rape being one of the traditional perks of victory. War is when guys like me could finally get some cooperation from the girls, like at swordpoint. Most women were sensible enough to deal with that, and usually signaled their, uh, recognition of the hostile takeover by baring their breasts. This told the victorious Goth or Saracen raider, "Hey, congrats on the victory, here's your peace dividend, no waiting!"

Maybe it wasn't the kind of deal Dianne Feinstein would approve of, but people weren't such wusses back then. They just tried to roll with the punches and stay alive. Africans still deal with reality like that, but the rest of the world goes around trying to pretend it just can't imagine such crude doings.

Well, just you do-gooders wait for the next big warquake, when the crude runs dry. You'll see the old ways come back fast—and you'll be amazed at how your most PC friends are the first to switch. People are joiners, just like dogs. Today's do-gooders will be the first berserkers to jump off the longboats and get down to the rape and pillage.

What's really funny is how the liberals are running two totally opposite lies about women and war lately:

1. War is a mean, bad, sexist thing, and besides . . .
2. Women have always been brave soldiers who were right there on the battle front!

To prove number two, a bunch of professors have been collecting stories about girls who dressed up as guys and went to war.

These so-called historians say all the big European armies of the eighteenth and nineteenth centuries were crammed with butchy girls passing as men. After reading a bunch of sites promoting this lesbian crap, I finally understood why the ancient Greeks went into battle naked: They were just trying to make sure their ranks weren't inflated with millions of dykes in drag.

I'm not saying it didn't happen. Until the twentieth century, most European armies were all-volunteer in the traditional way, meaning if a press gang caught you in a dark alley and you had two arms and legs, they'd knock you on the head and when you woke up, you were in uniform, having volunteered while you were out cold.

Soldiering wasn't an elite profession, more like a way to avoid hanging. Some armies, like the eighteenth-century Prussian army, were officered by local boys but soldiered by any scum the press gangs could grab.

Nobody was in a mood to ask you about your past, and since these people bathed about once a year, whether they needed it or not, a girl didn't have to worry about those embarrassing locker-room scenes you get in teen cross-dressing comedies.

So no doubt, plenty of country girls who didn't look forward to getting beaten by the hubby every night and popping out a kid every year must have stolen their brothers' clothes, smeared a fake axle-grease mustache on, and practiced lowering their voices an octave or so with a view to a military career.

Even in the Civil War—you know, the 1860s, the most sexually twitchy era in history—some women passed as guys and saw combat. One of them, a freaky girl named Jenny, called herself Albert D. J. Cashier (I just like her alias somehow, thought I'd put it in) and enlisted in the Illinois Volunteers. She served till Lee surrendered, and—I love this quote—"was never suspected to be anything more than likeable, shy, and very brave."

In other words, sharing a tent with hundreds of hairy vets for over three years, nobody noticed she was a girl. Which tells you a lot about hygienic standards in wartime.

Jenny, or Albert, liked the whole man thing so much she stuck to it, undiscovered, all the way into the twentieth century. In fact, that newfangled technology was what revealed her little game: At the age of sixty-six, she got into a car crash, and when they prepped him for surgery, some brilliant diagnostician noticed that him was a her.

So basically, what we've got is another reason to love war: It allowed the sistuhs back then to express themselves free of gender roles, and all that crap.

War was a great way for a Civil War–era girl with a taste for Melissa Etheridge and women's softball to break out of those old stereotypes, see the world, even go courtin' the girls—some of these butch chicks even fought duels over the "affections" of camp follower girls.

But after seeing pictures of some of the women who supposedly passed as guys, I can't help suspecting that desperate recruiting officers who were worried about making their cannon-fodder quota let them in, knowing damn well they were more or less female. Take a famous case, this British woman named Dorothy Lawrence who spent WW I reporting from the front line in drag. Check out a photo of her on Wikipedia, and tell me if you think she could pass for a guy, even in the mud and blood of the trenches. She's got big, wide hips, narrow shoulders, short arms, and small features. She couldn't pass for a man anywhere, even at a Democratic Party Convention.

Maybe it made her feel better to believe people took her for a guy, but I bet the Tommies started telling dirty jokes the second she moved on to the next trench interview.

This whole topic makes me kind of uncomfortable, so let's just move on to the Russian girls, who as far as I can tell are the only ones who were totally able to fight magnificently without turning into medical freaks who had to shave twice a day. I have to salute you Russian woman warriors for that.

The USSR mobilized its women more effectively than any other power. Nazi Germany was the least efficient, according to Albert Speer's memoirs. I guess all that old-fashioned ideology got in the way. Funny to think of the Nazis as softies, but in all kinds of ways, they actually were. It was the Soviets who were really tough.

Stalin wasn't squeamish. He got called a lot of things, but not squeamish. So once all the boys of the class of 1941 were dead (and that didn't take long, the way the Germans were rolling up whole armies that summer), he called up the girls. Russian women were the logistical base of the Red (later Soviet) Army. They drove the trucks, ran the trains, manned (so to speak) the communications networks. And saw plenty of combat, too, not only in partisan warfare, but in some of the Russians' most effective frontline units.

The coolest of all these units was the 586th Fighter Regiment, an all-female outfit that flew Yak-1s against the Luftwaffe's Ju88s and Bf-109s. At least two of the women in the 586th earned ace status before the war was over. And if you don't mind me being sexist for a second here, both these aces were pretty durn cute. I even have kind of a crush on one of them, Lydia Vladimirovna Litvyak, who was credited with eleven solo kills and three team kills.

When she was shot down in 1943, the Soviet command feared she'd been captured. That would have ruined her career as a Soviet propaganda symbol, because Stalin was a little bit prejudiced against Soviet soldiers who got themselves captured, as in he considered them traitors and was already warming up a nice, unheated barracks for them once the war was over. Luckily for Lydia, it turned out she hadn't been captured at all, just died in the crash, which was perfectly OK and patriotic.

Comrade Stalin had this generous rule that if you died, you didn't have to ride the G-for-Gulag Train to Yakutsk. In fact, if you could prove you were dead, you were automatically let off your sixteen-hour shift when the temperature fell below minus 65 degrees. So Lydia got to spend the rest of the war in a nice, comfy grave.

The other combat role Soviet women really did outstanding in was as snipers. Some of these Russian girls notched up serious three-figure kill totals and managed to stay cute doing it. The top gun among them was this really gorgeous Ukrainian girl named Lyudmila Pavlichenko. Dumb name, great girl—by the end of the war she had, get this, 309 little notches on her stock. Which shows you how incredibly effective a good sniper can be over the course of a long, mobile war like the Eastern Front, 1941–1945. They say that on the corpse of one of the Wehrmacht snipers she killed, Lyudmila found a notebook that listed more than five hundred kills. So she not only took out three companies of enemy troops, but by killing this ubersniper, also saved Lord knows how many Soviet soldiers.

You could argue that Lyudmila had the combat effectiveness of a battalion. And what a profile! The only negative on her is the song that Woody Guthrie wrote about her, and it may seriously be the worst song in the history of the world. I don't know why people think Guthrie was so great, but if you want to be deprogrammed from that notion, just read these lyrics he dedicated to Lyudmila:

> Miss Pavlichenko's well known to fame;
> Russia's your country, fighting is your game;
> Your smile shines as bright as any new morning sun.
> But more than three hundred nazidogs fell by your gun.

> CHORUS:
> In your mountains and canyons quiet as the deer.
> Down in your bigtrees [sic] knowing no fear.
> You lift up your sight. And down comes a hun.
> And more than three hundred nazidogs fell by your gun.

God, that's lousy writing. Too bad nobody ever gave Lyudmila clearance to take out ol' Woody before he got to that chorus: "Pliz, Comrade, I haff clear head shot at zees 'singer.' Pliz let me take it, or I must shoot self from ze agony of ze listening!"

I've seen pictures of Guthrie with a sticker on his stupid guitar reading, "This machine kills fascists." I hate commie posers like that, taking credit for kills he never earned. Just compare a phony like that to Lyudmila, who went to war, did her job brilliantly, and managed to stay a real woman right through it.

Well, we won't get anybody like her anymore. So much of what made war worth doing died in 1945. That's the Nazis' real crime, if you ask me: They ruined it for everybody except the damn suits.

From now on, women in war is going to be buzz-cut Hillarys with pictures of their girlfriends in their cockpits and a sex-bias lawyer waiting for their first disciplinary hearing. It's probably somebody's idea of a good time, but not mine. Just makes me want to make that move to Eritrea, where men are men and women still fight with babies on their backs.

THE DOCTRINE OF ASYMMETRICAL WAR

TAKE A HARD look at modern warfare—not Halo III or WarCraft, but what is actually happening out there. And you'll see it contradicts everything we were taught. For starters, no twenty-first-century war is purely military. The days when countries duked it out on the battlefield are over. What we have now is something very strange. It goes by a lot of names, from *terrorism* to *asymmetrical warfare* to *fourth-generation warfare*, depending on whether you're for it, against it, or just trying to sound cool. But whatever you call it, the key factor is that it never involves WW II–style conventional war between nation-states.

Oh, there'll be a few good, old-school, conventional wars from time to time. My favorite is the Ethiopia-vs.-Eritrea war of the 1980s. And you could include the Iran-Iraq War from that same decade.

But those wars are rare and will get rarer. Because there's a much cheaper, easier way to make war. This way doesn't require any of the building blocks of conventional war: You don't need industry, aircraft, armor, or massive armies. In fact, this kind of war can be played by any group of wackos who can round up a dozen or so bushwhackers. All you need is small arms and a grudge—and those are the only two commodities most of the world has a surplus of.

It's a heartbreaker for you hardware freaks, this idea that it just doesn't matter whether our tanks are better than their tanks (or planes or artillery, or whatever). But it's time you grew up, guys. Haven't you kind of noticed that in most wars, the other side doesn't even use tanks, or planes, or artillery (except mortars, which are so portable they can be considered small arms)? You guys are stuck in the dream about a classic NATO/Warsaw Pact sumo match in Central Europe, and you just don't want to think about all these brush wars. Well, time to wake up. The Warsaw Pact doesn't exist anymore, so this kind of war is never going to happen. The fact is, it never was. If the Soviets had sent the tanks into the Fulda Gap, it would have been a nukefest, not a tank battle like Kursk. Not exactly a war-gamer's dream: Before you can even get your corps deployed, the whole playing field would melt down.

So I'm preaching real war here. If you want tank duels, go replay the Kursk Salient, or project yourself fifty years into the future, where maybe, just maybe, the Asian powers will have a good all-out war. If you want to know about war now, then you have to jump into the weird world of *asymmetrical war.*

And I'll tell you: Once you make that jump, you find this kind of war is just as interesting, just as satisfying as setpiece battles. I made the jump back in the mid-1990s, when I realized my hardware research wasn't helping me understand the wars that were actually happening in Africa and Asia. And I'm glad I did, because I understand the world way better than most people. I knew Iraq would go bad, because I've studied this kind of war. I wish more people had. Maybe we wouldn't have jumped into this mess.

To get your head around this kind of war, you have to delete most of your ideas about warfare. That's right: Get your Black & Decker out of the garage, charge that puppy up, and do some brain surgery on the part of your cortex that stores your favorite ideas about war. Here's a list of War Myths, so you'll know where to drill:

1. *War involves battles.* Wrong! Most of the "armies" in the world right now avoid battle and focus on killing civilians.

This is the hardest thing for Americans to understand: armies that don't aim at victory and that actually avoid battle. So many war buffs who ought to know better just won't see this. If you read military blogs, you know the type: guys who say "we won every battle in 'Nam!" as if that proves we should have won. Boneheads! The NVA/Viet Cong strategy was classic irregular warfare stuff, based on outlasting the enemy, not defeating him in battle. When they did go for military victory, as in the Tet Offensive, it was a near disaster, as explained by the next key myth about this sort of war.

2. *You win by killing the enemy.* Wrong, wrong, wrong. In this kind of war, the enemy wants you to kill a lot of people. A lot of irregular warfare groups start their campaigns with a suicide raid, where they expect to be slaughtered.

3. *High-tech beats low-tech.* Not lately it doesn't. Here again, it's a matter of you hardware freaks facing hard facts. If we take Iraq 2003 as a familiar and painful example, you saw a classic outcome: Our high-tech beat their wanna-be high-tech in the conventional battles. Then we started getting picked off by low-tech ambushes where the insurgents used IEDs in combination with old, rugged Soviet weapons like the RPG-7 and Kalashnikov. After four years, those simple weapons are still effective—and they're actually getting lower- and lower-tech! Take IEDs: When the Iraqis started using them, the insurgents would hook the detonator up to a garage-door opener or cell phone so the devices could be set off by remote control signals. Our convoys started using jammers to stop those signals from getting through to the detonators. So now the insurgents are using wires or even string to set off the IED. You can't get much lower-tech than a string. And that's why it works, because you can't jam a string, either.

4. *Overwhelming force! Hit the insurgents hard enough, and they'll quit.* Wrong. Americans are pretty well antideath,

but lots of other tribes are in love with the idea of the martyrdom thing. Like the Shiites, whom I've written about already, some might say, with admiration. People who woof about "hittin' 'em hard" haven't thought cold and hard enough about what they mean. We have a problem with the Iraqi Sunnis; there are about seven million of them. All you need for an effective insurgency is a few hundred urban guerrillas (with a much bigger base of civilian supporters). So they're never going to run out of young men. And no overwhelming force short of neutron bombs will solve the problem. Which brings us to another very interesting question, the future of genocide and nuclear weapons. But as long as we're wimping around with this no-nukes rule, there just ain't no kind of overwhelming force that can convince every testosterone-poisoned Sunni kid to join the Pepsi Generation. Consult your own experience; remember what young males are like! Remember high school PE! How hard would it have been to get those guys, Beavis and Butthead times eighty, to plant a bomb or shoot a sentry if they thought they could get away with it, or better yet, be seen as heroes by their fellow countrymen? Teenage boys are the cannon fodder of any guerrilla war, and teenage boys are nothing but weasels who stand on their hind feet sometimes. Keep that in mind when media types try to hand you the following piece of total crap.

5. *People want democracy and peace and all that kind of stuff.* No. In fact, *Hell* no! Let me repeat your first lesson: Consult your own experience instead of believing the talking heads. Do you care about those things—I mean, compared with money and sex and taking revenge on the MR2 that cut you off a couple of blocks back? The only ideology I see around me is God. Most people in Fresno have a bad case of God. It takes up all their brain power trying to read the Bible and mind everybody else's business. They wouldn't

care if Charles Manson took power as long as he said *God* and *Jesus* every few seconds. Out of all the people I've met, I can only think of one who cared about democracy: my social studies teacher. But he was one of these decent old Minnesota Swedes, good-hearted, too soft for Bakersfield, committed to ignoring reality. His wife, another big secular humanist, left him for a dyke, his students called him "Gums," and he admitted once to our class that he'd lost his faith. That made him public enemy number one with the Christians, and he had to transfer to another school district. That's what believing in that stuff'll get you.

If this is a democracy, it's weird how the only people who go in for it are con men and closet cases, like Rove. No normal American would go near it. They know better. We all know local politics belongs to real estate developers at the civic level and to the corporations at the federal level. Which is fine with me, and with most Americans, but why call it democracy?

And as for peace, I was always against it. Peace is for people who have satisfying lives. The rest of us want that flood, that real rain. Like the man said, "Bring it on."

Look around the world, and you'll see that people are divided into ethnic gangs, as if the planet is one big San Quentin. All they want is for their gang to win. If they have any ideology beyond that, it's more of the God stuff, and you need Thorazine to cure that. God-fearing gang-bangers, that's exactly what we ran into in Somalia, 1993. Half the population of Mogadishu turned on our guys who were trying to provide aid for the starving. Those Somalis didn't want peace, democracy, or any of that shit. They wanted their clan to win and the other clans to lose. And if stopping the aid convoys from getting food to those enemy clans was the only way to win, they were ready to make it happen, ready to die fighting our best troops backed by attack helicopters and APCs. We killed maybe a thousand of these "civilians" and lost eighteen Rangers and Delta operators. And the Somalis made the anniversary of that fight a national holiday. It's worth taking a moment to let that sink in: These people fought to the death against overwhelmingly superior U.S. forces, because they wanted their clan to win by starving rival clans to death.

Yes, Grasshopper, you must meditate on the fact that people are superstitious tribalists. Democracy comes about 37th, if that. Nobody wants to face that fact: We're tribal critters. We'll die for the tribe. More to the point, we'll kill for it. We don't care about democracy. And I'm not just talking here about people in tropical hellholes like Somalia. I mean your town, your street. Most Americans are just like me: old-school nationalists. We want America to be Roman, to kick ass. The rest is for Quakers.

Just remember, everything they told you is wrong. Here's a quick list of the main points. Go and meditate upon them. Memorize them while I whack you with this stick like a good Zen teacher should.

1. Most wars are asymmetrical or irregular.
2. In these wars, the guerrillas/irregulars/insurgents do *not* aim for military victory.
3. You can *not* defeat these groups by killing lots of their members. In fact, they want you to do that.
4. High-tech weaponry is mostly useless in these wars.
5. "Hearts and minds," meaning propaganda and morale, are more important than military superiority.
6. Most people are not rational; they are *tribal*: "My gang yeah, your gang boo!" It really is that simple. The rest is cosmetics.